Cold Water Souls

Chris Nelson

Contents

It is February, the 1980s and it is sleeting. Northerly winds are biting at this time of year; straight out of the Arctic, they cut through everything with a pathological ruthlessness. The mercury has dipped well below freezing, wind chill is a concept we are yet to grasp and the brown rippled sea is about five degrees. I am wearing a damp, cold wetsuit. It has luminous yellow flashes down the sides – neon is still cool. This beauty, this 3/2 summer steamer has detachable arms, only the arms are not detaching. I am stripped to the waist, chest turning an alarming pinky purple, yellow sleeves still welded to my arms. It's a bizarre colour clash. My fingers are too numb to grasp the paper-thin neoprene. All I keep doing is nipping handfuls of white flesh. I look up, face reddening with frustration, and catch a glimpse of my friend who is desperately trying to zip up the fly on his jeans. He has given up on his anaesthetized fingers and is trying to use his knuckles instead. I look around the circle at the rag-tag bunch of half-dressed, dishevelled figures, hunched and stooped, involuntary grunts and moans emanating from one and all. What are we doing? We have just spent an hour in the frigid North Sea, our only protection an assortment of leaky wetsuits, holey gloves and cumbersome boots that were clearly designed by someone who'd never been near the ocean. Why? We are sheltering in the dark embrace of an easterly-facing bay, one dominated by towering Jurassic cliff faces, where huge slabstone reefs angle gently away into the brown folding ocean. Today, the swell was so big we surfed the inside reef, where head-high walls were ruler topped, where glassy faces begged to be etched by a trailing hand. We traded waves, watching as each in turn hooked into the relentless onslaught of feathering lines. Every paddle back out, thinking about taking time to rest up, to steel yourself; every new set bringing a burst of adrenaline to spurn that thought with the mantra of 'just one more'. And all the time, out back, the pitching barrels of Second and First Reef, each

bigger than the last. We watched with awe, as those empty caverns spun down the point, thinking one day that would be our playground. This was why we did it; this was why we shivered and mumbled blue-lipped in the line-up, minds numb, heads clasped in the vice-like grip of winter. We shared an experience, something we felt was unique, something we cherished. Little did we know then that around the globe, on the frigid shores of Nova Scotia, Iceland, Hokkaido and Alaska, there were others, others who shared this experience, others with whom we had a bond, others who were cold water souls.

Some debate the true origins of waveriding, whether it was ancient Polynesians or the Peruvian *Caballitos de Tortora* who first rode the waves. One thing is certain, it was in Hawaii that the Sport of Kings had its modern re-birth and from where it spread across the globe with phenomenal speed and voraciousness. *Gidget* spread the word, but it was Bruce Brown's movie that set us on our way; he brought *The Endless Summer* to the world, a phrase that over the years would become synonymous with the art of the glide. His hyperbole and cinematic magic captured the imagination of a generation and the search was born: chasing the perfect wave, a mythical place of sun, sand and surf. California boomed and surfing spread like a viral campaign, coursing up the coastline from Malibu to Santa Cruz. Oregon fell to the advance, as did the shores of New Jersey, Long Island, Cornwall and Biarritz.

Through the sixties and seventies, a hardcore brand of explorers redefined the boundaries of just what that search meant. They pushed deep into the jungles of Indonesia; G-Land and Nias were discovered and ridden. Bill Boyum, Peter Troy, Craig Peterson and Kevin Naughton were just a few of the seekers who hopped Indian Ocean ferries to far-off islands or scoured the fringes of Africa and Central America. *The Lost*

New England
Fresh delivery.

Ian Battrick
Cold water seacher.

Island of Santosha was beckoning and the *Morning of the Earth* was dawning. We were pushed ever onwards; it seemed a new discovery was always just around the headland: warm waters, crystalline barrels and new, empty line-ups. Then the surf camps arrived, the charter boats and the crowds. Communities of expats guarded their new paradises, skippers parked alongside other skippers as the line-ups became just as crowded as the ones back home. Was the era of exploration running out of new horizons?

The truth was that surfers from the cool fringes had already been pushing out to explore new regions. They lived a life encased in neoprene so, as fingers traced the coastline on the world map, cold water was no barrier to their search; it did not limit their scope. Scotland, Iceland, Alaska;

in an era when the globe spins ever faster, the centrifugal forces are pushing ever outward, offering a myriad of new opportunities. Surfers are looking at new destinations and the cold blue of northerly latitudes now sets pulses racing. However, pioneering missions did not always find splendid isolation. Often line-ups were shared with bands of hardy locals, communities forged in the cold fires of burning fingers and ice-numbed toes. It was a coming together of kindred souls united by a love of the glide, a meeting of those who chased swells through the depths of winter, when the white duvet brings a deathly quiet to the beach. These were places where travelling with respect was met with respect, for we all knew what it meant to don that still-damp wetsuit on an ice-glazed morning. For some surfers the cold is something to endure,

Sunset Hack
Santa Cruz.

something that needs to be overcome whatever the cost. Then there are those that embrace the cold; those that feel it is an integral part of the surfing experience, something to be celebrated. The shocking jolt of that first icy duck dive that makes you feel alive, the stunning clear lip that feathers overhead or the feeling of snow falling, tones and shades growing muted in the advancing quiet. Cold water surfing is not for everyone, but everyone who surfs in cold places is connected by a bond that comes from shared experience, from being in that car park, dribbling, freezing cold, hands too numb to turn the ignition and get the heater going, but knowing all the time that when the tide turns, you'll be back out there.

This isn't a definitive history and these are not, by any means, the only cold places to surf. *Cold Water Souls* is the result of a lifetime spent in cold places and a three-year journey to seek out some of those who share the same stoke and fire. These are the stories from surfing's frigid outposts, the waves that break there and the surfers who call these line-ups home. Along the way I've been privileged to share waves and split peaks, break bread and talk story with kindred spirits from Hokkaido to home. I have met first-generation pioneers who braved ice-filled line-ups with beavertail wetsuits and steely determination, big wave chargers who drop into the coldest, darkest pits in the surfing world, stoked groms, shapers, teachers, carpenters and oil rig workers, all who share a love of surfing, who go into their environments embracing the elements, whatever they hold. There is a binding connection that unites these places, these surfers. It is a shared experience, a shared purpose. It is a love of the glide and everything that entails.

The Endless Summer is over, a new era has begun. It is the era of the Cold Water Souls.

Top: Hokkaido
Across the tracks.

Bottom: Maine
Event.

Chris Clarke
Thurso local.

TIM NUNN

Zack Humphreys
New Jerseyite in Norway.

West Coast USA

DAVID PU'U

"Look dad, a shark!" Few things will tear a hungry man away from his lunch, but the cry of 'Shark' is certainly one of them. We are sitting above Steamer Lane, salt crusted, surfed out; basking in the last vestiges of warmth afforded by the late Autumn sun. I have a sandwich in one hand, hot coffee the other. The line-up is packed from The Point through to Cowell's where a horde of beginners and an armada of longboards vie for position. Mavs charger Zach Wormhoudt is on his way. The hustle and bustle passes us by as we melt into our seats, content with our day's work, until the shout of the small boy captured our attention. We look up as the boy's father approaches the cliff edge. "It's probably just a big sea bass," he says dismissively. "Oh no, that is a shark." The boy beams. "Good eye son."

We find ourselves on the edge, squinting down through the glare. Below, a grey torpedo glides along the bottom. The water is about eight feet deep, the shark about six feet long. Not a man-eater by any stretch, but it is an amazing sight to behold, especially from this bird's eye vantage point. It is a view into another domain. The predator moves slowly. The pack of surfers sit inanimate, barely breaking the surface tension, oblivious to the myriad of life below, the actions and reactions. Our territory is a thin film that clings to the earth's surface, separates the deep from skies. It is only when boundaries are blurred that we glimpse these other layers. The hold down, the dolphin's leap, the child's shout – these are the windows to the other realms. Zach arrives, a man who regularly transits the boundaries. I open my mouth to point out the shark but feel a Crocodile Dundee moment could be in the offing. "Shark? That's not a shark…"

AL MACKINNON

Green Day
California Coast.

It's a sunny morning, September 1926. The California coastline is virgin land, protected by armed cowboys. For nearly twenty years, the landowner, May Rindge, has been battling to prevent the new Pacific Coast Highway crossing her land, and the battle is all but lost. Sunlight glares off the sea and two wakes are visible far out, heading towards the point. 'Probably elephant seals,' decides the gnarled ranchero, squinting. He turns and spurs his horse back inland with a flurry of dust. The sea gives him the creeps. Tom Blake and friend, Sam Reid, are making the long paddle out to the point, profiles low. "In those days, cowboys with guns and rifles still rode the Ranch," recalls Sam. "The gate at Las Flores Canyon had 'Forbidden – No Trespassing' on it. We paddled the mile out to the beautiful, white, crescent-shaped beach. It didn't have a footprint in the sand." Three-foot high sets are rolling down the point as the two arrive in the line-up. They sit and survey the view, turning to see a man on horseback disappear over the ridge. A wrapping wall is feathering around the headland, ruler-edged and diamond sharp. Blake paddles, feels the momentum shift, then pops to his feet, trimming his ten-foot redwood board out on the face. The significance of this moment isn't clear. But the envelope has been pushed, the boundaries have changed and a new era is coming. Surfing has a new outpost and its name is Malibu.

Looking at a map of the Pacific coastline of the United States, its erratic boundaries and roving borderlines seem to show scant regard for the impasse of geography and the rigidity of geology, but these lines are not the random rambling of a pen, they are the result of careful study, thought, deals and counter-deals: the things on which nations are forged and identities cemented. The result is a region that covers a staggering seven thousand, six hundred miles of shoreline, ranging from the borderlands

NICK LAVECCHIA

of San Diego in the south, through the vast California Pacific belt, north through the rainforests of Oregon and Washington State, by-passing Canada before converging on the vast reaches of Alaska. It is a mind-blowing expanse of bays, beaches, reefs, coves, islands and inlets. It encompasses environments from the semi-arid to the temperate. In the southern reaches of San Diego, summer temperatures nudge over ninety degrees (30°C), while the ocean, somewhat tempered by the California current, stays between seventy-two (22°C) and a comfortable fifty-nine (15°C). In Seattle, on the Canadian border, mild wet winters see the mercury hover in the mid thirties (2-4°C) and, while the summer is generally warm in the high seventies (25°C), the ocean never truly looses its chill, peaking at fifty-two (11°C), meaning wetsuits are a year-round reality. The great wilds of Alaska can deliver balmy T-shirt-wearing summers and frigid winters spent indoors, refreshing cool-water dips or roving pack ice. However, the coastal region is buffered from more extreme changes in climate by the Pacific, which acts as a summer heat sink and winter heat balance.

The coastline boasts some impressive urban landscapes – Los Angeles, San Francisco, Portland, Seattle: a who's who of cool conurbations – yet huge swathes of this colossal fringe stand green and undeveloped, with lush forest headlands or dune-backed beach. This is an area racked by fault lines, fissures where the tireless creep of tectonic plates is brought to juddering life. There's anticipation that 'the next big one' could just be moments away.

For surfers, the next big one has quite different connotations. Checking charts, following the swell prediction sites and watching the weather forecasts, waveriders of this region are truly blessed. With such a huge body of water from which to draw swell and a westerly orientation, they see consistent lines arrive through the seasons. Powerful north Pacific storms generate intense swells that slam into the coastline during the winter months. Then the southern hemisphere acts as a swell generator from late spring to early fall. Autumn can be a golden time. Great things can happen when swell seasons meet: the water temperature is still mild, the long-distance lines can be perfectly groomed by light offshore winds, and those on a dawn patrol smile in the empty line-up as the sun cracks the horizon.

Green belt
Huge swathes of this colossal coastal fringe stand free and undeveloped, from lush forest headland to dune-backed beach.

Surfing was born in the Pacific. The origins of the glide has Polynesia interwoven in its chromosomes: the joy, the freedom, the respect, the order. It was more than just a pastime; it was an integral part of Hawaiian heritage and culture. The art of waveriding was virtually stamped out by early Christian missionaries, who felt the frivolity and sheer abandonment must in some way be ungodly. But for a small group of Hawaiian watermen, the sport of kings may have died out. These few still took to the waves on Alaia boards or in traditional outrigger canoes. The dawning light of the twentieth century shone on the hidden corners of the sport with the formation of Da Hui Nalu or 'Club of the Waves' on Waikiki Beach with members, including Duke Kahanamoku and Rabbit Kekai, riding traditional solid boards. As news of the Waikiki scene spread, Hawaiian beach boy, George Freeth, found himself invited by a wealthy industrialist to put on a surfing demonstration in California. Surfing had actually ridden onto the California coastline during the nineteenth century with Hawaiian crews of passing sailing vessels taking to the breakers there, but its arrival had been under the radar, not for public consumption but rather for personal pleasure. But when Duke surfed at Santa Monica and Corona del Mar, he drew and astounded the crowds that gathered to watch. Duke's stay on the California coastline and surfing forays with friends from Hollywood, brought more converts to the cause. One of those was a young man named Tom Blake who would go on to redefine the modern surfboard and in doing so, surfing. By the late fifties, surfing was

on the brink of becoming a fully-fledged phenomenon, a wave that would sweep up the youth of the Golden State and bring hordes flocking to the shores of Malibu.

The 1950s were the dawn of youth culture, when kids with cash in their pockets became consumers for the first time, hungry for music, movies, cars and clothes, for their own identities and icons, not just the hand-me-down heroes from their parents' generation. Riding in the vanguard of this movement were the counter- culturalists – bikers, beatniks, hot-rodders and surfers – rebels with their own causes. Through the decade, Malibu, with its perfect peeling right-hand point break had become the 'drop-in, drop out' centre of the surfing universe, the masters of which were the anti-heroes Mickey Dora, Tubesteak, Micky Munoz, et al. One of those drawn to surfing and this edgy Malibu scene was Kathy Kohner. When she told her screenwriter father of her exploits at the beach and those of the local

NICK LAVECCHIA

Right
Golden opportunities glimpsed across the channel.

crew, he quickly turned her tales into the 1959 movie, *Gidget*. Suddenly, the bohemian lifestyle of 'hanging out' at the beach and 'shooting the curl' – albeit a bastardised, sanitised version – had been beamed onto the mainstream subconscious via cinema screens from California to Kentucky. Suddenly everyone wanted a slice of the surfing pie. The first boom of the modern surf era had been fuelled.

1963, Rincon Point. A figure huddles, sitting on his baby blue Tiki board shivering, surveying the line-up. The wind has picked up and goose bumps spread over his arms. The sets are coming, bigger now, eight-wave trains bearing down like a relentless onslaught, almost too much for the senses. This is bigger than he's ever been out in before. To his right, he sees a surfer dropping own the face, angling, leaning. Like a muscle memory, he can almost sense the feeling of toes gripping the deck. The curl frames the rider's outline, towering overhead, a mane of water unleashed by the gusting off-shores. He realises that, as he watches, his hands are gripping his rails harder and harder, despite sitting in the safety of the deep-water channel. The waverider sets the rail and the wall begins to race, passing inside the gaggle who float wide of the impact zone; locked in, he disappears, just the back of the wave now visible beneath a sea of spray. The watcher closes his eyes as the cold water fizzes and showers him, the rumbling express passing. Looking towards the pebble beach, he can see the smoke of high-tide driftwood fires, but the promise of warmth seems out of reach. He decides it's time to go in. Next set. He nods to himself as if to cement the deal, takes a deep breath, lies on his board and paddles deeper, into the pack. No one is talking, everyone is focussed on the end of the point, looking for the tell-tale signs. A dark line rises. Everyone begins to paddle out. 'Shit, this is a big one,' he thinks. 'I've got to get out of here.' The first wall is swelling,

starting to feel the bottom, standing tall. He knows the waves behind will be bigger and, in that instant, decides to just go. Sitting up and pivoting the board round he begins a two-handed pull. The board launches forward and he digs again, feeling the tail rise, as he starts a lazy acceleration. This is it; he begins to pop. But, oh, something feels wrong; his brain is sending out a frenzy of impulses; he's too steep. Why? Panic starts to register; he is vertical now, pitching. He watches helplessly as his board twists; he is thrown forward, cart-wheeling. Eyes wide open, he sees a blue blur rotating, his board spinning magically like a top, caught by the wind, rising, pitching high over the crystalline curtain, a guillotine that is descending. Slap. He lands flat on his back, failing to penetrate the water. The impact knocks the air from his lungs and then the lip strikes, a viscous explosion that shocks him with its severity. It is dark. The earth is tumbling. Scrambling up the rocks, he stumbles on the slippery boulders. Cold, shaken, he collapses by the fire. His head is spinning. He needs to lie down. Eight waves of churning fury have washed him clean down the point. His knee is bleeding. His new board is gone. His baby blue, nine-foot-six Tiki. He will worry about that tomorrow. Today, he is just glad to be alive.

I t is a time when all animals are wild. The dog is wild, the horse is wild, man and woman are wild. One by one, the animals are tricked into becoming the servants of man. All but one. There is one animal that is too wise, too wired to be tricked, too clever to lose his freedom. 'I am the cat that walks by himself and all places are alike to me.' A grainy, sixteen-mil image fires up on the screen, scratches and hairs dancing around the bleached oceanscape. Dora appears on a waist-high wave, lays down a drop-knee turn and side-steps up to the nose. The line-up is peppered with a myriad of boards. Dora takes two steps back, sideslips the board around a kook

paddling out. Two surfers drop in on him. He grabs the shorts of the first one and yanks him backwards off the board. The other he dispatches with a single shove. Dora wasn't just the best surfer at Malibu, Dora was the Landlord.

Miklos Szandor Dora II was born in Budapest, Hungary, in 1935. His stepfather was Gard Chapin, a renowned surfer of the thirties and forties. Mickey grew up surfing empty Malibu. Greg Noll may have been christened Da Bull for his big wave charging, but Dora was Da Cat, a name awarded for his grace and style on the water. The moniker was more apt than anyone knew at the time. Dora was a loner, sometimes friendly, often charming, occasionally vulnerable, introverted, defensive, wary of new faces. He could disappear and establish a new territory. People were drawn to Da Cat, to the legend, the enigma. There was always a new board sponsor waiting in the wings to add the aura of Dora to their rider list. This, despite being known to bite the hand that fed him. He was quick to engage the services of his attorney, if he felt his image had been used without his strict authorisation, yet was happy to take paid bit parts in the Hollywood teen surf flicks that were murdering the scene. To the average surfer, it appeared that Dora never sold out. His faults were generally overlooked as he railed against what he saw as big business making a buck off the back of the ordinary surfer. He loved to say, "Thank God for a few free waves." But with Dora, the free waves often came courtesy of some other sucker's dollars.

One of Dora's cohorts from that era was John Millius, legendary filmmaker, writer of *Apocalypse Now* and director of *Big Wednesday*. He recalls, "Mickey was comfortable with the beatniks of the fifties Malibu era, but when surfing became really popular, it brought in a whole new crowd of people who he considered

Opposite top
Same as it ever was; Malibu wall.

Opposite middle
Da Cat: archetypal anti-hero.

Opposite bottom
Steely edge.

DAVID PU'U

Rincon
While Malibu was the media queen, Rincon to the north was the dark knigt, lighting up in the brooding winter swells.

bordered on Neanderthal. There were only a few of us who he considered were up to talking to." To anyone else the place was over-run; to Dora the place was over. As the post-*Gidget* era kicked in and the Malibu scene exploded, there were already those who were seeking out new territories, new places, away from the crowds and away from the limelight. The push north was on, the push into the cold.

Off Highway 101, Rincon straddles the county line between Santa Barbara to the north and Ventura to the south. The colder cousin to Malibu's summer playground, it is only truly brought to life by the brooding northwesterly and westerly swells that roll in with the chill winter months. Often referred to as the 'perfect point', it was here that the paradigm shift in surfing happened, triggering an overnight revolution. In 1968 local visionary, George Greenough, and Australian shaper, Bob McTavish, traded waves. McTavish was riding the first 'shortboard' to be put

through its paces on the American mainland. "We had pumping Rincon for weeks," says Bob. "George was on his four-foot-eight spoon and me on my eight-foot lightweight dream board. We were the only two guys in California on shortboards." It was across this canvas that a young Tom Curren honed his fluid style and flowing turns. Another reluctant icon, he would go on to claim three world titles riding the ultra-progressive boards of Santa Barbara shaper, Al Merrick. Rincon is a proving ground, a test site. It is the cutting edge.

Tucker Stevens is walking out across the rocks, hoping to hit some sand and avoid the barnacles. His balsa board is upside down, a stabiliser; he holds it with two hands as he wades in a foot of water, then out into two feet of water. He tries to sense if he is out of the rocks yet, if he is deep enough to avoid his fin snagging on the bigger boulders that lurk on the inside at Rincon Point. He wades some more before launching onto the cold Pacific. He lies flat to distribute weight,

Top: Bob Cooper; Hollister Ranch
Post surf resting on the tailgate of
Tucker Steven's 1939 Ford Woody.

Upper middle: Left turn
Kathryn Water Stevens, Hollister
Ranch boundary. "The owners of
the neighbouring Bixby Ranch
placed a barrier of cars on the
beach in an attempt to stop
surfers driving onto their beaches.
But of course, the tide came in and
moved all the cars around so we
could just drive past them."

Lower middle: Tucker Stevens
Little Drakes, The Ranch.

**Bottom: Steam Lane
Contest 1964**
"The New Zealand surf team were a
guy short so I was drafed in to surf
for them," says Tucker. "This is me
along with NZ surfer 'Ace Mowtel.'"

better for passing over hidden obstacles. Tucker is soon on his knees, two arms pulling in the cool water, trying to avoid getting too wet, too cold. Head up, he scans the waves. It is a random Tuesday in the late fifties and Tucker has Rincon Point all to himself, not another soul in sight. "There were some hot embers on the beach, so I'd collected some driftwood and got the fire going for when I came in," he recalls. "Often, when I was surfing in the winter, if I was edged too far out onto the wall, some of my friends would mock me for not getting close enough to the critical part of the wave. Hey, I didn't really want to fall off – that water was pretty cold. They'd say, 'You look boring out there.' So I said, 'I don't want to get cold.' They'd say, 'Yeah you do. You wanna get cold!'" When your crew involved the likes of Greg Noll, Rennie Yater and Dewey Weber, these were some pretty high standards to follow.

It was 1957 when Tucker Stevens started surfing. He and a friend discovered a hollow, plywood paddleboard made by Peterson and took to the waters. Having never seen any other surfers to emulate, their early exploits involved simply paddling around, they even tried standing on the board and punting it with a canoe paddle. Then, a chance meeting with John Severson, surf filmmaker and soon-to-be founder of *Surfer Magazine*, changed everything. Severson showed them film footage of guys surfing waves and the penny dropped. "All of a sudden we realised what we were doing wrong and we got really involved with surfing," he explains. "When I started, there were about nine surfers in the Santa Barbara area; by 1958 there were probably about fourteen."

Tucker is a bona fide cold water soul. There are those that probably consider surfing in this part of California as a pretty comfortable existence. For Tucker and his crew, in the pre-wetsuit era, surfing was an undertaking that took some serious application. "We would surf year-round, summer, winter, whenever there was surf. We would surf in just with our bathing suits, that's all," he explains. "The water would be around fifty-five degrees (12°C) and you kinda just got used to it." The key, however, to a decent length session was the avoidance of total immersion for as long as feasibly possible; the buoyancy of the longboards that sat high on the water line helped the cause. "Because our surfboards were so big – they were nine-foot-six – you tried to stay out of the water as you paddled out. You would paddle out on your knees, then when you hit a wave you would stand on your board to go over it. You could surf for about thirty minutes, then you'd go in, build a fire on the beach and go back out as soon as you were warm."

For the fledgling crew, it became hard to differentiate between the surfers when watching from the shoreline, to work out just who was getting the best rides. They came up with an ingenious idea. "You'd try to make a bathing suit that would be an unusual colour, so that everybody could tell who you were," he explains. "If you saw the bathing suit, you'd say, 'Oh, that's Tucker,' or Greg Noll – he had the black-and-white zebra trunks – so you could tell your friends by what they were wearing. This would

be Greg, Velzy, John Severson, Hobie Alter; they were the people we'd go surfing with." For the Santa Barbara guys, surfing was a year-round endeavour; on this part of the coast, often the best swells would coincide with the coldest times. "We would surf every month of the year," says Tucker. "Water temperatures could be as low as fifty Fahrenheit (10°C). We had this wonderful cold water existence, no wetsuits and we just loved what we were doing. We had the Rincon Beach, which was a public beach, and then we had the Hollister Ranch, which was closed to only fifty surfers. I was one of the fifty."

Covering an area the size of Santa Barbara, the Hollister Ranch was a farm that wound its way north. There was pristine, unspoilt coastline with only a few dirt tracks traversing it, over ten miles of beaches, reefs and points, and no one to surf them. The Santa Barbara crew would head up the coast onto the beach at the Ranch, and just drive. But the surf boom was coming; they could feel it in the air, like the crackle before an electrical storm. They saw what was happening at the old Malibu Ranch down the coast and wanted to keep the Hollister for the Santa Barbara crew. "At first, to go to the Hollister Ranch was no problem, you just drove there," Tucker explains. "Nobody would stop you, no problem. Then somebody thought, 'you gotta find a way to close it down,' so Arlen Knight talked to the owner. Dr Hollister said, 'Put a lock on my gate; if you form a club then you may go into the Ranch.' We told him we'd keep it at a membership of fifty people. We started out with twenty-five, then by 1960 the membership was full." Arlen became the enforcer. It was surf elitism and door policies, separating the mainstream from the core, the locals from the 'incomers', order from disorder. Breaches of rules could see you thrown out of the club; at the very least, you'd get a visit. In reality it was almost self-regulating. They knew that this was something to be cherished and respected, that

Card carrying member
Only members of the SBCSC had access to the Hollister Ranch and the miles of beaches, reefs and points hidden there, away from prying eyes. For a California surfer, there was no more sought after ticket.

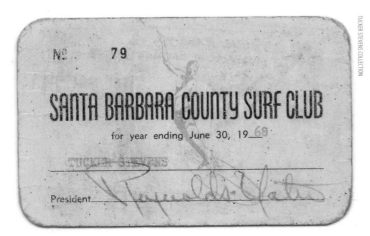

No 79

SANTA BARBARA COUNTY SURF CLUB

for year ending June 30, 19 69

TUCKER STEVENS

President

DAVID PU'U

access to this wonderland was a privilege. While the landowner may have been happy to accommodate a small band of well-behaved surfers, a mass invasion would result in the place being locked down. They certainly didn't want to see their privileges revoked.

These were the halcyon days. They would drive out to the Ranch, take their sleeping bags and stay for the weekend, build their own driftwood shacks on the beach. "Then we were able to sleep in a bit more comfort. It was like a Disneyland. You'd drive a hundred yards and you'd find a surf break, then another hundred yards, another surf break, and so on." Getting a pass into the Hollister Ranch became one of the most sought-after things for a California surfer. "We had a waiting list of 200 people. Then it opened up to seventy-five members. Membership was twenty-five dollars a year; it went to a hundred dollars a year! We were allowed to take one guest, because if you wanted to take your wife or girlfriend,

they wouldn't be members of the club." If you were one of the faces, you might get an invite; the best surfers in the state could regularly be found in small groups, sharing waves on the Ranch.

The guys from the Santa Barbara Surf Club knew the dream would one day crumble and that, quite possibly, the Hollister Ranch would too – this was prime real estate on a blossoming California coast. "We knew Dr Hollister's heirs would not want to keep it closed," explains Tucker. "They'd want to make money out of it. When he passed on, the Ranch went to the heirs, and they started selling these parcels of land, a hundred-acre increments, for a hundred thousand dollars each." Surfers pitched in together to buy lots, meaning membership of the Ranch and, ultimately, the right to surf the waves. The subject of the commodification and ownership of a wave, where private access is paid for by the privileged few, is a contentious, complex global issue. But back in the early sixties, the Ranch was simply the playground of a group of surfers who'd charge the cold, empty peaks.

"I don't know how I surfed in that cold water," says Tucker, casting his mind back to the days before wetsuits. "I just had to turn my mind off, just like when I was in the army. We'd go for a surf, stay in for twenty minutes or so, then warm ourselves up by the fire, telling lies about how great our waves had been," he laughs. The advent of the surfing wetsuit was a slow process and many were reluctant converts to the cause, feeling the small gains in warmth were compromised by the lack of mobility afforded by the rigid garment. "Old wetsuits, they were really cumbersome," recalls Tucker. "They went over your legs, your head, we thought they'd inhibit your surfing too much; we didn't want anything to do with that. One of the surfers from Los Angeles came up and showed us this suit, it was called a beaver tail, where you would wear a wetsuit for the top part of your body and you would have a flap like a diaper. We said, 'We could do that,' because your legs and your arms weren't so inhibited." One of Tucker's extended circle was a certain Jack O'Neill. "Jack was an inventive guy. He would make these prototype wetsuits and say, 'Try this, see if you like it.' We'd give them a go and often we'd tease him because some of the wetsuits started turning pink and green and yellow when we went in the sea. There was another guy in Santa Barbara called Don 'The Wetsuit'; he was also making them. Back then they were extremely thick: a quarter of an inch. I was never a wetsuit guy, because they were so hard to put on. We'd have to buy baby powder and then either put it in the wetsuit or on the top halves of our body just to be able to get them on. But Jack found a way to make them thinner and better." The time of braving the chill armed with nothing but a sturdy pair of shorts and a driftwood fire was coming to an end. The wetsuit era had begun, and surfing would never be the same.

Jack O'Neill was born in Denver Colorado in 1923. He moved to San Francisco in 1949 and, having developed a love of the ocean, could often be found body surfing in the frigid shore break at Ocean Beach. In 1952 he opened up the original Surf Shop, selling balsa boards and wax. The surfing population was tiny at that point, but O'Neill kept his store going until he relocated to Santa Cruz in '59, at Cowell's Beach near Steamer Lane. Jack's overriding passion was to find a way to stay in the chilly waters for as long as possible, and that meant experimenting with new materials for surfing jerseys and wetsuits. "When we first started making wetsuits, they used to laugh at us," admits Jack, "but then they could see the first in with the wetsuit was the last out. First in, last out. That was my philosophy. I just wanted to surf longer."

There were already wetsuits out there. Divers had already taken the plunge in their quest to explore the deep, but their suits were rigid and built for warmth not movement. "Because of the heaviness and how restrictive they were, you couldn't really go out and surf in them, " says John Hunter, Head of Design and Product Development at O'Neill Wetsuits. "You were basically in prone position, wiggling your feet." The needs of the surfer were different; it was all about keeping the flow, engaging with the energy and having the ability to respond to it. "Jack's original thing was to come up with materials that not only allowed you to be in the water longer but also allowed some movement." Initial experiments with wool jerseys proved unfruitful; the tops quickly filled with water becoming heavy and, ultimately, did little to keep the cold at bay. New ideas needed to be explored. "One of the first neoprene-like materials that Jack came up with was foam out of an airline seat. He customised that into a vest. It was thick but the insulating factors of that – even though it's just a vest – meant he was able to jump

Research and Development
"Part of my deal is not just designing, but I spend a lot of my time in the water actually testing the wetsuits," explains John Hunter who has been invloved in O'Neill wesuit design since '82.

off the cliff here at The Lane and stay out there for like an hour-and-a-half, where most people were doing a fifteen- or twenty-minute session."

In putting up barriers to the cold, the door to surfing's new frontiers had been thrown wide open. The wetsuit expanded people's minds to the surf potential of the planet, pushed their physical limits and opened up the possibilities for year-round surfing, enticing those who may not have otherwise endured the cold to put a toe in the water. As surfers, we take neoprene for granted. Most can't remember a time before this foamy, black material cloaked our world in an insulating blanket of air pockets and microscopic cells. "The primary insulator used in the world today is air. Think windows, home construction," says John. The first neoprene was rigid, less flexible. "It had some air in it but, because there was less than we use today, it needed to be worn a little bit thicker," he explains. "Neoprene is waterproof. As the years have gone by, we've worked out the proper amount of air cells in the neoprene that conduct the most amount of heat but then also give you a decent amount of durability." It's about formulating Nasa-like equations, striking the right balance between warmth, stretch, softness and durability. John has seen a lot of advances over the last two decades, quantum leaps in wetsuit technology in a relatively short period. "We're working on some really futuristic stuff, but it's still a bit down the road – for example solar, or other things that I can't really talk about. Today, there are times when I'm out there on the road, testing the product, and I have to let some water in to cool off," says John. "It's incredible to be able to go out into those conditions and be toasty; now it's more like getting changed is the issue, 'I don't wanna get out of my wetsuit – it's cold.'"

I opened my eyes at one point to try to orientate myself and it was just pitch black. It just seemed like forever. I was just like, 'well, I'm doing OK just holding my breath, but if the next wave is bigger, I'm going to be in trouble.' It was definitely the longest hold down of my life. I had a guy call me today that was doing water patrol rescue, and he said, 'I can't believe that.

That was the most crazy thing I've ever seen in my life.'" Zach Wormhoudt is recalling a wipe-out he took at Mavericks, the world-renowned California big wave spot, where he is one of the most respected regulars in the line-up.

Zach wears many hats. Father, brother, XXL-winning big wave charger and a guy who is quietly shaping the world of skateboarding from his office in Santa Cruz. Zach's dad, Ken, built his first skate park, Derby Park, in Santa Cruz in 1974. This was the era of Dog Town and the Z-Boys, the time of Tony Alva, Jay Adams, Stacey Peralta and Santa Monica's Zephyr skate shop; it was the time of Rich Novak and Santa Cruz skateboards. Sidewalk surfing was about to pass from the realm of the disaffected grom into the mainstream; it was about to go global. Zach's life took an abrupt change of direction when his father passed away. "I was doing an O'Neill Europe tour in Belgium and we were teaching kids how to surf, and I got a call that my father was sick and probably wasn't gonna make it," he explains. "I ended up jumping straight into the business and taking it over. I went from surfing full time to managing a business full time and trying to keep it going." Today Wormhoudt Incorporated is the leader in its field, acclaimed designers and builders of skate parks across the globe. Derby Park, with its snake lines and concrete bowl, remains the oldest public skate park still operating in the world.

Growing up in Santa Cruz, Zach thinks it was inevitable that he would get into surfing. "They have the junior lifeguard programmes here; my parents kind of treated it like summer school for us," he explains. "Growing up in Santa Cruz you had to do junior lifeguards whether you liked it or not. Fortunately we liked it. That was probably the major factor in getting myself and my friends in tune with the ocean at an early age, maybe like five, six, seven years old."

Right: Zach Wormhoudt, 30 minutes south of SFO
"There's 30 to 40 guys out on a day that's forecast, that's been going on for 8 to 10 years. Almost the crowd's now are more dangerous than the waves. There's a lot of risks just surfing Mavericks, so if you throw in a whole bunch of more risk by guys potentially raining down on you when you're going down the line, you can see why some people are kind of done with it."

Opposite: Shades of Zach Wormhoudt
Steamer Lane to Derby Park.

Right: Santa Cruz Blues

Opposite: Richard Schmidt, Santa Cruz
Everyone needs a role model – someone to bust down the door. Richard Schmidt was the man who inspired the men who are currently the most inspirational big wave riders today. "There were so many really talented surfers, guys like Richard Schmidt," says Zach Wormhoudt of his home town surf scene. "The kind of guys that were the cutting edge surfers on a much bigger scale than just Santa Cruz; for all of surfing."

The set-up at Steamer Lane looks as though it has been lifted straight from some how-to surf manual. There's a natural hierarchy, a natural route of growth and advancement up the point, always pushing, always promising new challenges, always just that little bit out of your comfort zone. "The way The Lane works, all the way down to Cowell's, through Indicators, it's such a perfect progression," Zach explains. "There's a world-class beginners wave through to a pretty big wave spot, through one point. That was a big factor. If I'd learned at a normal beach break, things might have turned out a bit different, but the fact that you could always see a bigger wave out the back, a little bit further up the point, set it up so that you're always day-dreaming about going out a little further. And then, actually progressing – that was pretty cool."

"There were such good waves during the winter that we were just captivated; there was no stopping us," recalls Zach. "It was cold, it was tough. Just to bike home after surfing, your fingers would freeze. It was torture, the whole deal where you can't button your jeans when you get dressed, your hands are too frozen, or you can't turn the key in your car. When we were kids, that cold factor was tough. It didn't stop us but we definitely paid into it dues wise." But as well as conditions to challenge, surfers need a figure to look up to – be it in the form of a poster pulled from a magazine and taped to a bedroom wall, a favourite sequence on a well-worn DVD or in the flesh – something to push their waveriding. "There were so many really talented surfers who were five, ten, fifteen years older than us, guys like Richard Schmidt and Vince Collier, the kind of guys that were the cutting-edge surfers on a much bigger scale than just Santa Cruz – for California, for all of surfing. We were surrounded by so much talent that it was just inspiring. It influenced us more than we

Ken 'Skindog' Collins
Trying to outrun an avalanche and
the inevitable.

realised at the time. We thought, 'Wow these guys are ripping,' but now I look back and little did we know just how hard they were ripping. The bar that we were looking at was way higher than we thought. This wasn't just the best guys on this side of town; they were world class."

Today, Mavericks is revered as one of the most hardcore and best big waves spots in the world. The fact that so many of the chargers out there hail from the Santa Cruz area is no coincidence. "Most people get to surf eight to ten feet, but it's a big jump to then go surf twenty foot," says Zach. "To surf at Santa Cruz, it sets you up as you can surf twelve-foot waves, fifteen-foot waves; it helps your transition. That was my experience." The fact that the set-up in town provides so many aspects present at Mavs certainly helps.

"It's cold water, bit of a shark factor, big waves, rocky coastline, wind, it's like the ultimate big wave training ground," he explains. Then he pauses, as if remembering just what it feels like to take that drop, chase that giant wall. "But to be honest, practise all you want, wherever you want, there's nothing like catching a wave at Mavericks."

For Zach, there is nothing that compares to dropping over that ledge, into the pit at Half Moon Bay. The rocks, the deep, the cold and, now, the crowds. A potentially deadly mix. But it's the cold that seems to bring the most challenging element, as if altering the very molecular structure of the water. "The years I've surfed Waimea, that's where I've noticed the biggest contrast," he explains. "The water feels less dense. When you wipe out it feels lighter; it still can be brutal, just as deadly, but it definitely has a different feel to it the warm water. I know a lot of guys from Hawaii who say, 'I'd surf Mavs but that whole cold water thing is too much.' It's true, you're only adding a few millimetres of wetsuit but you're compromising so much flexibility that if you put on a pair of six mil booties, you're giving away a lot in terms of surfability and dexterity. For me, it's not always just a matter of keep layering up. I try to surf Mavs in the thinnest suit possible, just to be as loose as possible. But it's a trick to pull off. I think that's one of the hardest things to figure out. Sometimes I'll sit for ten minutes when I get there and try to work out what thickness of wetsuit to wear. There so much paddling, it can get tiring if you've got too thick a suit on. But then a lot of suit is nice for coming back to the surface."

Having surfed Waimea, Todos Santos and tow-surfed up at Nelscott Reef, Mavericks is still pretty much at the apex of big wave surfing for Zach. "It's so gnarly. I have a lot of good friends who film up there for a living and they're always telling me, 'Dude, the wave's just so gnarly. I can't believe it.' And I say, 'Yeah but you've been filming it for 15 years, quit saying it ,'and they say, 'But it's true. I can't believe it. How loud it is. It's going right through the rocks, every wave.' Every time you go out there, it's totally breathtaking how heavy a wave it is. A really bad wipe-out can either chip away at your confidence or it can make you feel somewhat invincible – which is probably not a good idea because you're not, obviously. It can pump you up or it can just as easily send you to the hospital. The sport is so weird – I can't believe what people do, to tell you the truth, all the things people are doing: making it and not making it and coming back for more."

The silver ocean is oily and slick. The boat cuts through the calm, a gentle rising pitch, the wind off the bow creating a refreshing breeze as the sun fights the high cloud. Fifteen miles to port, the coast of Alaska makes for a hazy green margin, a low dark edge to the bright sea. Mount Edgecumbe is visible, white and gleaming, marking the way home. Some trips see the wind so bloated with rain, or the air so thick with fog that the volcanic peak slips by

Reasons to be fearful 1,2,3
Cold, sharky, local.

unseen as they motor into the sound, but today is a rare bluebird morning. Looking out from the deck, a dark shape is visible, a large fin rising above the surface. A shark? Its progress seems slow. They turn the wheel, curious, divert the fishing boat to check it out. Getting closer, an idea begins to take hold. The engine kicks into idle as the boat glides alongside. It is a jumbled mass of Neptune's beard and dark scribbles of matted life but sticking out of the back, a large glass fin. They lean over and heave the heavy object aboard. It must weigh over a hundred pounds. Dumping it on the deck, they stare down. It is a floating colony of life, a slick of seaweed stubbled with clusters of barnacles. Somewhere in there is the rarest of migratory creatures: one born in Ventura, California; one that escaped the clutches of Rincon Point, that has traversed the open seas for over twenty years, rounded the jagged peaks of Hawaii and ridden the Japan Current north, heading for the cold. Somewhere, beneath this leafy coat, lies a surfboard. The first surfboard they'd seen. "Now what are you going to do with that?" asks the friend.

"They brought it by my house and asked me if I could glass it," explains Charlie Skultka, recalling the day in the early 1980s that would change his life. Charlie lives in Sitka, Alaska, a small town of over eight thousand people, nestled in an inlet off the Pacific coast. At the time, he was working in a boat yard, so he knew his way around fibreglass. "After stripping all that crap off and cleaning it up a bit, the board itself was pristine," he says, "but the ends were worn through. I dried it off for about two or three weeks, got it down to about thirty pounds; it seemed to be pretty dry inside, so I glassed the thing up. The board is a nine-foot-six Tiki pop-out surfboard with a huge clear glass bi-plane fin on the back. It has a baby blue gel coat bottom that wraps up around the rail with the same coloured blue racing

Alaskan gold rush

TANE SKULTKA

Charlie Skultka, Sitka
"I just finished skinning the deck and bottom with locally cut and air dried Alaskan red and yellow cedar. I'm gonna throw on two thin pinstripes of alternating red and yellow cedar and then its ready for solid yellow cedar rails and some shaping and glassing. It should finish up around 8'6". I'm really looking forward to getting this one wet."

Opposite top
Mountain white.

Opposite middle
Into the blue.

Opposite bottom
Air borne.

stripes on either side of the stringer. It has no leash plug and a real cool Tiki man logo towards the tail that was barely legible. It sat around my house for about a month."

A few hardy souls had been sneaking to the area for waves since the mid sixties and Charlie had heard of the places they'd been. Having seen surfing on TV, he figured he had a good idea how it was done; he decided, why not give it go. "I dragged the board down to the beach and I caught my first wave and rode it all the way to the beach," he says. That first wave had Charlie hooked. The only problem now was that every time he tried to get to his feet he fell off. "It took a lot of skill to finally learn how to turn the damn thing." When it came to wetsuit technology, Charlie found his options were about as modern as his newfound board. "For a wetsuit I had a summer john with a beaver tail," he laughs. "It didn't fit very well, so I had to cut the arms off, so that I could paddle. Then I would put the sleeves on my arms for some warmth." Initial forays to the one local beach with a swell window were solo missions, but soon Charlie had an accomplice. "I surfed for two or three months before my brother-in-law started coming out with me. It took him a while to get a board and stuff, but he took his honeymoon in Hawaii and brought one back with him."

The fledgling surf community in Sitka was met by puzzlement and incredulity. "When we first started surfing, they all thought we were nuts," explains Charlie. "I remember one early time I went out, it was a pretty good swell and a cop car and an ambulance turned up at the beach. They were so certain I was gonna get hypothermia that they stood by for about a half hour. One of them was on the beach. When I rode all the way in, they told me they were there to save me. I told them I was alright and after twenty minutes they left." For most of the local population, entering the water willingly seemed crazy; after all, this was Alaska; the majority spent a lifetime trying to stay out of the water. "It took about a decade for people to realise it was safe to go in the water. The number one killer of Alaskan commercial fishermen was the simple fact that most of them didn't know how to swim. Because of the water temperature, they never really spent much time in the water. Here in Sitka, it's a requirement in school that you cannot graduate unless you learn how to swim. That's made a difference to how people view surfing."

Charlie takes a step back and looks down the plan shape, lifting the tail, studying the subtle shadows cast on the base, following the smooth contours with his gaze. He is in his workshop at the Cultural Centre in Sitka; a warm rosy glow cocoons the room. Outside, there is a steely blue to the cold. "The hardest part was finding the wood," he says. "There's no balsa up here, so I decided to use red cedar and yellow cedar. Then, finding planks that were ten feet long was kind of an issue. I work here in the culture centre doing native metal work. Across the hall there, the guy is a totem pole carver and he just happened to have some long lengths of cedar, so we milled it down." The board already looks like a work of art, something to be cherished. "We've seen the red and yellow cedar used before; there are several people in the area who do wooden kayaks, and when it's been glassed, it does look nice." His first board, the Tiki, had been a long-term partner, his companion through many experiences and many adventures, and he rode it for about ten years before looking for an upgrade. "That was kind of like stepping out of a Volkswagen into a Lamborghini," he smiles. "It was amazing, the first board I bought; it turned when I wanted it to; you were able to manoeuvre it; it was just a real learning experience." But Charlie still has that Tiki board. "Overall it surfed well, once it got rolling, but took every

ounce of energy and careful planning just to make a successful bottom turn. If you could master one of these babies, you could probably surf on anything. It still has no leash, most people say it belongs in a museum, but I feel it really needs to be restored and surfed again. A boat in the harbour is safe, but that's not what boats are made for."

The landscape is cloaked here, a thick blanket of richly verdant rainforest smothers the contours of the peaks and lines the sounds to the high-water mark. Such dense foliage and a rugged landscape mean getting around by car is limited to a network of only thirteen miles of road. The surfing real estate that is easily accessible is pretty limited. If you wanna get ahead, you gotta get a boat. "Life around here is pretty dry without one," explains Charlie. "We've got three boats and two cars; just about every family in town has a boat, or access to one." With just one surf spot in town that works maybe twenty or thirty times a year, boating in to the breaks is standard. The Pacific side of Kruzof Island is the destination for many of their voyages. "The only way to get there is by boat or by sea plane," says Charlie. Striking the right balance of swell is crucial. "That's a big issue – it's often too big. As you head out into the sound, it's less and less protected; there's been quite a few times when I've paddled out and looked over the shoulder and paddled right back to the boat – it was just too big: surf or die kind of stuff."

For most, do or die is a slogan, a motto to stoke the fire, a mantra to push them into more challenging situations. Up here, get things wrong and it's a very real possibility. "I almost drowned out there several times," Charlie explains. "It's totally different: there's no peanut gallery on the beach, there's no lifeguards, there's nobody out there but the people that you bring. If you were to get into trouble… I remember one

NICK LAVECCHIA

Alaskan Highway
Twin outboards.

day I did lose my board and I drifted probably five or six miles down the island. I was coming up on the last beach where I could make it ashore and was on my way out when I spied my board in the same rip. I got on to the beach and had to walk for about three hours to get back to the camp. When I got back to the camp, my brother-in-law was there and they thought I drowned. They saw me take the tumble and that was it, that's all they saw. After I ate crap, I was in the soup bouncing around; as I got closer to the beach, the tide was ripping and it was on an outgoing tide: the closer I got to the beach, the faster I was going out. On that particular island, it has an extinct volcano, Mount Edgecumbe, and, on the outside, it's all lava reef, so there's a lot of sheer walls and stuff, lava flats that we surf on. There's only a few places to get ashore there. I actually panicked for about three seconds, then I realised, 'I'm in a wetsuit, I'm not going to sink.' I just started swimming sideways with the current, aiming towards the shore and, eventually, made it." Not that this brush with death kept Charlie out of the water. "I was back out there after we'd camped."

Though some people call this part of Alaska the 'banana belt', it is a relative term. "Years ago, I had to have a push-button installed on the dash of my Chevelle because when I got back to the car I didn't have the finger strength to actually hold the keys in the crank position," explains Charlie. In the biting cold, it takes more than an iron will to see you through. You need tactics. "When we surf the winter months, sometimes we bring thermoses of hot water to pour down your suit. Surf for a couple of hours, go to the beach, pour hot water down your suit, that'd give you another hour of surfing." Chasing waves is a year-round pursuit here. "If you waited for all the good days to go out, you wouldn't surf very much," says Charlie. "A lot of times we're surfing in the rain, snow, hail and, occasionally, we get a

Top: Grizzly
"On a surf trip, when we do go ashore up here we definitely bring a gun. Sometimes several. Some guys will bring bear mace. Other guys will rely on what we call dinner bells – or bear bells. These little tinkly bells. There used to be a joke up here 'How do you tell if it's bear shit? Bear shit has the bells in it." Charlie Skultka.

Bottom: Alaskan Byway
4WD.

Opposite: Yakutat
Peaks, trees, lines.

few days in the sunshine; it doesn't happen very often but, when it does, it's really a treat." It may seem like surfing in Alaska is just about as extreme as waveriding could get. There's the cold, the bears and the fact that every surf trip is truly an expedition into the wild: a full-on adventure. "In Hawaii, every time they have an epic north swell it's left-overs from here; the closer you get to the source, the heavier it gets. Winds can bring down trees, seas can be roving mountains. No wonder they call those north swells the Aleutian Juice." But, for Charlie, there is a something about Alaska that goes beyond the vistas, the wild landscape, the passing killer whales, the sea otters, the eagles and the towering elegance of the Sitka spruce, or, perhaps, it is a combination of all of these factors. "Everybody needs to come to Alaska at least once," he says. "It's really unique; it'll change your life – or at least the way you look at it."

NICK LAVECCHIA

Vancouver Island

TIM NUNN

Stop!" I screeched to a halt, pulling over to the side of the road. "There," said Richie. Looking through the side window, across the shiny tarmac, nestled in a small dip: Twin City Auto Parts. It was a huge expanse of metallic carnage, a graveyard of vehicles disfigured and destroyed, blinded faces glimpsed through razor wire, rust bleeding into the rich soil. A beige Chevy Blazer, laid to rest beneath a pile of orange drums; no more school runs, no more fishing trips. An old Toyota Land Cruiser waiting for attention, a pile of assorted wings and fenders resting on its hood. I wondered whether it would still start. Probably. Here was a scene of automotive devastation, like a vehicular battlefield after the great war. Cadavers left to the carrion crows.

We had been on the island for over a week, our senses had been overawed by the vistas, the huge swathes of perfect coastline, the virgin forest, the green. The valleys had unfolded as we travelled, waterfalls spilled spray across the roadside, glassy lakes like fields of chrome. Yet here was something that jarred, that demanded our attention. It seemed so at odds with the sights and sounds of Vancouver Island. But why? For this isle is not a biome, a bubble, a stage where sea eagles and killer whales perform on cue, or sand is swept clean by an army of unseen stagehands. It is a living, breathing, functioning place, with jobs and initiative and industry. It is a functioning society, not an idyll from a brochure. Richie jumps out into the rain, grabbing his camera bag. He focuses on the ugly yard, beneath the lofty cedars; it is the perfect dichotomy. "We would be a tourist board's nightmare," he says with a smile. "We always find the interesting stuff." He begins to set up his tripod as the drizzle intensifies.

Point in Time
A moment of clarity.

I slands are one of the few places in life where you literally reach the end of the road. Go far enough and you will run out of places to turn. You'll run out of options. Jay Bowers turns off the engine. There hadn't been much of a road to start with, just the broken rubble of a logging trail that cut through the towering cedars. But it stops without warning and ahead lies nothing but dense forest. For the last half an hour the pick-up has been bumping down a rutted track, heading to a rendezvous with purpose, a point in time: a right point. Then the road ran out, like a wrong turn, as if the forest had simply taken back what rightfully belonged to it. The intense green spreads as far as the eye can see, graduating into a silver grey as it reaches the horizon. There is no path or trail to guide the way forward. Occasional white patches of mist cling trapped in the treetops, like kites snagged in the branches, pulled and stretched by the wind before breaking free and spinning off into the ether. To the east, steep mountains disappear into the clouds, the coastal plain to the west sweeps for miles before ending abruptly at the boiling fringes of the Pacific. Everywhere is smothered by huge, living architectural masterpieces. These trees can rise over two hundred feet, concealing hundreds of densely packed rings stretching back to the times before any European set foot on these shores. The sun breaks through the clouds for the first time in a week and Jay begins slipping and clambering over the immense fallen trunks and through the dense undergrowth. There is a deep rumbling echo of the ocean, yet no sense from where it emanates. There is a base smell that underlines the forest. The smell of damp cedar pervades everything. It is the smell of Vancouver Island. Scrambling to the bottom of a steep bank Jay stands silhouetted by the sun on the fringe of the forest, breaking through the last branches and out onto the rounded, volcanic boulders that line the point; pupils constrict, eyes adjusting to the sudden brightness. A sudden moment of clarity – there it is.

Vancouver Island has come a long way. In fact, it's come all the way from the South Pacific. Over the millennia it steamed in a northeasterly direction until it finally careered into Canada's western coastline. The impact caused the mainland's Pacific seaboard to buckle and crumple, forcing up a mountain range that is now home to the legendary powder fields of Whistler and Blackcomb. The two-hundred-and-eighty-mile long geological battering ram has recoiled to rest just off the coast, clothed in dense forest, shrouded under a hanging mist. The ferry crossing reveals a snow-capped ridge

Below
Douglas fir and western red cedars preside over the isle.

Opposite top
Moving in dark spaces.

Opposite bottom
Beneath the waves.

that tops out at seven thousand two hundred feet, a cool white line, stark against the green, bisecting the island into a rain-drenched western coastline and dryer eastern shore. The Pacific side is riven with deep fjords, inlets and bays, the vast temperate rainforest spilling off the land out onto myriad rocky headlands and low-lying islets. Dark sand crescents are squeezed between waves of blue from the vast, angry ocean and towering walls of Douglas fir and western red cedar. The Pacific coastline seldom sleeps. It is swell rich and surf drunk. A belligerent westerly flow brings moisture-rich weather patterns spawned over the sea. Winter sees the vast open plains of this great ocean roamed by outraged depressions that vent concentrated energy at the shoreline's passive stance. The dark seasons bring the personal encounters of raging storms, as well as those sweet long-distance pulses of groomed groundswell that arrive like a whispered apology. Aleutian lows skulk in the Gulf of Alaska, dominating the cold months, while fast-moving coastal lows spin towards the shore, drawing in the cold northerly air as they rapidly intensify. These swift storms may deepen quickly into malevolent gales within hours, transforming the ocean with sideways rain and violent squalls. Summer ushers in a quieter time, temperatures rise into the twenties, small waves roll ashore onto the sandy bays punctuated by the occasional lined southwesterly. 'Fogust' can be a misty and hazy month, while the fall strikes a perfect balance, with warmer waters and plentiful waves.

Relief maps of Vancouver Island show swathes of green, unblemished by the purposeful meanderings of red streaks. Major roads are few and far between. The spinal scrawl of the Nineteen wends its weary way up the east coast from Nanaimo to the northern outpost of Port Hardy; the Four traverses the interior, winding through valleys and leaning to run a finger in glassy lakes before making a ruler-straight dash

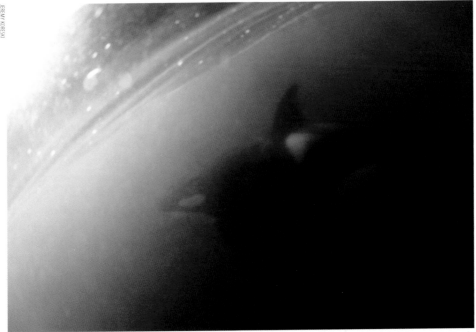

Top
Vanouver City Scape.

Upper middle
Sunrise ignites Ucluelet skies.

Lower middle
Plane view.

Bottom
Still waters.

along the western coastline of the Pacific Rim National Park into Tofino. Tourist destination, surf town and home of luxury beachside lodges, Tofino is a crown perched casually atop four square miles of the verdant peninsula, home to a population of less than two thousand. The humid rainforest, freed from exploitation, acts as a natural break on the town's growth rings. Forty kilometres to the south, Ucluelet has traditionally worn a collar of a darker shade of blue than its close cousin, but the tourist boom is precipitating a change of tone. The town has roots planted in the seal fur trade of the 1870s, nourished by whalers, fishermen and lumberjacks that followed. This area is the homeland of the Yu-cluth-aht, the Ucluelet First Nation, casting a watchful eye over the expanse of Barkley Sound, but the influx of holidaymakers and second home-owners is seeing a proliferation of new builds and new boundaries. Between these two poles stretch twenty-six miles of towering old-growth, vast open beaches, mountain backdrops, cougars, killer whales, black bears and white water.

Showers, drizzle, sleet, hail, snow, fog, mist and condensation: this can be a wet place, the wettest in the whole of North America, with up to two hundred and sixty inches of precipitation falling, mostly through the autumn and winter seasons. If you call this shore home, you have to learn to love the rain. "I remember once it rained non-stop for a whole month. That was a bit of a strain." Krissy Montgomery is leaning on the counter of the bright, modern, glass-fronted boutique, as another dark squall blows down Campbell Street. Surf Sister is an archetypal Tofino success story, a thriving girls' surf school, café, hang-out and focal point. "We always expect rain in the winter," she explains. "At this time of year the most popular shoes around here are gum boots." This section of the main drag into town reflects the multifaceted prism that is modern surf culture. On the western side sits the girls' emporium: bright rails, hibiscus decor and the smell of fresh coffee grinds. On the opposite side of the road is the traditional wooden slat building that houses Long Beach Surf Shop: old skateboards fill the walls, racks are loaded with shiny white foam, the smell of neoprene and coconut wax fills the air – geographically close, culturally distant. "Surf Sister was started back in 1999 by local surfer Jenny Stewart," explains Krissy. "Jenny would give lessons on a weekend and take small groups of people out. They would come over here from Vancouver to try surfing. Today we take bookings all through the year, even in the winter. I mean if it's a poor season for snow in the ski resorts, we get busier, as a lot of people decide to come down to Tofino to give surfing a try instead."

Beneath the shiny façade of the store displays and warm spotlights beats a heart of pure stoke. The women surfers of Tofino are a hard-core crew. Up to a third of the bodies in the line-up are girls, not that you'd really notice. With the whole pack encased head to toe in democratic neoprene, the jostling peaks are a competitive place, no quarter given, none asked. "The thing about the girls who surf here is that they are really committed and serious surfers," says Krissy. "It's too cold to kind of just hang around the beach. The girls here surf year-round and the advances in the design of girls' wetsuits mean it's easier to do that. The standard of surfing is getting quite high here too. Put us in some warm waves, like on a nice point break and we can certainly hold our own." The concept of women surfing in these frigid waters is not new; what's different about the scene here is the way in which it has developed. Blossomed. With roots planted in the early seventies, the scene has flourished as in no other temperate surf locale. In an era when female surfers charge giant Mavericks and drop into the warping terrors of Teahupoo, the beaches of Tofino have been the arena for an

altogether quieter revolution. "After Blue Crush, it was like the flood gates opened," says Krissy, who grew up in Nanaimo, a town three hours away on the eastern side of Vancouver Island. "I got into surfing during high school. My friends and I were immersed in the snowboard and skateboard scene; it seemed like a natural progression. We first began with weekend road trips to Tofino. After high school I packed up my car and moved out here for the 'summer'… that summer never really ended."

The group of kids look up at the bewildering array of stacked ply in the Victoria lumber yard. It's 1965 and three thousand five hundred US Marines have just disembarked in a far-off land called Vietnam. "Hey, check this out," says the tallest. The air is thick with the heady scent of pine and cedar, the floor dusted with a spindrift of fine shavings. In

Island reflections
Pete Devries by the light of the camp fire a boat ride from home.

Wayne Vliet
"We used to follow the old logging tracks out to some of the isolated breaks that were secret spots and you'd hike through the woods with your board. It could be interesting if you lost your board and you had to swim in among the floating logs at high tide to get it back. These cedar logs would be smashing together."

Top
Shades of light.

Bottom
Rainbow's end: Tofino docks.

JEREMY KORESKI

RICHIE HOPSON

amongst these towering isles lies the knowledge: a stacked library of instructional sheets unravelling the mysteries of an adolescent universe and answering all important questions, from how to build a kayak to constructing your own sailboat, in step-by-step detail. "Here," says one, holding the sheets at arms' length, as if to get a better look at the sacred leaves: "How to Build a Surfboard Paddleboard." Intuitions tweaked and shins scabbed by homemade skimboards, minds expanded by finger-worn copies of *Surfer* magazine and now the means to an exciting new horizon. Soon they are armed with two heavy, hollow paddleboards and heading for the water's edge at Jordan River. To their surprise they see half a dozen surfers, bobbing out back. A silhouette is up and riding, casually leaning back as he zippers along the curl, the spilling white collapsing as the surfer turns and straight lines to the beach. As he exits the water, the kids eye up the board he is holding: bright stripes, rounded fin like a shark, shiny foam and glass glistening wet. "Wow," they all say in unison, as he saunters by, carrying the future in his hands.

"After seeing that, we quickly made a deal to get our hands on foam boards," says Wayne Vliet. He looks up from the arm of the couch where he is perched, a fifty-year-old Gibson resting on his knee. His features are obscured behind a huge white beard, yet his eyes betray the smile as he skilfully bends warm notes through subtle pressure on time-weathered frets. He is backlit, framed in a huge picture window that looks out on the glassy waters of Ucluelet Inlet and, beyond, to the verdant mountains erupting from the far shore. The wild deer grazing on his lawn give the scene an almost surreal edge. "They were still nine-and-a-half feet," he says. "This was '65. People brought them in from outside. There was a dive shop and many of the surfers up to that point were recreational divers. The dive shop, would bring in the odd surfboard, but they were not good." Wayne and his friends soon discovered the closest surf shop was in Portland, Oregon, some three hundred and fifty kilometres south, and fixed on a trip down there. "But then, almost immediately, the shortboard revolution was on," he explains. Free-thinking kneeboarder George Greenough and radical shaper Bob McTavish had condensed decades of board evolution and changed the way every surfer thought about waveriding overnight: charging shortboards with curved fins, deep in the pocket in classic California point surf. The gig was up. "We only surfed these boards a couple of years before we were chopping our boards down to keep current," explains Wayne. First he was cutting his own board down, then he was doing it for other surfers, before glassing them in the back yard. "That's how I got into shaping. Eventually we got a source for some blanks. A friend of mine brought some up from California with cloth and resin. The blanks then were big chunks, they took a lot of shaping. The first board I wanted to shape was something a little over six foot – things had gone down in size that rapidly." Winters were cold, the frigid Pacific kept at bay by rigid second-hand dive suits and a familiar resourcefulness. "We didn't have decent booties, so we had to put oversize running shoes on," explains Wayne. "We had no surf wax so we used to steal my Mum's paraffin wax and heat that up and paint it on the board so it had enough texture so you didn't slip."

The late sixties and early seventies saw surf culture wash upon these shores with visiting surfers. Sure there were dog-eared magazines, *The Endless Summer*, but in the pre-video era incomers brought new ideas, new designs and new possibilities. By 1970, Wayne had obtained a student grant to run a surf school and water rescue operation at Long Beach. "During that time we had itinerant surfers come through," he explains. "We had our little squat shack in the

Above
Port Alberni: precipitation.

Opposite
Fluid undertones.

bush and we'd see some California plates with boards on the roof so we'd go up to see what's going on. One time it was California film-maker Bud Browne, and he had some surf stars in tow – Corky Carroll and Jericho Poplar. My buddy and I played guitar and found out that Corky was a reasonable musician, so we had a jam session. Other surfers came through like Mike Purpus, one of the faces of the Hermosa beach scene." In an unspoken reciprocal agreement, a fresh influx meant a fresh place to explore, a new destination to surf and place to crash. "We went down to visit a lot of the surf buddies we'd made," explains Wayne. "All the way to San Diego, but mostly up north. Guys came from Oregon, guys from Santa Cruz – lots of guys from Santa Cruz."

The drips rain down incessantly, drumming on the Gore-Tex hood. Standing under the fringe of the old-growth cedar, looking out towards Frank Island, the dividing line is clear between the curve of North Chesterman's and the arc of South Chesterman's. It is dark in the trees, moss wraps a verdant blanket around fallen boughs, breathy smoke signals lead a broken vapour trail away in the light offshores. The swells arrive here unhindered, full of wrath and power, long fetch, Pacific-bred. The noise is relentless, like a battlefield, like a heartbeat in ears plugged against the cold. The surf isn't in Tofino or Ucluelet – you gotta get out of town, down the coast, out onto the beaches. The road into Tofino only arrived in the late fifties, linking the two settlements with Port Alberni and the outside

Above
The forest bleeds down to the water's edge offering shelter, protection, concealment.

world. Out here, shoreline shacks at Chesterman's Beach and Wreck Bay were home to the first-generation surfers and their families. Some bought parcels of land, close to the pounding sea, in the tree line, under the cedars and firs. The Nuu-chah-nulth, the First Nations who occupied these lands, considered these bays to have little to offer: the sea was rough, no safe water to launch canoes, no salmon rivers to fish. The fishermen from Tofino and Ucluelet weren't much interested in the beach, in living away from their boats. The lure of the sea drew a specific community out here: people like Jim Saddler, Ralph and Ruth Devries, Henry Nolla – surfers, artists, musicians, carpenters, wood carvers, free-thinkers. "There were a few guys around here," says Wayne. "Jim Hudnall – his daughter Jenny went on to start Surf Sister; Jim Saddler – his kids were just young then. We'd hang out at Florencia Bay, known as Wreck Bay. It was a nice beach and sunny. There was a hippy community down there too. It was in the late sixties and just at the start of the seventies; then the 'Park' kicked everybody out."

LBJ did not seek re-election. The war still raged in Vietnam under the new Nixon administration and tens of thousands of young American lives were lost by the start of the seventies. 'The Manual for Draft Age Immigrants to Canada' sold a hundred thousand copies, as the country saw an influx of those avoiding the conflict; young, mostly college educated men transplanted across the border to start new lives in Toronto, Halifax and Ontario. For some, Vancouver Island was paradise found. "The young Americans were on the road doing their Jack Kerouac thing," explains Wayne. "The Vietnam War was on, they were all leaving the US and they built a bunch of driftwood shacks down the beach. Some of them surfed. Most of those people were fairly low profile. There was maybe half a dozen that surfed. Some have said they were a fair influence, but they were pretty low profile." When the newly formed Pacific Rim National Park cleared the settlement at Wreck Bay, some moved up the coast into vacant plots for sale at Chesterman's Beach. Hand-crafted shacks, ocean side, pristine beach-front lots: it didn't take long for people to cotton on to just what was on offer on the west coast. And, with the Park limiting the land available to build on, it meant one thing: land prices were on the rise. The temptation and, sometimes, pressure to sell became strong.

The line-ups of Chesterman's, Cox Bay and Long Beach must have seemed a million miles from the bustling points of Santa Barbara, the hectic beach breaks around Santa Monica – all sun-hazed afternoon, grommets cruising the boardwalks on plastic skateboards, neon wetsuits, tight boardies and skinny tees. "There was no outlet for any product here," says Wayne. "I guess to some extent we didn't really have any role models – in the beginning we were pretty much in a vacuum. If you're tracking a similar lifestyle, your needs are similar somewhat out of practicality, so you would wear similar clothes. But, back then; we didn't have all the surf brands. The clothing industry surf wise wasn't huge – it was in its infancy. But I'd often be surprised to find some prejudice just in everyday stuff, like, if you had to go and do business at the bank, you'd get attitude, just because of the way we dressed or our long hair." In the water there was little growth in numbers. "For ten years we probably surfed with not much change in the surfing population," Wayne explains. "We would go to Cox Bay and there might only be three of us surfing. People worked at whatever: fishing boats – tourism wasn't very big then. I worked for the Park – firstly collecting all the camping fees, which was good. You got to meet all the women. Go camp fire visiting later," he says with a smile. "Carpentry has been my trade for years. It's a common one with surfers all over the globe. You can make your own hours."

The small, gravel car park is surprisingly busy in the mid-morning early winter drizzle. Paul Horscroft is already waxing his board. A transplant from the UK, Paul moved to Vancouver Island and, with a few years under his belt, he has the same vocal lilt as everyone else. "Most people here are in a six-mil suit with a fixed hood in the winter," he explains. Another truck rolls alongside. A dark figure leaps out, neoprene-clad, jogging towards the surf, board under arm. This is no place to linger with a damp towel around your waist. Forget your hood and that first duck dive will bring that familiar grip of an ice cream headache. The ocean has a green marble translucence and a remarkably low salinity – salt water lite. "I think it's the amount of fresh water run-off from the forest," says Paul, as he sits on his board in the line-up. "From the rain." There is a clean shoulder-high swell running, fanned by off-shores. The surface of the ocean morphs from dappled excitement through to the sand-weathered matt of sea glass, indicating that the rain has eased from heavy downpour back to light drizzle. The silhouettes peppering the bay face out towards the horizon, scanning for the next set. The panorama from the water is like a jungle vista in Panama or Java, the rainforest harasses the very fringe of Chesterman's Beach. An isolated cedar stands like a watchtower near the point. A huge shadow launches into the sky, lazy wings loping powerfully as it sweeps over the line-up, its white head scanning back and forth. The eagle arcs out towards an offshore island as a blazing gold flash streaks the horizon. The sun breaks through the cloud, and the mountainous interior is splashed with sunlight. Lost deciduous trees shout their presence amongst a sea of huge evergreens, the reds, burnt oranges and browns of their broad leaves brought to life by the morning rays. Snow-capped peaks are revealed for a short, fleeting moment before the clouds descend and the scene fades once more to muffled grey.

From an eclectic domain of beachside shacks, Chesterman's now finds itself home to some of the most sought after and expensive real estate in the country. Set along the shoreline, muscled in the tree line are the huge designer homes, massive wooden boxes, glass-fronted, illuminated beacons of success and wealth that pierce the night. The rich and the famously rich reside here now. Tofino has boomed under the influx of tourism, a market eclipsing the waning vestiges of manual labour. The town is smart and clean, compact yet open and airy. The shops and boutiques betray the driving forces here.

November 2006 and the remains of the Pacific Surf School lies compressed under the weight of a red JCB, a cloud of black sooty smoke billows from its exhaust as it crabs over the flattened debris, picking through the carcass. It seems a fitting analogy for the environmental changes taking place here in Tofino as well as the changes that have taken place in the local surf scene. This crushed emporium, not a symbol of failure, but of growth. Just as the last piece of the old building comes down, Pacific Surf founder Jay Bowers explains that soon a new, bigger unit will sit here, like new growth in a forest clearing. For an island once driven by logging and fishing, the changing socio-environmental climate means tourism has taken over as the principle economic force. The resources that once drew men to exploit the landscape now draw in tourists and holidaymakers. Even the raging winter weather is marketed with 'storm watching' retreats on offer. The island's surf culture is also stretching its wings within the local economy. Surfers are no longer an embarrassment, dwelling in the shade of the fringe – it's mainstream, accepted. "Pacific Surf Co is going into its fourth season in its new digs," says Jay, just off the jet from a trip to New Zealand and Australia. "Business is going well and surfing in general here has gone through the roof! The level of surfing has

Opposite top left: Paul Horscroft
Transplanted to colder climes.

Opposite top right:
Jason Pickton
On islands large or small pulling together is the key to change. In Tofino the community banded together to campaign for and raise funding for a new skate park.

Opposite bottom
Noah Cohen.

Jay Bowers
The boulder headland is home to one of the island's best waves, but its location is guarded well. Back from the water's edge of this semi-secret spot, a small community of shacks and rough-built cabins have sprung up somewhat organically from beneath the trees, owned by local surfers looking to quell the numb between sessions and take in the wide vista as the sun sets.

Raph Bruhwiler
"Surfing on Vancouver Island is a challenge and I like it. To get to the good, far out of the way surf spots it's not easy sometimes – in a small boat, rough seas, pissing rain, fog,cold. Then when you get there: get firewood, build a big fire, keep bears away then you're ready to surf. You have to survive first then you can go surf. A lot of things can go wrong, and they have, but you learn a lot on how to be prepared for trips into the wild and to survive in the cold. There are still so many good waves to be discovered up here on the island and it's always an adventure when you set off for a trip. The fishing is good and you can live off the land, the air and water is clean, there is no one around and you're surrounded by beauty."

jumped dramatically, but it is great to see those kids taking it all to the next level. The business has also changed a lot. We have a lot of new programmes for special needs kids and young adults and are involved with a few colleges and universities to offer co-op programs for their adventure tourism sectors. I have two full-time managers that have taken over daily chores and staff." It's clear Tofino is no surfing backwater, it has developed a sophisticated scene. There are media-savvy professional surfers, backcountry free-surfing explorers, photographers and film-makers, board builders, surf schools and boutique shops. Surfing here seems to have found the common ground between tapping into the mainstream and keeping its core integrity.

This is however a community coming to terms with the spotlight of the outside world falling on its isolated piece of paradise. House prices have rocketed and property tax has followed. Accommodation is devoured by the tourist sector through the summer months, meaning a shortage for the young who work in the service industries, including surfing, a universal theme common to areas from California to Cornwall. "You can find places to let through the winter and spring," explains Jay. "But they want the space for the summer so they can capitalize on the influx of tourists. Many are forced into caravans or tents." The exploits on the 'Tiltin' Hilton' houseboat is the stuff of local legend. Surfers from as near as Vancouver and as far as Australia are also crossing the Straight of Georgia to sample what is still a pretty unique surfing experience. Not everyone is over the moon with the growth in numbers. But some take a more philosophical view. "The thing is we are not losing the magic of the area," explains Jay. "It is getting busy but it really is all inevitable. The next generation is in the water and they are killing it! One thing that has changed is the way the township looks at surfing. After the Cold

Top
Two wheels are a popular mode of surf transport on the island

Bottom
Jeremy Koreski: the other side of the lense.

JEREMY KORESKI

Above
Snow falling on cedars.

Water Classic they have finally accepted the fact that we are a solid clean industry in this town and it is not going to go away any time soon."

Pete Devries must have flashed back to himself as a skinny kid, exiting the water here at Chesterman's, driven ashore by the bone-chilling cold, shivering through the shallows, no crowd on the beach, no noise, no PA, no flags or tents. Just a short jog up the sand to home, a beach-front house with perfect views across North Chesterman's. "My dad came over from Holland and met my mom at the Wickanninish Inn," explains Pete. "They both worked there for a few years, before they bought a lot here on Chesterman's Beach back in the early seventies. It had a great view of the whole

beach. My dad surfed, so I guess it was inevitable that I would surf too." Pete's first memories of surfing are kind of hazy. From as long as he can remember it's been there; almost his first memories are standing on a boogie board, riding the white water, living on the beach, the ocean part of his summer playground. Surfing wasn't a conscious step, it was part of life. "Every year I would get an ex-rental suit that was only warm enough for the summer," he explains, "until I was twelve and I could fit into a woman's winter suit. My first real board was five-foot-four-inch Fish that I paid for with money saved from doing chores around the house" – the house that stood on Chesterman's Beach, a quiet beach, a community, a sanctuary. Today is Hallowe'en, 2009. The crowd has swelled into the hundreds, huddled on the wet sand, wrapped in heavy coats and scarves, cheering, amped, warmed by the stoke. Striding through the shallows, he waves. This morning he knocked Corey Lopez out of the semi-final of Canada's first ever WQS event. It didn't matter that just a couple of years before Lopez was considered a world title contender; this is Pete's beach. Growing up here, Devries was inspired by the performance of the Bruhwilers, brothers Raph and Sepp. There have always been good surfers here, but the Bruhwilers were the first to make the quantum leap, evolving from local stand-outs to international names. Local surf photographer Jeremy Koreski synergistically recorded the brothers, the epic waves they charged against a wilderness backdrop. At a time when magazines were hot

for the tropics, these snatched moments of cold-water poetry captured the imagination of the international psyche. Koreski's film *Numb* gave a hint at the amazing potential on offer around this Pacific coastline. Pete aimed high with a shot at the WQS Tour in 2006, boarding flights for far-off contests, the goal a berth with the elite forty-four. It's a hard slog even for seasoned pros; doing it alone, without the support of fellow countrymen along the way can be soul-destroying. Pete didn't win a heat. Today, however, the 'QS has come to him, and, as he wades ashore, he is hoisted overhead by good friends and local chargers Noah Cohen and Ole Atkey. It is a change of tide and fortune, the ultimate 'local boy done good'. Burleigh charger Jay Thompson, one of Australia's best, was the

Below
Sepp Bruhwiler.

JEREMY KORESKI

Opposite top:
Wayne Vliet shaping decisions
"We put our brains together, decided we were going to make ourselves surfboards. We went back down to the lumberyard and in the plywood section there was all these instructions about how to make a kayak, how to build a sailboat and how to build a surfboard paddleboard. So with the help of his Dad we built ourselves a couple of heavy, hollow paddleboards. We took them out at Jordan River and then we found out there was maybe half a dozen other surfers out there that had real surfboards. We quickly made a deal to get our hands on a foam and fibreglass board – but they were still 9 ½ ft."

Opposite bottom:
Raph Bruhwiler
"Taylor Steele videos started coming out when I was young and I watched those all day over and over again then I would run out to the surf and try the moves in the videos. I had no one else to push me with my surfing but the videos."

clear favourite on paper, but in the final, out in the water, Devries was unstoppable. The O'Neill Cold Water Classic Six Star Prime has gone down in the record books, a first. It is the first ASP contest in Canada, the first WQS contest won by a Canadian, an achievement that will be hailed across the Canadian mainstream press. It is certainly one of surfing's greatest upsets – the son of Chesterman's thrust into the spotlight as one of Canada's sporting heroes.

Wayne Vliet holds the blank at arms' length and looks down the stringer, then tilts the matt white foam to gaze down the rails. The booth is illuminated by the bleached glow of the neon strips. Shaping booths have a universal feel, from Hawaii to NYC. Form follows function. Only the images pinned to the walls change. "We used to follow the old logging tracks out to some of the isolated breaks, and you'd hike through the woods with your board," he says, pausing to slide his work-in-progress back into a rack next to a pea-green fish. "I remember surfing this rivermouth bank, and it wasn't working very well, and looking up the coast at a point, and the swell was wrapping in perfectly, so I decided to go up there and give it a try. Now it's a popular spot but back then very few people would surf there." The rolling points of Vancouver Island have a mythical aura. They are boulder-lined, tapering perfection. The erosion of time has left a tangled stack of cedar trunks along the high-tide mark; some snatched from the forest by rampant storms, some slipped from the ranks of huge floating rafts corralled by the logging operations, the hardy grain seemingly impervious to the weathering forces that abound in this environment. "It could be interesting if you lost your board and you had to swim in," explains Wayne. "In among the floating logs at high tide, trying to get it back. These cedar logs would be smashing together in the white water." The points are still the domain of the few. A challenge to the best, many are still closely guarded secrets. It is the beaches during the summer season that have begun to feel the pressure of numbers. "Sometimes I look at it and just drive away," he says. "Having had it pretty much to myself, it's pretty disconcerting, but, when it's good, the people are spread out. That's the thing on Long Beach, you can spread out and find your own spot, find a wave."

But Vancouver Island is over two hundred and ninety miles long and the region around Tofino and Ucluelet is but a small part. The coastline is rich with possibilities. Camping trips along the coast mean taking precautions against bears or cougars, a very real threat when venturing into the wild. Trips to offshore worlds accessible only by boat or jet ski, eating and surfing what nature supplies. "There are some fertile waters north of Tofino," explains Wayne. "A good surf partner of mine, Bruce Atkey, he was a pioneer all over this island. He did the research, got out there, did early exploration. I've been on a lot of forays with him. We did them in boats. One break we built a cabin at, and we would land the boat and drag it up the shore. We'd take off our clothes, jump in the water and haul the boat up the beach and we'd be there for a week maybe. You're at the mercy of the elements. Conditions can change quickly here. We took a guy named Lloyd Kahn along, and he was blown away. He was from Northern California – he said, 'It's a cakewalk back home compared with what you guys go through to go surfing.'" Today, north is still the buzz word, the area at the forefront of the island scene. On good swells, guys like Raph and Sepp and Pete Devries will be gone from town, away from the crowds, charging gaping barrels in splendid isolation, hollow waves where only the towering firs watch on, where the mountain backdrop frames a scene viewed only from the line-up or the boat deck. "These spots are getting a lot of exposure and they're getting quite busy," says Wayne. "We were up there one day when it was blown out from the southeast, and there was three or four boats cruising round frantically looking for spots. It's people from the Island – Tofino and Victoria." This isn't a place that welcomes the novice or the inexperienced. These waters can be cruel. "There's lots of obstacles and rocks and stuff to run into. And rough water conditions. I was amazed to see people on a jet ski bucking it back into town, and it must have been a hell pound. It doesn't strike me as a favourable mode of transport. There's not a lot of margin for error, and you're travelling alone through rough water." But then the rewards are clear. "My most memorable session is probably one that happened up the coast," says Pete. "In all the trips I've been on I've never surfed waves that good. I've never had days on trips where you just go out and get barrelled all day. The most barrels I've had in a session has been in Canada. That's the best thing in surfing, to sit in the tube and just look around, the colour of the water. The sun's behind you, look out the back and it's just the greenest green."

Vancouver Island offers so much surfing potential, from the tight line-ups at Jordan River, to the miles of empty peaks at Long Beach, to the reeling cedar points and deathly grinding reefs. Yet, in a way, it is sheltered from the true impact seen elsewhere in the surfing world. Buffered by the ferry journey from the big city, cosseted by the rainforest's embrace and wrapped in a winter chill that deters all but the true believers. "I think that the cold water weeds out the people that truly love surfing from those who only like the image of it," says Krissy Montgomery. "It's easy to sit around on a tropical beach with a bikini on and a board beside you, looking the part… but no one really wants to put on a six-mill wetsuit, boots and gloves in snow, hail or rain, unless they really love it. Our cold, remote location helps to preserve the beauty of its so for the year-round locals we have a strong bond – we're lucky to surf in pristine clean water with a backdrop of rainforest behind us. Vancouver Island, it's probably the most stunning place I've ever surfed."

JEREMY KORESKI

Below
Breathing space.

Right
The mighty have fallen.

JEREMY KORESKI

The surfer stands in the shadows of the cedars, board under arm, an outline against the ocean's green luminescence. From behind, no age is discernable, no sex or nationality is revealed by the stickerless white board. The line-up is quiet in the winter's cold, rain thrums through the canopy above and a biting chill cuts the air. The figure watches the peaks, scanning the moving water, examining the pack and the peeling walls. The ocean has a pale green glow under the dark brooding sky, the waves a chunky, heavy edginess. Suddenly the figure is off and running, throwing pulses of sand up in their wake, arrow straight towards the fizzing white water. Leaping and skipping through the first few steps, almost stalled by the resistance of the weighty shallows, the shadow launches over an approaching hurdle of foam and is suddenly free — gliding. Stroking out in the discordant current, the dark silhouette rises, before gracefully sinking beneath a pitching wave, trailing leg held high before melting into the onslaught of the emerald face. Soon they are at rest, sitting upright, bobbing on an empty peak, scanning the horizon in anticipation. On a day like today, with just a handful of souls scattered like jetsam through the curvature of the cove's green baize, one could easily be back in the early seventies, when Vietnam blazed and Paris rioted, when hand-crafted beach shacks were home to a community of artists and surfers and carpenters. When it rained so much that it could almost drive you crazy, when the roar of the sea was a relentless auditory onslaught. For all that Tofino is labelled a 'surf city', branded a 'happening place', a 'tourist draw', a few strident paces away from the parking lot transports you to a scene that has changed little over the last half a century, has lost none of its essential magic and drama. Time and tide have not blunted the impact of the ocean's rolling thunder, nor dulled the landscape's shock and awe. Standing alone on the beach, one can still draw breath heavy with moist sea air, rich with the taste of salt and cedar and dark earth. This is the smell of Vancouver Island, this is its very essence.

Nova Scotia

RICHIE HOPSON

The grass is waist high and glistening wet, the ground a sponge saturated by the drizzle. My feet are sodden. Although I have hiking boots back in the glossy black people carrier, I left them behind in my haste to get out onto the point. With them sit my camera and DV. I plough on through the tangle, skirting the pines that lie to my right. The ocean is no longer visible through the trunks, the bobbing surfers are down there, somewhere. But now I am guided only by the boom of the rolling sets as they steam down the boulders. So I wade on, in my wet trainers, camera-less, because when the excitement of the chase kicks in, sometimes adrenaline over-rides logic.

Fighting through the damp grass I finally emerge onto a narrow path. It's barely a track, more like a centre parting in the foliage. I can see a clearing ahead, beyond it the sea and beyond that the horizon. I tramp out onto the top of a red cliff at the very end of the point and peel back my hood. The coastline is a layered zig-zag of colours that stretches to the far north and south, each headland lighter and less defined in the rain, as they fade away into the distance. Swell lines are rising and pitching towards peeling points. A reef leaves a telltale triangular footprint of white-water. Below a wave is rolling through and I notice a scramble path down the cliff to the small pebble beach. I reach into my pocket for my camera and find only the residual warmth left behind by my hand. I smile. Sometimes it's best to let such panoramas go unrecorded. I turn to make the trek back to the hire car. It's a big, ugly Chevy, with out of state plates – I hope it's still in one piece.

CHRIS NELSON

A sheen of cold sweat glistens on the bonnet of a grey saloon, camouflaged against the grey tarmac on a grey day. The mist has leached every hue and chroma from the surrounding environment – only the serpentine double yellow lines tracing the middle of the road seem to cling onto any tonal value. A bank of tired boulders arcs out along the point fringed by conical pines, arrow straight, edges blurred by the advancing gloom. A black silhouette bobs alone in the melancholy, rising and falling with the advancing lines, watching on as pale glassy blue transforms to spilling white. Occasionally the speeding wave face warps and bowls, distorted by an unseen imperfection, before clarity returns to the wrapping curtain. No rush here, except for that of the drop and trim; time to wait for the right one, the slightly bigger outside sets. No noise here, except the rumble of the ocean; no passing cars to distract, just the endless traffic of right hand walls. Somewhere on the coast, away from the towns, away from the hustle and bustle, away from the others, this is a point with a name that only a few share. Not hidden, but right here, by the road. Not hidden, but right here, on the map. Yet this is a point few come to ride. Localism doesn't guard its virtue, it is just another curve in the coastline, just another lay-by on the road, like so many others along the rural shores of New Scotland.

The province of Nova Scotia dominates the eastern seaboard of Canada, an embryonic curve of low-lying ground tethered to the mainland by a thin umbilical of land, bathed and nourished by the turbulent North Atlantic. The region is home to the indigenous Mi'kmaq, and it is here that many scholars believe Leif Erikson and his band of roving Vikings set up the legendary camp of Vinland nearly five hundred years before Columbus landed in the Americas. Nova Scotia was bickered and squabbled over by the British and the French, a prolonged row that is written across the land, marked in place names such as Truro, Liverpool and Yarmouth or the region of Cape Breton in the north. Provincial capital Halifax is the largest city and a vital port, the population of the metro area just under three hundred thousand; about forty per cent of the province live within its reach. Two bridges traverse the inlet, linking the Halifax Peninsula with Dartmouth to the north. The town's urban grid system blends European and US influences, while, rising at its heart, Citadel Hill looks down over the wooden housing, commanding views over the harbour and guarding the waterways.

Nova Scotia is a hard place with soft edges – if you count the texture of drifting fog or tumbling snowflakes as soft. Winter temperatures can drop so low that the sea steams like a hot spring and the rounded boulders of the shoreline become glazed with a vicious frosting of frozen seawater, making the tidal zone a treacherous place to tread. A wind chill of minus thirty degrees can combine with a northerly sea flow that sees bays transformed into a Slush Puppy of ice water. Yet, in the summer, the thermometer often climbs over the twenty-five degree mark, with long sunny days and barbecue evenings. But it may just as easily draw a misty curtain across the city, for Halifax can see two hundred foggy days in a single year. The region's low

Above
Grayscale.

profile is swathed in a mixed forest of pine, fir, spruce and maple. A confused shore is riven with inlets and fjords, headlands and islands, scattered boulders and shattered stone, grassy bluffs and tree-topped cliffs, rock-lined points and sandy beaches. Villages of wooden slatted houses are planted back from the shoreline, at locations such as Lawrencetown Beach and Seaforth, token shelter offered by spruce and pine. Warm lights glow from within cedar-clad homes on achingly cold days. It is a place where Scottish, Breton and Nordic explorers washed ashore and in this Celtic landscape felt at home.

The points and reefs that litter this coastline are pathological, indiscriminate; they lie waiting for passing ships and Atlantic swells alike, waking the tidal zone, sending cartwheel lines spinning into the bays. For the waveriders of the province, surfing is a waiting game. There can be long flat spells even in peak season, but, when the waves come they come, in many forms. At one extreme, short fetch windswells may blow in to liven up an otherwise flat week and allow the groms a chance to chop hop a few, maybe attempt to bust some air. Ground swells generated by the spinning lows that track away towards Europe can bathe beaches and points with lines, while the autumn hurricane season is when the gravy arrives: corduroy, groomed and travel weary, long period, short tempered. Fall is the golden time.

There are few waveriding communities that can pinpoint the exact day surfing arrived in its waters, but Nova Scotia can trace its genealogy back to day one. Ground Zero: 7th July 1962, Rod Landymore and his brother paddle out at Lawrencetown Beach. "Their father was Rear Admiral William Landymore and he was in charge of the whole fleet here on the eastern coast," says Jim Leadbetter, first generation surfer, Seaforth local. It seems the Landymore brothers got a taste for surfing while their father was stationed on the west coast, so when they moved to Lawrencetown, they immediately recognized the potential – all they needed were boards. "Their father made an arrangement: if the Admiral of the American fleet came to visit, he brought in two surfboards on the main aircraft carrier. It was a Saturday afternoon in July 1962 that they got their boards from the ship in town, and they started surfing Lawrencetown that day." It all seems to have a slight *Apocalypse Now* undertone: the US military command shipping the surf lifestyle from the shores of California into a new outpost, but it was more like a plague ship arriving in a new land. The US fleet delivered a virulent strain of counter-culture to a susceptible section of society; once exposed even the harsh environment would not halt its spread.

"They call them 'weather bombs' here," says Jim. "We get the snow storms, sometimes rainstorms. They go into the Gulf of Maine and they start off as a meek low pressure and, in the middle of January and February, they just explode into an intense depression. The Perfect Storm, that was an example of what they call a weather bomb. They blow up and then they come by us. They're every bit as intense as a tropical storm, if not more so. I've seen winds of a hundred and forty kilometres an hour from one of those weather bombs – they develop quick and they move quick. They give us huge waves for a day or two and then the raging north wind afterwards.

Cold light of day
Right here, right now, in glorious isolation.

JEREMY KORESKI

CHRIS NELSON

RICHIE HOPSON

RICHIE HOPSON

Top
Left out in the glooming depths of a winter's depression.

Upper middle
Halifax cityscape.

Lower middle
Backcountry reflections.

Bottom
All Hallows Eve.

Some winters they never stop." Jim swings open a giant hinged window in the roof apex and the mist-fringed Atlantic is revealed, greying in the retreating afternoon light. The outside air, laden with moisture, drifts into the room, fine droplets condensing on his face. "There's The Right over there." Jim sweeps his arm towards the tree-covered, rock-fringed headland to the south. "Probably one of the best waves around here," he says, lowering his voice in an almost conspiratorial way. "And that point to the north we called The Left, and in the middle of the bay sits The Cove. We weren't very original when we named these spots," he smiles. He turns again to admire the view. Jim's house sits back from the coast road, enjoying an elevated stance, tucked in behind a screen of wind-weathered pine. He caught the bug in the mid sixties, when surfing here was just a couple of years old. "We never thought we were doing anything that 'out there'. It was just fun." In the early days, Lawrencetown Beach, or to be more precise The Reef at Lawrencetown, was the place. The two classic point breaks that fringe the bay seemed to be beyond the focus of the embryonic crew. "We weren't surfing the points and we weren't surfing real big waves because, when it gets big at The Reef, there's clean-up sets and you can't get out," explains Jim. "Then we gradually started to migrate out and start surfing the points. A couple of guys came in, Australians, like my next door neighbour Paul Camilleri from Sydney, and he had surfed all over the world, and so he and a couple of the other guys said, 'Let's go over here, this looks better.' Now The Reef's a fun spot, but it's not anything compared to the points."

As with most surf communities out on the fringe, equipment was hard to come by. Boards were 'pawned' to locals by visiting US surfers lured north during the fall hurricane season, cross-border raids replaced broken sticks, while recon missions to the promised lands of SoCal brought back new designs. Ex-Navy dive suits were sourced from a surplus store near the Dartmouth dockyards – two-piece neoprene that had seen better days. "They'd worn out essentially," says Jim, "but we could pick them up for like twenty bucks for the two pieces. They were horrible for surfing in." Getting rinsed in quarter-inch neoprene wasn't a great experience. Suits designed for underwater use weren't built to resist the water ingress a four-foot set on the head delivered. "When you were on the surface with those heavy suits they stiffened up really bad in the cold temperatures," Jim explains. "The rubber wasn't flexible to start with and it got worse in the cold water." Not that this kept the crew out of the line-up. "There were times when you were out there, middle of February, minus 32 wind chill; often we went out without hoods. Back then a lot of us had long hair, and you'd have chunks of ice frozen to your hair as you came out, like dreadlocks. A lot of us had trouble with our ears and stuff. We tried dry suits for a while – some of the guys still use them. I used one for about four or five years. They were like a ballistic nylon – thin. You wear a heavy pair of woollen underwear underneath and you do stay dry – except when they leak. You stay quite warm, but you're awful buoyant. It's really difficult in bigger surf to get under the wave at all. The air will come up and bunch around your neck. I got tired of feeling like a beach ball and getting thrown around."

As the first generation of waveriders from urban Halifax and Dartmouth got a real taste of life at the coast, so they wanted more. Drawn away from the suburbs, they gravitated to the villages of Seaforth and Lawrencetown. For guys like John Brennan, Paul Camilleri, Jim Leadbetter and Joe Reardon the whole beach lifestyle proved an irresistible draw. However, these small, tight-knit, conservative communities weren't quite ready for an influx of long-haired hippy types. "We were

from the outside and I can't say that immediately we were accepted," says Jim. "There was a view from a lot of the local people that maybe most of the guys were into drugs and that sort of stuff. And I'm sure a few of us used to… have some… puffs and stuff like that, of course, but it wasn't what they thought." In small places, socially dry from years of tradition, rumours can take on a life of their own; like a California brush fire, sometimes

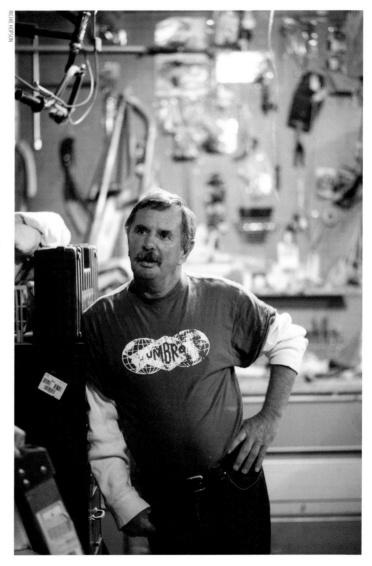

Jim Leadbetter

"The guys here who have been surfing a long time are really committed to it and would have a hard time going anywhere else and living without it. Of the twenty guys that were surfing twenty years ago, probably eleven or twelve are still doing it of our original group. I think that is unusual. In other places some of the old guys are coming back to it; born again. Here most of us never really left it."

they can be started by the most innocuous spark. "I'm sure you've heard of Surfer Joe," says Jim. "I guess the guy who still surfs and has been at it longer than I have by a year or two. He's always lived in this whole area, in trucks, in vans. They were convinced, all the local people, that he was running drugs. He used to walk – he's kind of a recluse, a very smart guy – but he used to walk along the headlands a lot wearing one of those ponchos, and locals were all convinced that he was signalling the drugs to come in to drop off, and the other surfers were coming and picking them up. They were convinced that the surfers were drug runners. We weren't accepted, in a big way, for quite a few years."

The sea here was the domain of the local fishermen, tough men who made a living in tough conditions. These men didn't take kindly to these 'boys' who were suddenly in their midst, parking in their spaces, weaving along the glassy breakers, whoopin' and hollerin' near their lobster pots. "Their job was cold and rough and dangerous, and the sea was not a place where you played – the sea was a place that you earned your living at a great cost," explains Lesley Choyce, a New Jersey-born surfer who transplanted into the fledgling community nearly thirty years ago. "I think they were wondering 'what the hell?' They had a hard time figuring out what the hell we were doing." Long-haired youths arriving by the combi-load seemed like an intrusion and the fishermen weren't the kind of guys you'd want to get on the wrong side of. They responded in a direct way. A temperamental van left at the beach over night was found filled with boulders. There was intimidation, disagreements, even the occasional fight. The fishermen were the original watermen here, and they were quickly becoming fluent in the language of localism. It took time for the two sides to integrate, time for the flames to dissipate. Some

surfers found work as fishermen, brought their skills as carpenters to the quayside; new bonds were formed and levels of trust forged. A deep appreciation of the sea that had at first pushed the two sides apart, eventually brought them together.

Twin points stand sentry over Lawrencetown Beach, the southern headland streamlined against the chill wind, steep sides shaved with a central Mohawk crest of pines running along the ridge. The northern diadem, a stained drumlin, gouged red till scoured by glaciers from a base rock more then fifty kilometres to the north. The long scythe of copper sand is backed by high-tide pebbles and a road-topped bar, a combined barrier that keeps the open ocean at bay, back from the flat expanse of Porters Lake. The reeds and grasses that grow at the lake's shores were harvested by early settlers to nourish livestock, while abundant moisture feeds the atmosphere, growing the June gloom that settles here through many summer days. Low hills bowl around the loch, dotted with occasional houses, while a small estate grows steadily on the southern ridge, ocean panoramas en suite. A narrow dusty lane skirts the northern bank. The house is powder grey, wood-slatted, single storey, southerly facing windows staring lazily across the lake towards the landmark MacDonald House, when the rolling mist allows. New swells at Lawrencetown Beach announce themselves as a bass percussion at the wind-weathered door, the waiting waves a thirty second car ride away. Fibreglass tails and fins protrude from beneath the house, a sure tell for those with a keen eye. Lesley Choyce sits by the window, illuminated even on an overcast day, reflected light angles through the modern pane. Leaning back in his wooden chair, he sips from a white mug cradled in cupped hands. Born in 1951, a product of the New Jersey streets, he developed an interest in surfing just as the Beach Boys were extolling the

Opposite top
Voglers Cove.

Opposite bottom
New generation: Isaac Norman in from the cold. This sixteen year-old from Liverpool is a veteran of three World Pro Juniors.

Lesley Choyce

"There can be days when I can look at all the weather charts for the north and south Atlantic and say that there's no way there should be a ripple in that ocean, but there'll be a window of three or four hours of phenomenal waves. By the time the city people and the crowds start showing that wave has been and gone and there's nothing left but choppy little six inch waves. I think that's part of the magic of the ocean."

virtues of the California lifestyle. His first board was a Greg Knoll 9' 6" slot bottom. "I think I was twelve or thirteen," says Lesley. "I couldn't carry it to the ocean, so my dad had to hold one end of it to get me to the water. When you got hit by it, it was heavy duty. It was probably the year I graduated that I came up here with a friend on a surf trip; rumour was that there were waves in Nova Scotia, so we came up here and it just blew my mind. I grew up in New Jersey so that was my standard. Beach breaks, sand bars, maybe jetties or piers or something like that, but there were no point breaks unless you went out to the end of Long Island and Montauk. So coming to Nova Scotia, I don't think I fully realized what a point break was. I guess I saw them in a magazine, but to see them peeling perfectly down the line, that was almost too good to be true."

Faded photos tell stories of endless barbecue parties, summer sun, flared trousers and lawns strewn with single fins, lying scattered like a bag of brightly coloured boiled sweets burst by a child's greedy rummaging. All are scenes that could have been played out on a lazy afternoon on the Gold Coast or any NorCal autumn Sunday. "Most of the surfers at that time had moved here to Lawrencetown or Seaforth or Chezzetcook," says Lesley. "Sort of five or six people, names you'll come across like John Brennan, Paul Camilleri, Jim Leadbetter, those are the guys I remember most. And people would come and go within the surf community. The priority was let's get situated by the waves first and we'll figure out the rest later. There probably were three summers that I lived here before moving up for good," he explains. "It really just stuck in my head that this was gold. I went to university and went to graduate school in New York City and then when Ronald Reagan got elected, I thought, 'I'm going to be really unhappy for at least a decade living in the United States,' so tried to emigrate to Canada, got

Top to bottom
Faded images from halcyon days tell tales of single fins, clay wheels and surfing the snow fields.

turned down about fifty times, until this guy at the consulate in New York said, 'Just go to Canada, we'll let you in – just don't call me anymore!'"

Outsiders weren't just drawn here by the promise of wide open spaces and a sense of adventure. Anyone could jump in a van and head for the easy rides and comfortable warmth of Cabo, but those drawn to the points of Nova Scotia were looking for more than just waves. "People would come here and they would say it was like California in the 1950s," Lesley says, smiling. "It had that feel to it, which it really held onto for quite a long while. I loved it. We were into the eighties and nineties and it was still like the fifties and sixties of surfing. People who travelled here, especially from California and other places, would fall in love with the fact that it felt like surfing before surfing became commercialized." Out in the world, Tom Carroll was signing surfing's first million-dollar contract, Tom Curren's silky smooth bottom turns at J-Bay were redefining technique, while Occy and Elko were trading gouging snaps across the competition circuit. Yet the community here were about as far removed from surfing trends and the changing face of the contest scene as they were from the beach at Pipeline, where Barton Lynch had just been crowned world champion. "We were here, we were on our own," explains Lesley. "It was always interesting to know what was happening in the larger surf world, but I always felt that it didn't really have much of anything to do with us. All I wanted was a good wetsuit that didn't have a lot of holes in it and was somewhat flexible. So cold water gear I would jump on – whatever was new. We were young people, drawn together by the surfing, and we were raising our families at the same time, so that pulled us together."

Sole surfer
Autumn gold.

JEREMY KORESKI

A small group of girls huddle together under an awning outside a bar, smoking cigarettes and shivering. Downtown Halifax is reaching the end of a working day, light spills out from shop windows and steam spews from restaurant vents. A fine drizzle makes the sidewalk glisten below the sign for the Dacane Surf Shop. Lance Moore, second-generation surfer, owner of Halifax's first surf shop, is half way through a story about going to the World Surfing Games for the first time. "It was the '92s in France. It's probably one of the most memorable experiences I've had in surfing. We were going to represent Canada, but man, we were like the Jamaican bobsleigh team. I know how to surf, I can hold my own, if the waves are good and we're on points – but beach breaks? I am not a champion of the beach break. One year we stayed at Robert August's house; we were staying there with the Guatemalan team, and they were asking me to sponsor them, and I said, 'Hey we're not rich, I run a surf shop, I'm not a big wheel here.' But you meet some great people and you see surfers that are the best in the world. Last time in Huntington Beach this lady who worked at the surfing museum said, 'I have a condo, you can stay there'; we stayed in this great place, she was proud to be a Canadian. I said, 'You realize we came like twenty seventh out of thirty four!' I guess that's why I'm so hard on my personal surfing because, when I try to explain whether someone is good, you gotta look at it on a world scale, because that's the only way you're gonna get better. It's tough, but it's true."

"When I first started, there were probably about forty guys, mostly older guys who originally started surfing at the beach. I was like the generation behind them. Oh, they abused me, or they tried to." Lance Moore is the kind of guy who could just as easily entertain a room as a single guest. You get the feeling that Lance is the unofficial mouthpiece of the Halifax surf crew. His shop is a brightly lit capsule, wrapped in the blanket of late afternoon darkness. He sits forward on the leather sofa and pushes his baseball cap back slightly. "We had no car, my parents were divorced. I bought this crappy scooter for like two hundred bucks and I used to sit on my board and go to the beach. It only went sixty and the speed limit was seventy at Lawrencetown, so there'd be cars behind me, giving me the finger. Sometimes I'd pull over and sometimes I wouldn't. Guys would leave notes on my scooter, give me crap in the waves and I was like, 'Whatever' – I was definitely cocky. But as you know, anyone who goes surfing in the middle of winter, at minus ten, and goes out there and actually surfs, you gotta at least give them respect for doing that. So after a while, I just kept coming back, and eventually they put up with me." There's still an element of the cheeky grom about Lance, even though he's now a somewhat central character in the surf community. He started out borrowing a board and wetsuit from his brother – until he wore them out. Then he bought another board from a neighbour. "I got it from him really cheap, although surfboards were really hard to come by, it was a really nice 6' 4" Byrne," he explains. Lance is imbibed with a determined streak and an entrepreneurial sprit that soon saw him running a surf store out of his mother's basement in Dartmouth. "I would sell stuff to my friends; I had a gangster cell phone, people would call me up for stuff. I was working at this Star Wars bar for all these crazy people – the kind of place you'd drive past with your Mom and she'd say 'Never, ever go in that bar.' The bar went out of business, and I had the surf stuff at my house and it was like 'Now or never.'" Lance found a location in downtown Dartmouth. "I opened a shop in the hood, no idea what I was doing, absolutely no idea. I had three hundred bucks and I struggled it out, made a lot of mistakes, moved across the street, then we moved to Cole Harbour, paid a lot of rent, didn't know what I was doing. Signed a lease when I was twenty five. Then

Top
Lesley Choyce dry suit session.

Upper middle
North Atlantic sunrise.

Lower middle
Lance Moore.

Bottom
On the shelf.

opened the store in Halifax; realized there was more people, we can sell clothes, we can do all that stuff."

Halifax Metro may be a large urban area with a bustling heart, but it doesn't have the feel of a compacted jumble of high rise. The orderly spread of three hundred thousand has a texture more akin to the weathered wood and ocean of San Francisco than the glass and concrete of Vancouver. There's a vibrant student scene here, art, music and a twenty-minute drive to the beach. "If you break it down, the number of surfers is still really minute," explains Lance. "But the thing about it is, surfers are their own best, or worst, advertisement. People who are over eighteen really want to try it, but they don't know how or where, if it's scary, whether there's sharks, all that kind of stuff. It's slowly just gaining momentum. The biggest thing out there is the Internet, and that's totally changed everything. People are looking for different kinds of surf spots, people are looking for new geography. Where we are, and England and Ireland and Scotland, they're the new places. I also think there's the novelty. People still love the palm trees, the beach, that kind of stereotypical thing, but I think to see images of surfing in the cold, the snow looks more exciting sometimes than the regular stuff. The upshot is, more people are going to the beach."

The mini-van pulls into the clearing at the end of the road, the fractured rubble terminating near the end of the point. The sense of isolation is palpable, the remoteness hangs in the air like the distant rumble of the surf. There is one other car, one other fellow waverider, somewhere through the trees, out in the line-up. Local plates, a single signifying sticker denotes that these aren't just the wheels of a lone walker. The traveller turns off the engine, then waits, remembering a conversation from the previous day. "It's a really

friendly place, and Canadian people are really friendly in general, but there has been some stuff that has gone on here with people going to spots that some people think they shouldn't, and vehicles getting torched and tyres slashed and windows smashed and violence and fights and things like that." For most surfers, modern day localism probably means getting vibed in the line-up, dropped in on or taking some verbal. In Nova Scotia, at the breaks where localism exists, it's old skool. Like the weather, it can be frigid.

For Lance, the localism has escalated beyond a point of proportion. "I think people think, 'Hey, I live here, I wait all year to surf here.' I don't personally do that stuff. I'm in the surf business, it doesn't look good on me. Also, I believe in portraying surfing as a positive thing. I mean, if you're coming here and you're dropping in on people and being a jackass, I'll just send you to the beach. I'm like, 'You're out'. Certain people, they're like, 'This is my thing, this is what I live for, this is where I stand my ground.' I have told those people, 'I can see if someone's being an idiot and getting in your way, but if they're being respectful, what's the use of it? Enjoy your day. You're gonna have kids, they're gonna go surfing, do you want that to happen to them?' I think the best thing people can do for their education – whether it's surfing or whatever – is to travel. You go somewhere else, you see what it's like. You be the outsider and quiet for a little while. When all those guys are staring at you – when Titus Kinimaka is staring at you, trying to figure out if he knows you, or if he's gonna kick your ass. I think that's a good lesson. And some people who live out at the beach don't experience that. I think you need to travel to understand that. There's always going to be that ruffling of the feathers. You belong to a golf course, they call your name and you go up and you get to play. Surfing's not like that. There are rules in

surfing, but, you wanna get better? You gotta catch more waves. People get bitter. And I say to people here who are like that, 'Why? Just quit man. Go to the gym, become a meat head. Just quit.' I think it's important to go and enjoy it. We're lucky to have it here, we're lucky to be able to go. Whether it's five minutes, twenty-five minutes or an hour away, we're really lucky to have it. Go to southern California on a south swell, then you'll be much more appreciative of what we have."

For many of the first-generation surfers, the irony of localism going full circle isn't lost on them. Just as they themselves had to endure acts of sabotage and intimidation from the incumbent fishermen, so a new generation of surfers find themselves subjected to the same treatment – only this time it's from fellow waveriders, just because they strayed out to the wrong point, surfed the wrong wave. The level of protectionism also seems to be linked to the remoteness of the spot, after all it's easier to keep a grip on an isolated point than a large open beach. For Lesley Choyce, this all runs against the spirit of the surf community, the spirit of the area. "A few of the guys are still feeling territorial," he says. "There's a few of these breaks down the road, places that a few of them tend to surf on their own, nobody knows too much about it. If you walk out there you might come back and find your windshield waxed or four flat tyres. This is very non-Nova Scotian, it would be more like America."

Nico Manos stands dwarfed by the huge wooden skeleton, its frame shrouded in a clear polythene coat. The harsh bass of hammers and rasping staccato of saws reverberate around the structure. As the wind blows across the plot, it catches the plastic sheeting, causing waves to ripple across the hollow structure. "Built with surfer labour," he explains. "There's no way I could afford to build here if it weren't

RICHIE HOPSON

Jesse Watson

"My first press I made using car jacks, when I was seventeen," says Jesse Watson, CEO of Homegrown Skateboards. A stack of finished decks lie on the bench waiting for designs to be applied, while opening the woodstore reveals a vault of precious materials, creamy auburn hues and criss-crossed grains. Jesse could spend hours telling you the difference between East Coast hard rock maple and their American and Chinese siblings. It takes that kind of passion to stay in a small town and build a company, build a scene. Homegrown's indoor ramp acts as a focal point for skaters from across the region. "It's become like a hang out centre over the years. It's a harsh environment here and there's little pavement to work with." You need a refuge like this when the wind chill hits minus 30 and the sea begins to freeze.

Dorian Steele

Huge wooden poles hang suspended from the ceiling, levitating four feet off the ground, illuminated by a ring of arc lights aimed into the central space. Dorian Steele works in long sweeping brush strokes as he lays the final coat of varnish on the masts of his Essex Fishing Smack, a 29 footer that used to ply its trade on the Thames estuary. This warehouse lies south along the jagged coastline, away from Halifax, out into the green and the serene wilds. Here, the line-up is whoever comes with you in the pick-up. "There are some excellent points around here, yet there's only a small crew. Sometimes Nico and the boys will come down, but mostly there's just a handful of us. We haven't really seen a growth in surfing numbers here. But then there are always other breaks. Breaks we've been using a boat to get to. But that's another story."

for my friends all pitching in: carpenters, plumbers, electricians – it's a real community." Nico is the modern face of Nova Scotian surfing; Quiksilver-sponsored, making pages in the international surf magazines, building his own house overlooking the beach. He has the squat solid build of a pro surfer and an easy, confident smile. Like most locals here, he wasn't introduced to waveriding at a young age. "Fifteen. Pretty late. Even right now there are only a handful, literally five surfers, under the age of twenty. It's cold and it's miserable and you have to be that much more driven to want to surf."

In an area of such pristine wilderness and empty waves, it seems strange that localism has risen its head here at all, let alone in such a high-profile way. Nico treads a fine line, being the name associated with surfing in Nova Scotia, going out into the surfing world and having images printed in the mags, proud of the waves back home yet not wanting to bring the media spotlight here. "I don't know if people know who's making the waves more crowded. There was a lot of discussion, on me for instance. I show up in magazines here and there, and is that leading to our line-ups getting more crowded? And I bet you some people would say definitely that's the reason. It's because more pictures are getting published of the place, but then you look at how few visiting surfers came here this year. I think it's probably the influx of people from the city discovering surfing. I think it's the surf world getting exposure as a whole and putting surfing in people's minds that's driving our three hundred thousand population out to the beach to surf, not the local exposure we've had. A lot of people would probably argue with me and I could be wrong. That's just my guess. Surfing is getting bigger and people know about it so they come out to try." Rising to the ranks of professional surfing is not as straightforward for the crew here as it is for those blessed with sunnier, more wave-rich environments. "No

RICHIE HOPSON

Left
24 carrot.

Opposite top
Nico Manos in the house that surf built.

Opposite middle
Cold rush.

Opposite bottom
The White Point Crew. Isaac Norman, Andrew Crouse and Connor Marsh divide their time between the ice hockey rink and the local breaks.

matter how on it you are here, you can't improve as much as someone who's surfing every day," explains Nico. "The cold is one factor, but that's something that can be overcome. You can get a good suit and surf three hours in the morning and three hours in the afternoon, but if there aren't waves you can't. You can skateboard and snowboard – and that will help you, but not as much as being able to surf every day." To compensate, he has developed a hunger for surfing that drives his development. Like many top athletes, Nico has used visualization techniques, like a Beckham free kick, like a Tiger Woods putt. "I lie in bed and think surfing. I feel like that may be helping me, visualizing certain turns. If I'd just been surfing for six hours, I probably wouldn't be thinking about it. I may have never started skateboarding or snowboarding. Who knows, maybe those things help me more than I knew."

The black pick-up sits ticking in the small gravel parking lot, wipers running, windows steaming. Outside, the moose stands with his back to the surf, head proud, contemptuous of the small gathering, rain trickling in rivulets down his metallic torso to the darkened concrete. The small waves on offer at Cow Bay today lie in the range of quiet contemplation, rather than hopping-around-the-car park stoke. Drivers and passengers in the handful of cars calculate odds, while watching the small gaggle of surfers paddle around in the modest left-handers peeling out front. The mathematics of reward versus pain, the probability of pay-off against effort. For the grommets in the water the equation is always skewed, for the older surfers in the cars the consideration takes longer on a marginal day like this. Cow Bay is considered 'Town', with its own local crew and its own scene. Lawrencetown is 'Country', different crew, different feel. "The boys out at Lawrencetown have their parties and poker games and hunting trips," explains Nico. "And the people in Cow Bay have their skate ramp parties and their beach clean-ups, and the people in town see each other at the bars. So it's a little bit divided, because it's not just one tiny stretch, there's seven hundred kilometres up and down the coast. Country boys have six waves and five of them are 'theirs'. They're kind of off the beaten track a little bit. And then there's Town. You gotta understand that five years ago no one lived at the beach. Maybe ten guys lived where you can see the surf. Now there's probably close to fifty or sixty that live between Cow Bay and Seaforth – that live within eyesight of the surf. That's something that's changed."

No one surfs White Point beach in the winter. The soft sand curves away towards the distant low-lying point; its waves are empty. When it's minus ten, duck diving is best avoided. White Point Resort is like a movie set, all *Dirty Dancing* and holiday rebellion. A framed sepia print hangs in reception, an image captured in the 1930s, when this was a draw for the hunting, shooting, fishing crowd. Between tall pines a collection of dark wooden lodges skulk, topped with green felt, their porches face the wide expanse of the Atlantic. Tennis courts that throng in the summer embrace the cold silence frost clings fragile to the fence. Behind lies the surf shop, a russet wooden boathouse reflected in the still waters of the lake. Inside, the chill winter air is immediately forgotten. A classic old Hobie hangs from the rafters above the green baize of a pool table, a twenty-five dollar ride brought back from the US back in the day. A huge sofa has settled by the plasma screen that displays a boardshort-clad surfer enveloped in a huge, azure barrel. Afternoon light angles through the picture windows, illuminating the dust as it dances on thermals spiralling off the matt black woodburner

that commands centre stage. "I started at seventeen/eighteen, came out here to the beach in the summer without a wetsuit, froze, lay on the rocks to try to warm up." Jeff Norman teaches at the school, runs the surf shop and combines the two to help bring through the new generation. Jeff's son Isaac is carrying the torch – at sixteen he has already attended three World Surfing Games. "For local kids going to the world contest, they see guys who are going to be pro surfers, the way they are surfing and that pushes their standards," says Jeff. "We've had guys go to California, Portugal and France, local boys who have worked here at the shop and have developed enough talent to get on the Canadian team and have gone to the Worlds. It's really good for them, a good experience. I got hooked when I went to university. I took a year as a transfer student to Florida. After school I'd go down to Sebastian Inlet – that's how I got the bug, when I was about 19 years old."

It's a small crew around the White Point area. Initially winter surfing was off the menu – until they started surfing the points. Fewer duck dives, better waves and better wetsuits all added up to more water time. "Our breaks are pretty accessible, even in the snow," explains Jeff, "because they're right next to the road. The guys have been pushing out, finding new points to the north and south over the past few years, but we don't have a lot of surfers here, and the breaks that are good are close, so we tend to not explore. Why spend time driving an hour to a break that might be good when there's waves that are good here and working?" The remoteness and beauty of this region is proving a draw for surfers from the US keen to escape the crowds and rat race back home. "Guys that are moving here are buying land specifically," explains Jeff, "but the guys that are doing it are pretty laid back and they fit in with us. They don't come in and try to take over; they enjoy what's here. They're here for a

Walter Flowers
"There was nothing locally, you had to go a hundred K's each way down to a shop in the sou'west there, or up to Halifax. The selection was real slim and prices were really expensive because they were the only game in town. I had the building here, and lots of space, and I thought 'I'll open up a shop,' got on the phone and started calling suppliers."

RICHIE HOPSON

Above
White Point.

reason, because of what we have for a culture. So they're working out well. We've had guys move here specifically to surf; we've had professionals like doctors who surf, and they say, 'I wanna bring my family up here, because it's laid back; I can still surf and it's fun.'"

The alloy bars are matt cold, blue-grey, leaden. The structure stands incongruous outside the warehouse, backed by forest, marooned in the gravel parking lot. Walter Flowers leans on the hood of his classic Jeep and folds his arms. "Ah, the shark cage?" he asks. "It's my brother's; he takes divers out. They see mainly blue sharks. They have caught great whites around here, back in the fifties. I don't like to think about it. There's only a couple of spots that we surf that have seals. I wouldn't surf Sable, I've heard there's some big sharks out there. It's an island about a hundred miles offshore. I know some guys who work on the supply boats for a bunch of oil rigs out there, and they've seen whites breaching before." Walter runs a surf shop in Lunenburg, a small picture-postcard town on the south shore. It's a surf community where he knows virtually every person he'll meet in the line-up. "The scene around here has always been

tiny. Watersports have never been big in Nova Scotia. There's not a waterskiing community, wakeboarding community to speak of – none of that. Windsurfing, there's a few people; it's just too cold. Four years ago around here there was maybe five of us who surfed. There were a couple of guys who were older than I am who have since given it up because of their backs and what have you. The core crew was like, myself, Dorian Steele, Jay Mews, Craig Fielding, Dorian's wife Sally – she's from Australia. So it's gone from five or six to like, I don't know how many now, but I have a shop and I wouldn't be able to keep a shop going if there were just five or six of us. For us a crowd is like ten people – I see that, I just keep going, there's plenty of other places. I can't even imagine these places where there's like forty people in the line-up – that's just insane."

The advent of new wetsuit technology has made life easier for Walter and the crew. "Ten years ago, you'd do an hour if you were lucky, you're all bundled up in the shit, chafed to death, but now the gear's so good," he explains. But then there's still the tricky subject of getting changed in a blizzard. "We were shooting the shit one day, wetsuits round our ankles, blowing minus ten and icicles hanging off your bag. We thought, man this sucks! We said, 'Ah we need a Winnebago, we need a semi-truck and we can install a couch, a heater and a TV' – just goofing. I was in town one day and I saw this trailer, it was behind a building. I said to the owner, 'What are you doing with that trailer?' and he said, 'I'm thinking of selling it.' So now we got 'The Shack' for local guys – trailer, heater; we can surf all day at minus fourteen and it doesn't matter. It's a great rig – rain, wind or snowstorms. A plough on my pick-up truck and we plough in, serious. Ploughing our way to the breaks. Snowplough driving with 'The Shack' on the back in the middle of a fucking blizzard. No fooling. It's not like tow-in – it's plough-in!"

There's a sharp reality to surfing here that hits you like a slap across the face. Sitting in a warm room, heating cranked, melting into the soft sofa, looking through the double glazing at the comfy white blanket outside is scant preparation for the shocking, stinging realism of an ice-laden sea. "We get full on ice flows come right into the area, not icebergs as such, but big chunks of ice as big as this room," says Jim Leadbetter. "They'll drift in and they'll all pack in. That doesn't happen often, but some winters that does occur. Then we get the slush ice; that's really interesting. To watch a wave move through that is incredible. It's a whole field of slush and you can see the wave pattern coming through it. There was a couple of times when there was ice flows and you could surf, so you had to watch out for the big ice pans. We used to get up on the ice pans and when a wave came you could run off and dive in and catch the wave. Kind of like a little island out in the middle of the surf break. I used to have to sit in the tub for an

hour to warm up – I was borderline hypothermic after," he explains. "I wasn't alone – everyone would. You'd get the woodstove cranked up so you knew you'd be nice and warm when you got out." That degree of cold carries with it an inherent danger, a quiet threat that lurks ever present. It waits for that one mistake when responses are slowed, when co-ordination and judgement are slipping. Just one bust zip during a mid-winter duck dive can start a fight for survival. "When I look back, the elements of danger are there for sure," says Lesley Choyce. "Heavy duty, hold down wipe-outs. There's a big headland left that seems to only break when there's a northeast wind and there'll be a huge swell coming in. The winds wrap around this headland and it's all rocks. Big boulders out there and just rocky shoreline, so when you wipe-out, you end up getting dragged along the rocks. The current will pull you and you can't get out to the deep water easily, so you're just banging away on these rocks. I had one winter out there where I

JEREMY KORESKI

Dawn
The warm glow cast over empty peaks.

Above: Lawrencetown Beach
Icy fingers; nimble feet.

Opposite top
Overhead under grey skies

Opposite middle
Drawing lines.

Opposite bottom
Making tracks.

tried to get away from the shoreline. On the sandbar there was this heavy pounding wave, unfortunately for me right where there was a rip. I thought I was going to catch this white water and zoom on into the beach, but it didn't happen. I wiped out and it was a really, really cold day; water temperature about freezing. I got caught in one of these dead zones, where the water was pulling me back out into where this big wave was breaking, and it was pounding me down. Going under, coming back up. *Really* cold water. You have only a few seconds under the surface in subzero temperatures before your head is exploding and your lungs are screaming. It's nasty brutal stuff. That would have been one of the three or four times, I guess, that I thought I was going to die. It scared the shit out of me."

Out of the water, the environment can be just as cruel and harsh. "Ice-covered boulders – where water freezes over the shore," says Lance Moore. "It's at its most dangerous when it's been warm and then it gets cold, and then it gets really cold. You're walking back from the points in Cow Bay – you're walking twenty minutes and you're against the wind, and those freaking rocks are insane. Worse than being on a reef on the North Shore. You slip, you slide, it's hard on your feet and it's hard on your body. You can slide, you drop your board, you freaking swear so much you almost want to cry. And, of course, you're tired, your body temp has dropped, all those things. And you don't realize it 'cause you've probably got some adrenaline running through your body from surfing. I see people and I'm like 'You're shivering cold man, you should go in.' That's the one thing I've really been trying to say to myself is go in after two hours. When it's like four or five below and you get cold, go in. That's when you get sick. But we always do that, we always stay out for that one more wave."

At the end of the chase
Mind surfing the first set.

The Nova Scotian winter delivers a terrifying beauty and a mesmerizing romance found in no other outpost of waveriding. An experiential draw of dense, raw oceanic energy, combined with a visual collage of light refracted off crystalline spray, a myriad tiny prisms scattered through wave faces and islands of sculpted glass floating through the line-up. Even at its most painfully cold, even when it carries the heavy weight of threat, so it delivers that unique sensory reward. "I always felt that there was something different about waves when you're surfing in the middle of the winter," explains Lesley. "Into the winter realm, air temperature ten degrees or more below freezing, water temperature right at freezing or slightly below, sometimes surfing with big pans of ice in the water down in Seaforth, or surfing in slush ice. There's something different about the waves you ride when the water's that cold, it's more dense. When you get ice crystals in the wave, it's a sunny day and you're looking through a wave – you're seeing all this light and crystal and ice actually glistening in the wave – it's spectacular."

JEREMY KORESKI

Northeast USA

LUKE SIMPSON

Toes on the nose, wind biting against my face. The water is dappled with side chop, though we are riding smooth. Ahead I see the Statue of Liberty rise; an azure colossus, pointing skyward, enigmatic elegance in the bustling sound. Riding the ferry is something everyone says you have to do. I've never found the time before but now I get it, now I see why it's a must. To my right, Brooklyn reclines along the riverbank, just a jumble of dark buildings today; but the name excites. Brooklyn. The bridge traverses the divide, stridently crossing boundaries, meeting Manhattan with its steely span, web of cables fanned out in a pleasing lattice. Manhattan waits aloof; a chess board of noble figures, sculpted pieces standing tall in pleasing red brickwork and dazzling glass that deflects the gaze. It is a place of many faces.

Toes on the deck, rail biting into the face of the wave. The wind is offshore, dappling the surface. Paddling back out, the line up bustles and hustles, crackling with energy, anticipation. Surfers on their lunch break, those who've ditched college, wives, boyfriends, called in sick or scheduled vacation time all compete for the head high barrels. The lucky ones have hit the road, following the fury, chasing the swell, pursuing the dream. This is the hurricane season and everyone has been on standby. Phone calls have gone unanswered, emails have been ignored, work goes unfinished – everything is sidelined. The beaches of the Northeast are alive – animated by this pumping swell, born of a spinning swirling depression, generated off the coast of Africa, delivered, at Rockaway Beach, New York City. A place of many faces, and this one is turned oceanward, seeking out my next wave.

TOMMY COLLA

RICH MCMULLIN

The dark silhouette stands on the beach, alone in the white, back to the boardwalk. The brown ocean folds into oval barrels, spinning on a speed wash towards the strip of sand that has been cleansed of snow by the surging tide. The figure is devoid of detail: just a black outline against a blank canvas. A trail of footprints lead to this point, the only sign that this is no passive shape sculpted by the hands of Gormley, placed to weather and rust in situ, a statement – an Angel of the North Jersey beaches. He crouches, gathering his board that has lain white on white, and, sprinting towards the oily ocean, he launches into the waters, planing into graceful motion. On the beach, his form was inanimate, but in the water it is transformed, jolted into life. The surfer paddles out through the channel towards a pitching peak, where scattered silhouettes wait, backs to the shore, scanning the horizon. The rumble of the inside, the memory of waves past and lost, is muted by neoprene hoods. They focus only on the now, on the approaching sets. The air's sharp edge is dulled by the light dusting of flakes, cast across the murky ocean. Away to the north, the metropolis waits, inhaling, drawing in its life blood. A fresh influx is sucked along the arterial blacktop, mustered by the imperative of appointments, schedules, deadlines. Another day is dawning in New York City and the channelled chaos and rising rhythm of the commute is underway, as unstoppable as the tide and as regular as the sun's traverse. But, for this huddled group of bobbing shadows, there is nothing but the approaching lines and the ocean's rise and fall, the pull of the riptide, the thrill of the drop and the joy of the glide. At this moment, everything else is merely muted background static.

The US Eastern seaboard appears out of the darkness of the North Atlantic, a billion points of illumination, lighting up the night, rising to

Cold front
Dark Silhouette.

greet the incoming intercontinental flight. The wave of golden brightness spreads as far north and south as the eye can see, a giant ocean of life viewed from above the surface, a glow of countless teaming ribbons and innumerable pulsing grids. The megalopolis of the northeastern states is a core of urbanisation that runs through this coastal heartland, encompassing many of America's great cities. From Washington DC through Baltimore, Newark, Philly and New York City, the concentration of humanity here is breathtaking. And yet, for so much brightness, there are still massive tracts left unlit. Even within the reaches of the Big Apple, there are places where the sprawl and expansion have not seeped, where carpets of sand see few footprints and night skies are illuminated solely by the bright heavens.

The Northeast boasts a population of over fifty-four million souls; if it were a country, it would sit just behind Italy in the world rankings. This is a region that sees great contrasts through the seasons. During the summer, the mercury soars to nearly 84 degrees Fahrenheit (30°C), while, in the winter, a frosty blanket can draw the temperatures below 23 (-5°C). Air conditioning fights the August highs, while snowploughs battle the January blizzards. This is a land that drew the early settlers. After the Vikings there came wave after wave of Europeans, drawn to the promise of new beginnings and boundless opportunity. This is a rich and diverse region, a complex tapestry of states, from the fertile farmlands of Connecticut, Maine, Massachusetts, New Hampshire and Rhode Island through to the bustling urban sprawl of New York and New Jersey, and, at its heart, is the Big Apple, a true icon. Generations have been enthralled by its celluloid image and changing face. It was a platform for Keaton, a backdrop for Allen and a gritty stage for Popeye Doyle and the countless heroes and anti-heroes that followed. The Bronx,

Brooklyn, Manhattan, Queens and Staten Island. The eastern seaboard is the engine room of the US, the gateway to the promised land.

They were the dog days of the administration of President William Taft. Former New Jersey Governor, Woodrow Wilson, was on the verge of sweeping to power. West of Washington, Model T Fords were rolling out the new Highland Park plant at the rate of one every three minutes. 1912 was the dawning of a brave new world, where mechanisation and production lines were the catch-phrases for an awakening super power. However, in Virginia Beach, James Jordon was launching a craft of an altogether more ancient and less complex nature. The nine-foot Waikiki redwood board had been sculpted by grain-worn fingers in time-honoured fashion, using knowledge handed down from generation to generation. While rickety motorised carriages chattered out onto the tracks of America, Jordon's lines were quieter, more graceful. Onlookers were transfixed by the oceanic dance, shooting the curl, gliding on white water towards the sun-warmed sand, his lifeguard friends eagerly awaiting their turn. The hook was set; surfing had arrived on the East Coast.

"My first board was actually my mother's ironing board," explains Mike Howes. "It was the right length and size and shape to ride the waves on." By the early '30s, waveriding had drifted longshore onto the beaches of New Jersey. Mike was among those who could be found gliding through the shore break, proned out on whatever craft they could utilise. "We used belly boards until we started building surfboards in 1937." It is no coincidence that this was the year Duke Kahanamoku and Tom Blake came to Atlantic City to put on a surfing display. Duke was a confirmed Waikiki beach boy and prolific Olympic swimmer. His events took place across

Opposite: Illumination
Top: Frozen Maine.
Bottom: Kevin Richards; golden moment, New Jersey.

NICK LAVECCHIA

RICH McMULLIN

the globe, from England to Australia, designed to promote the surf lifestyle, to bring new converts to the sport. That was a game changer for the young Mike Howes. Then, Blake's seminal article in *Popular Science* magazine on board construction sealed the deal, setting Mike out along the path of making boards for himself and his friends. Tom Blake was a visionary. He took board design through two quantum leaps: not only had he invented the hollow board, cutting the weight of traditional designs in half, but his introduction of a skeg or fin caused surfing to change direction, bringing consternation to many in the insular world of waveriding. Blake was also instrumental in bringing the surfing lifestyle to the US mainland. His casual dress style, adopted by him for form and function, were taken on by many of the new breed of surfers, unwittingly creating the surf style of fashion that remains familiar today. "We had a couple of Tom Blake's boards that he had built," explains Mike, "but they were a little bit wider and longer than our boards. Instead of having a sharp tail, they had a rounded tail and they didn't work too well in New Jersey surf." Blake's ethos of evolving surf design had taken hold and locals were soon creating boards for their own waves, their own conditions. Fuelled by an infectious fervour, Mike Howes and fellow surfer, Stretch Pohl, formed the Malolo-Akula Surf Club. A local infrastructure was spawned and surfing began its slow ascendency.

The 1960s blossomed into a decade of brilliant colours painted to the rhythm of a burgeoning youth culture. Beatlemania had crossed the pond, and the infectious beat of Motown became the soundtrack to the turmoil of racial integration and the rolling thunder of the Vietnam War. Yet, out in coastal towns from South Jersey to Montauk, a grassroots movement had taken hold with the determined grip of Japanese Knotweed. The dry central plains proved to be a scant barrier

Tom Petriken
Deep recesses, safe havens.

for the Malibu scene: garage surfboard factories sprouted along the northeast shore. Ron Jon Surf shop in New Jersey, John Hannon in Great Neck and Charlie Bunger on Long Island fed a habit that craved fresh lines and devoured new sticks, a movement thirsty for its own cultural references, its own local heroes.

By the seventies, downtown New York was in a state of flux. The hedonism of Studio 54 and its cult of fame and coke was rampant on West 54th Street. Punk, spawned as the antithesis of all that was disco, was finding its legs at the CBGB, with the Ramones and Patti Smith performing short sets with strutting arrogance. Meanwhile, among the shattered ruins and empty lots of the South Bronx, gangs like the Savage Skulls, Ghetto Brothers, Black Spades and Seven Immortals vied for turf, and the seeds of hip hop germinated, ready to proliferate across the world, propelling a one-time street corner art into an all-conquering global phenomenon. However, out on Long Island, away from the thrum, the raised voices and the screech of fan belts, the warm summers were a magical time, and the ocean seemed like the only place to be, the perfect refuge for those looking for a home away from the urban grind. The surfing lifestyle was always there, the practitioners of the glide fully visible to the big city's glare, but they were overlooked by its inward-looking myopic focus.

Brian Heritage, Winter 1980. Smashing the lip at 7th Street, Ocean City, NJ. Air temperature 25°F; water 40°F

"My dad began making boards in 1962," says Brian of his father Dan Heritage. Having seen an article on board building in *Popular Mechanic* the seeds for Dan Heritage's future as a shaper had been sown and two years later he had opened The Little Wave Surf Shop in Sea Isle, NJ. By the end of the decade, self-taught Dan was manufacturing boards full time, passing on all aspects of the process to his team. "So I rode longboards when I was five, then on to the twin fins, and then the thrusters," recalls Brian. "I've pretty much experienced every aspect of surfboard design. I've been brought up through it all." It didn't take Brian long to be initiated into the ways of the shaper and by the age of 16, he was making boards. Brian continues to shape and today is at the helm of the family run Heritage Surf and Sport, at the heart of the South Jersey scene.

Charlie Bunger Snr, the finer things in life

At the vanguard of the East Coast's surf scene, Charlie started shaping boards in the early 1960's, turning a garage hobby into a burgeoning surf business. "We had no one to teach us anything because nobody really knew how to do it", he explains of the trial and error beginings of board design. When consdering what it means to be a Long Island surfer he says, "We might not all fit into the cookie-cutter model of what a surfer is supposed to be, but the surfers here are down to earths. I just think about the kids that are out there in 38° water in the middle of the winter, and that alone lets me know where we stand. It's diehard."

No dreamlike corduroy today: no endless, mesmeric train. Overnight an angry wind has descended, whipping through the line-up, scouring the spindrift on the beach. Feathering peaks are laid waste, their spray driven into jet-streams of fine white vapour trails. Viewed from the boardwalk, the beach wears a fine white coat, a frozen dusting unsullied by the random furrow of a dog's erratic ramblings or the train line of its owner's steady trajectory. It's the start of the Walkman decade; the two grommets jump up and down with excitement. Just into their teenage years, Jamie Breuer and his buddy Brian are embarking on their first winter as hardcore surfers. Until now, their adventures into the big blue have been cut short by the snap of winter's frosty embrace. No longer. The Breuer grandmother's Long Beach home has become advance base camp for this first expedition into the unknown. Prepped for a scheduled competition, they had their hopes dashed by organisers who felt the one- to two-foot side-shore chop was a waste of time. Man, what did they know? Jamie and Brian aren't yet fully equipped summiteers, but they figure the burning stoke will see them through. Jamie stands clapping his gloveless hands, fingers marbled blue, warming them at intervals with steamy breath. Brian stamps his naked feet, hopping as he surveys the line-up. "Lets just get in there!" he says with an edge of impatience. They cavalry charge down the white – leashes trailing, feet skidding. The usual momentary scrunch of Velcro proves more problematic than usual : Jamie's anaesthetized fingers are stubborn collaborators and Brian's neoprene-fattened digits fumble for the leash's tag. They glance at each other before rushing with raised steps into the white water. High-pitched hoots and low-pitched growls emanate involuntarily from the brothers in arms as they emerge from their first duck dive, heads racked with icy shards, paddling with an increasing fury and vigour, as if pursued by some demon from the deep.

Twenty minutes later, the boys sit huddled under the boardwalk, shivering in damp wetsuits. All their determination, all their pig-headed willpower could not overcome the eventual realisation that defeat was inevitable. They were frustratingly close; they had tasted victory, but not even their youthful enthusiasm could overcome the frailties of their neoprene vestiges and the biting cold of the Atlantic winter. Back on dry land, a moment of Zen-like clarity begins to crystallise in the minds of the frozen grommets. "What if we could take it in turns to surf, taking it in turns to wear the gloves *and* the boots?" says Jamie. There is an ancient eastern parable about Heaven and Hell. In loose terms it tells that those in Hell are confronted by a banquet of irresistible delights and are invited to eat their fill. The drawback is that they can only eat using the chopsticks provided, and these are six feet long. No matter how hard they try, they cannot feed themselves. In Heaven, diners are confronted with the same banquet, the same chopsticks, the same conundrum. They, however, choose to feed one another. In a world where some find it hard enough to share a peak, two young surfers reached a moment of enlightenment under the boardwalk of Long Beach. One stoked grommet sprints towards the oceanic playground; one huddles, towel in hand, to hoot and cheer on his friend, while waiting his turn. "When we finally came in, we felt pretty triumphant about it," says Jamie with a smile. "It's funny because I'm a teacher now, and the emphasis is trying to get kids to figure things out for themselves rather than just filling them up with information. I always thought surfing broadened me, helped me learn things I wouldn't otherwise be interested in." Epiphany or not, Brian's mother was none too happy at their quasi-hypothermic initiatives, and there is nothing quite as frosty as a mother's fury – not even the frigid North Atlantic.

Same but different
The familiarity of the sunlit scene, the bluebird day jarring precisely with the neoprene figure.

They say that words can change the world: be it the spirit-lifting inspiration broadcast to a generation by a great leader, the pumped-up metronomic repetition of some motivational life coach or the dark voices that creep into a troubled mind on a wild winter's night. Tyler Breuer's life was changed by the printed page. *Stories By The Fire* was *The Surfer's Journal* feature on Kevin Naughton and Craig Peterson's travels through the seventies. They were *Boy's Own* adventurers who scoured the planet in a quest for waves, penning tales of their escapades to pay their way. The fourteen-year-old grommet now knew what he wanted to be: "A surf journalist. I went to school for writing, focused on a lot of surf journalist stuff, and read tons of surf magazines, and really studied waveriding culture," he explains. "My older brother Jamie and I, because we didn't have a lot of interaction with other surfers, we'd get that fix from surf movies and magazines and we just studied everything voraciously. Then, one day

when I was older, I met writer Alan Weisbecker, author of *The Search for Captain Zero* and I said to him 'I wanna do what you do.' He said, 'Don't bother kid, it ain't worth it.' I was about fifteen so I was like, 'Screw him.'"

Tyler grew up bouncing between Long Beach and the sands of Robert Moses, where he was the only grom, apart from chief surf-pusher Jamie. "My brother really got into surfing when I was about seven years old; he was about twelve," he says. Being the only one of anything doesn't sit well in the classroom environment. Red head. Tall. Freckles. Anything. Here, to stand out is to put your head above the trench. "At my school, kids would make fun of me for being a surfer; I was the only one there," explains Tyler. "I had some friends that I made at the beach, who I'd see during the summer, like Michael Machemer; we met when I was, like, twelve or thirteen. I'd do the amateur contests, meet kids from all over the island, but they weren't people I knew well or would call up to go surfing with. During the winter I'd be watching surf movies and that would be it. From fifteen on, it changed; then I had friends who drove, so I got to see people who surfed on a more regular basis."

The shortlists have been drawn up, the panel assembled, the screenings and Q & As scheduled; Tyler Breuer is in the eye of the storm, a sea of calm as the preparations swirl. As a kid, Tyler remembers older sibling, Jamie, utilising a Karate Kid-style discipline and focus to drum in not just the routine of surfing, but the importance of style and culture. "He kind of forced me into it, made me watch all the surf movies and memorise everyone's techniques. 'That's Tom Carroll, not Tom Curren!' That was my induction." The irony is that Jamie's 'media training' paid off and today, as founder of the New York Surf Film Festival, Tyler and his close crew of cohorts are on the eve of their third annual event. "I just love surf movies, but I hated always having to go see them in a bar or, I remember one time going to see one in a seafood restaurant," he explains. "It was cool looking back, but we wanted to give film-makers the opportunity to show their movies in the proper place and push surf films." The idea took hold after a chance visit to the International Surf Film Festival in St Jean De Luz, and Tyler turned his creative focus on bringing something to the New York scene that was lacking. Based at the Tribeca Cinema, the weekend of features, shorts, art and culture takes place every Fall, drawing in big-name movie-makers and aspiring independents. Amidst the din of this cultural megalopolis, surfing now has a very clear voice.

Jersey is culturally and physically distinct from New York. Millions come here for the sun and the sands; generations owe their existence to those summer romances that blossomed and grew from the boardwalks and beaches. The stereotype may be Springsteen,

Ocean City, NJ
Ice-packed wonderland.

RICH MCMULLIN

RICH MCMULLIN

wise guys and run-down vacant lots, but the modern face is high-end beachfront cottages and the sandy straits of Wildwood and Cape May. A dichotomy of high-brow and low-end, real estate is inhabited by both bona fide Hollywood stars and reality show wannabes. The Jersey Shore isn't just some cheap, dumb MTV construction; it's a patchwork of cultures with a diverse heritage, a vista of herringbone walkways and temple-like casinos, shiny clean from the re-generation of the region. The Jersey Shore is a collage of beach tags and Ferris wheels, fairs and stalls, summer madness and the smell of hotdogs wafting over the noise of a thousand voices. There's the hustle of Atlantic City, the bustle of Avalon and the sports bar cries of the north-south divide, whether it's Phillies versus Mets, or Giants versus Eagles.

The coastline is a chain of barrier islands, compressed urban grids fronted by ruler-straight walkways, where towns run out of land and groomed sands buffer the ocean's fury. Places like Long Branch, Asbury Park and Belmar pulse and change with the seasons. "Ocean City is my home town," says New Jersey pro, Andrew Gesler. Lying in the southern reaches of the island chain, this seven-mile-long town is alcohol free – a dry zone surrounded by water. Founded in the 1870s by Methodist ministers, the resort pitches itself as a family summer retreat. "I'm, like, five blocks from the beach," he explains. "I ride my bike around the town; it doesn't take too long to ride from the north end to the south. There's waves all along it, but I'm fortunate enough to live on the most swell-receptive end of the island." The surfing gene was not something enshrined in the Gesler DNA. Andrew's parents grew up in land-locked Delaware, two hours from the water. Without his family's move, his life may have turned out very differently. Today he can chase down storms or enjoy some of the coast's finest waves right on his doorstep.

Condensed and constrained by the waters that surround it, the island is tethered to the mainland by an umbilical highway. "This island is like a little city," he proudly exclaims. "There's shopping from whatever you can think of – clothing to tourist stores, to thrift stores to bike shops, to Sub Shops – right there on Asbury Avenue, main street Ocean City. This town goes back; it's been here for a long time and it's always been a resort. Families come down here in the summertime on vacation to the Shore." With summer sun and water temperatures into the mid to high seventies, Andrew naturally grew up at the beach. His family threw him on a boogie board almost before he could walk. "I'd seen people riding waves standing up, so I wanted to do that," he explains, "so there was always that influence from my peers." At the age of ten, his uncle bought him his first surfboard and he never looked back. "There was a small surf scene on this island, which dates back pretty far. We've got some pretty great heritage right here in Ocean City, Sea Isle. I just thought it was cool as a little kid; I wanted to do it for my own self. You know what happens: all of a sudden, I'm skipping baseball practice, bouncing on soccer practice, thinking, 'Hey I'm going surfing.'"

This part of the East Coast endures a schizophrenic rollercoaster of seasons. Though summers may be all boardies, romance and warm evenings, the winters can be five-mil wetsuits, three-foot snowdrifts and empty streets. "Every season here is so contrasted," says Andrew. "Summertime is crazy; it's hard to hear yourself think. In the winter, it's a whole different story. All you can hear is your own thoughts." The changing seasons are a classroom of new experiences for every young northeast surfer. "I think I was about eleven or twelve when I bought my first winter suit from a friend," explains Andrew. "I rode the bus with an eighth grade surfer called Lee Asher; he sold me my first five-mil wetsuit. It was used;

Andrew Gesler
Top: Ninja suits, quiet contemplation.
Bottom: Breaking through the background noise.

it let water in; it was freezing; it didn't work hardly, but I used it. The main thing was it had a built-in hood; that was the difference. Before, I had an old 3/2 that wasn't making the cut. Just having that hood on, just putting that ninja suit on made me feel so awesome, like I could do anything! I think that kind of put an exclamation on my passion too: having the heart to paddle out in that cold shit. My mom and my dad were like, "You're crazy; there's no way we're gonna go stand and watch on the beach; it's too cold out." For Andrew, this was that defining moment where he made the transition from someone that goes surfing to someone who is a surfer.

Andrew was part of a small crew that snowballed as they progressed through school. "One or two of us started off surfing in the winter," he explains. "By the spring, the rest of our friends were like, 'Woah, dude, you got good, I gotta step my game up,' so we started recruiting winter guys. The next winter there were three or four, the year after that, there were five. Today, I'd say there's like eight tight, close-knit guys that I surfed with and hung with and partied with and did everything with. Back then the line-ups weren't too bad in the winter, now they're pretty much filled. There's a big contingent of surfers that are year round and wanna learn to chase surf and chase swell and know when and where to be when the surf's pumping."

As spring rolls into summer, as the heat haze dances on the blacktop and traffic is siphoned onto the coast roads, villages and towns are transformed. The annual pilgrimage of holidaymakers begins and the summer rentals spring to life. Window boxes bloom and shutters come down, bars begin to fill and a buzz crackles in the air. It's a time of great anticipation. "It does make it an exciting place to grow up," admits Andrew. "It's a real test on your soul, you know. It's such a contrast. In wintertime it's a ghost

RICH MCMILLIN

Above: And the day is done
Ian Bloch.

Opposite top
Fins out, Jersey shore, Gesler.

Opposite middle
Kevin "Kevmo" Morris.

Opposite bottom
Bay Head, Rob Kelly & Kevin
Richards; surf bound.

town here. There's, like, five thousand people on the island. With the snap of your fingers, the summer is here and you're in the midst of tourist madness, more like fifty thousand people. The beaches go from empty to where you can barely get to the water because there's so many people sitting on the beach. As kids growing up, we had fun with it though. You'd meet new people, meet new girls…" he says trailing off with a smile. "It was crazy."

On the Jersey Shore, vacation time is not all laid-back lazy days at the beach, lolling in the line-up, trading cool summer peelers with buddies. "The water's beautiful, it's warm, the air's warm, you get long period swell coming up the coast," says Andrew, "but then you've gotta deal with the downsides. You've not only got people and crowds, but there's the lifeguards and beach taggers." The use of the beach environment is one example where the term 'Land of the Free' seems to have got a little lost in translation. Beach Tags are a tax, tickets allowing access to a particular stretch of sand for the day, but not just any beach. City rules regulate and demarcate zones for specific activities: sailing, fishing, surfing, swimming. On top of this, there are the lifeguards who can shut down huge stretches of shoreline, denying access to the water; life as a surfer can sometimes be anything but free and easy. "You can see why hurricane season is like a double-edged sword down here," says Andrew. "It could be going mental somewhere and lifeguards could be telling you that you can't paddle out. They work on a prevention-based mentality, so it's like, 'The waves are up; nobody goes in the water. No surfing allowed, except on the surfing beach.'" But therein lies the problem: being the only surfing beach, everyone will be on it. "Every year it gets more crowded. As for the officials, you could run past them, but then they can simply call the cops. Dean Randazzo has been carted off the beach in the paddy wagon

Roll call
Top: Dean Randazzo.
Upper middle: Andrew Gesler.
Lower middle: Zack Humphreys.
Bottom: Sam Hammer.

Looking back
Bay Head line-up.

for surfing in the hurricane when the lifeguards told him not to. You run past a thirteen-year-kid on the boardwalk who's asking for beach tags, he radios in and some hot-head beach tag manager calls the cops."

"The summer is fucking nuts," says Alex De Phillipo of the barrier islands. "There's so many people down here, you can't get around. You pick New York and Philadelphia, two of the biggest cities in the United States, and bring them to these small beach towns and you can imagine how populated it gets." Alex is a surf filmmaker from Atlantic City. His film, *Dark Fall*, follows the year in the life of a group of New Jersey surfers. "On the one hand, we like the summer because a lot of us surfers, we can't make

a living just on surfing," he explains. "So we work bars, we work restaurants; that's good, because we need to make money too." Alex has travelled, spent time filming in Hawaii, and has encountered the question common to east coast surfers from England to New England: "You surf there? Really?" So, Alex set about documenting the waves and the surfers of the Jersey Shore, educating the blissed-out ignorant. This is a tough balancing act. After all, as surfers we want it known that the waves we charge are good, we just don't want everyone to know and we certainly don't want everyone turning up to the party. In a digital era, with a lack of self-censorship, that is a balance that's getting harder to strike. But Alex's endeavours were keenly tuned to this. "My aim with this film was not to

RICH MCMILLIN

showcase New Jersey as a place to come and surf," he spells out. "The film was more about the people, their story."

One of the central figures in *Dark Fall* is Dean Randazzo. "Dean is a legend," sums up Alex. "He's the only guy from New Jersey, or from the Northeast as a whole, ever to make it onto the ASP World Tour." Randazzo was born in Atlantic City and grew up surfing at Margate Pier. By fourteen he was focused on becoming a full-time pro and by 1996 he had achieved his dream, making the cut as one of the world's top 44 surfers and qualifying for the 'CT. Dean's time on the tour was halted prematurely by the diagnosis of Hodgkin's Lymphoma. "He fought cancer four times," says Alex. "He's sort of the Lance Armstrong of surfing." For many of the East Coast crew, Dean is not just a role model, he's an inspiration both in and out of the water. "Dean's the guy that really committed," says Andrew Gesler. "He busted down the door as far as New Jersey getting into the professional scene. He's got this well of determination; the fact he's a four-time cancer survivor just adds to his legend. He's got heart. It's that heart that all in Jersey share. We're determined. It's about coming from the underground and making an impact on the international scene. Some people just wanna surf, dig the lifestyle and have fun with it, but for the select few that wanna get out and do this professionally, Dean is the mentor and the big brother that sets the precedent."

Some names barely register, lost in the mists of time, overshadowed by more glamorous rivals. Others become famous, infamous, media stars whose deeds and actions draw awe and fear. Colin did his own thing, was hardly noticed. Then came Danielle, bitter, angry. A balled-up whirlwind of depression with no fixed abode, she roamed on a seemingly random trajectory. Viewing her from a safe distance you could admire her simple beauty, her purity and passion, but Danielle stayed detached, far off. Earl was next, up close and personal, then Igor. To the uninitiated these names passed unheard, for these are no movie starlets or X-Factor wannabes; they are the cast of the 2010 Hurricane Season, and to practitioners of the glide, these names equate to moments of joy or frustration that will live long in the memory. Spawned in the warm waters of the tropics, these spinning storms intensify, tracking either into the Caribbean or north up the Atlantic coast, a wave-generator extraordinaire. The season kicked off in classic style, a stream of storms driving swell up the East Coast. Each forecast sent surfers scurrying to the garage to pack up the SUV, ready to hit the road, to chase down the swell at some of the Northeast's most hallowed breaks.

Cape Cod coils out into the North Atlantic like a giant beckoning arm. It lies on the coast of Massachusetts, north of New York City, south of Boston. Luke Simpson lives in Eastham, out towards the end of the Cape. It's a relatively small year-round community. This is low-lying, sandy land, tree-covered and wind-swept. Luke got into surfing in the mid eighties, as soon as he could persuade his parents or older surfers to take him to the beach. As the hurricane season rolls around, Luke finds his attention increasingly drawn to the weather forecasts. "One of the neat things about the hurricanes is the anticipation," he explains. "Living on the east coast of a continent, where all the weather goes away from us, it's the only time where we can see a storm that's generating swell coming towards us. For those who live in Europe, they can see a pressure system out in the mid-Atlantic and know that it's going to push swell towards you, actually see the pulse in the water for several days before it hits. We don't really get that. In the wintertime, we're calling in sick and waxing our boards to surf waves from a storm that hasn't even generated a

LUKE SIMPSON

Luke Simpson, Cape Cod
"To surf with any kind of regularity here, you need to consider all of New England and regularly drive to Rhode Island and New Hampshire. The special part is when you score really good waves with your friends, find that out of the way sandbar. That's what it's all about. The difficult conditions are just something you need to deal with to make that happen."

Opposite top: Ramping up
The start of the 2010 Hurricane Season.

Opposite middle
Shaye Cavanaugh, Cape Cod, MA.

Opposite bottom: New England
Peak District.

swell yet." For conventional low pressures, the surfers of the Northeast have to become oracles of the weather charts. They have to master the art of predicting the future and manipulating time, so that they can be there when swell and winds magically combine. "You're checking the forecasts hourly to see if it's changed," says Luke. "When it does switch, it's really about being in a place with the right local winds. We're watching low pressures over Canada or over the mid-western states. The best ones are the storms we call 'nor'easters', that's a low that comes off the mid-Atlantic states and sends a couple of days of really strong northeast winds. When those clear out, it brings the offshores and cleans up the surf. Some of our best days are nor'easters. The problem is they don't last; you'll get a day of good waves, if you're lucky, and you'll cross your fingers for leftovers."

While winter groundswells can produce a day of solid juice, it's the hurricanes that really get the East Coast fired up. An ideal scenario can produce a week of waves. "For this you clear out your schedule," explains Luke, "get permission from the wife, and then go down and meet it." For some, the chase can even go as far as the Caribbean, flying down to the crystal blue waters to catch the first blush, before winging it home to ride the same pulse. But chasing a hurricane isn't as simple as jumping in the car and heading for the nearest beach. There's an art to knowing just where the conditions will conspire to deliver offshore winds and pumping swell at a break that can handle the power. It can be a strain, even for seasoned hurricane trackers. "It's so frustrating. This last one, I put close to a thousand kilometres on my truck and I was never more than a hundred and fifty kilometres from my house. Just driving around everywhere. On our coast it's pretty easy to travel long distances on the highways, but then there's a lot of the places that are at the end of windy country roads; it's pretty time-consuming.

Left
"As the snow settles white,
There's a fire burning bright,
In Massachusetts." Arlo Guthrie.

LUKE SIMPSON

You make a couple of bad calls, you can miss the bulk of the session." With any swell there's always the nagging doubt, the worry that just around the corner the surf might be that little bit better, more hollow, more perfect. It's the drive that urges us ever on. With hurricane swells, the prize feels bigger, the search more pressured. "A lot of local knowledge and a lot of luck goes into it," he admits. "When you're in the right place at the right time and you've forecast it'll do exactly what it does, you've definitely earned that. I'm almost forty and with my contemporaries, we did things the hard way, learned by trial and error, made a lot of dumb mistakes, really had to work to figure out all these places. We earned our keep. Now there's so much in surfing that is handed to people on a silver platter." With swell-forecasting sites, GPS and texting, many are getting the instant information, but that doesn't equate to knowledge. For this there are no short cuts. "But then, surfing's so much fun, you can't blame people for wanting to try." The northeast coastline can be a

fickle mistress, but the rewards are there. "We always say, we can have a good season, but we can never have a good year. If we have a great hurricane season, chances are we won't have a great winter. The special part is when you score really good waves with your friends, find that out of the way sandbar. That's what it's all about. The difficult conditions are just something you need to deal with to make that happen."

A pulsing bass emanates from nearby Kent Street, but here the road is quiet, devoid of traffic. To the south a metallic web rises above the roof tops. The Williamsburg Bridge stands tall, its grey tower casting a gaze over the neighbourhood like a tottering, metallic invader, a striding giant spawned in the mind of HG Wells. Here, on River Street the vestiges of old graffiti fade, while vibrant murals run riot across weather-worn brickwork. This part of the riverside is still warehouses, beaten-up loading docks with flaking paint and small industrial units. This is a distinctly urban environment in the most metropolitan of cities: Brooklyn, NYC. Johnny Knapp is opening the shutters on Mollusk Surf Shop. In an era when the 'battle for the corners' has climbed the political agenda, this is one block were the only turf war is waged by the tufts of grass competing for light through cracks and fissures in the pavement, and the only marks left on the sidewalk are from sandy feet heading for the store. This is not your natural habitat for a surf shop, but, then again, Mollusk is not your average surf emporium. Opened in 2007 by John McCambridge and Chris Gentile, it's a small corner store with a big reach. It doesn't merely peddle the products of the surfing machine, it is more a purveyor of the wavesliding lifestyle. It is the eye of the NYC scene, a focal point. "Mollusk

is a huge cornerstone for our community," Johnny explains. "They'll do BBQs in the summertime and do flicks or have a party at the shop. People are able to meet one another. It's interesting how – maybe it's because it's the city – but everyone's real accepting. It's a nice vibe to have. Some places, people are real judgmental, but here everyone's stoked on meeting one another."

Johnny is 25, New York-born and raised. Coming from a surfing family, it wasn't long before his dad was pushing him into the Long Island white water. "I grew up right before the Hamptons, the Fire Island area," he explains. "It's kind of cool where I grew up because it's only accessible by boat, so you can kind of chase down the sandbars. If you've got a boat, you're

Goldsmith
Jeff Sullivan sets to work on Cape Cod.

LUKE SIMPSON

Mollusk Surf Shop
"Mollusk is a huge corner stone for our community," says Johnny Knapp. "They'll do BBQ's in the summer time and do flicks or have a party at the shop. Here in New York, to get your surf stoke, that might come in the form of a book or a video, that may be your only access to surf culture for the day."

surfing by yourself." While spots like Rockaway and Montauk have seen a boom in the numbers, Johnny managed to avoid the packed line-ups and heavy competition so close to America's most populated urban area. "The kids growing up at spots like Montauk have that exposure and have that mass of peer groups," he says. "I definitely didn't have that, which was kind of cool because you get to find things out on your own. I remember going out there when I was young and I'd see these kids in the pack and they were surfing so good; I would try and imitate what they were doing and then I'd go back to my isolation on the beach and try and do my best."

East Coast swells can be a lottery. Even during the peak swell season there can be the flats; in the summer there can be weeks without waves. In a city with a huge population of surfers, there was a need for a drop-in centre where the dry could go and slake their waveriding thirst. "Here in New York, to get your surf stoke, that might come in the form of a book or a video," explains Johnny, "that may be your only access to surf culture for the day. When I went to live in Hawaii for a while, the surf is so accessible, for a lot of guys there's not much thought about it once they are outside the ocean. They have a board they know will work, a Thruster; they have such good waves; that's all they need to know. But here, it's like, 'I've only got a two hour window and this is going to be my only time to surf, I need a board to adapt to the conditions.' Dudes are way more into design and different board features." Johnny loves the diversity and the rich surfing scene on offer here. There is also the sheer number of places to surf. "One advantage of living in the City is you can do the split and head out to either Long Island or New Jersey, depending on the winds," he says. "For me growing up out on the island, I could cruise there, but to get to Jersey would be a hike. But then, if you really wanted to and you had the

Top
Surveying the scene.

Upper middle
Tripoli Patterson: Hamptons surfer, curator and gallery owner.

Lower middle
Rooster tail frozen in time.

Bottom
Coast guard training – ensuring the teams can respond in some of Long Island's most critical conditions.

TOMMY COLLA

time, you could cruise up into the Northeast and there's a whole different bunch of spots up there. But that's a different story."

The ribs are exposed, naked, bleached. The spine is thin and ruler straight. It is a familiar shape, a pleasing symmetry. The air is dry and a million tiny particles dance in the thermals, caught in the glare of a low afternoon sun, which angles through tall windows. A low rasp accompanies the hand plane's sweep, riding with the grain. A pale shaving rises from the blade, rolling and spinning into a curl before falling to the floor. The final form is discernible; this skeletal framework is carefully clothed in cedar, shaved, sculpted, smoothed and polished. "We're really into the whole idea of working with your hands and creating something that's really unique, special, something that you can be proud of," explains Mike LaVecchia of Grain. And, in this workshop special things are being created. Or, not created – they are born. Every Grain Surfboard is handmade from locally sourced cedar and each takes about fifty man hours to craft. The Grain philosophy is to make beautiful boards that demand to be ridden. But it goes beyond that. "It's going against the traditional consumer approach of buying a surfboard," explains Mike, "then using it, breaking it and just throwing it away. Yes, we sell finished boards, but we really try and get the customer involved in the process. Customers can build a kit or they can come up here and take a class; it's all about being involved.

Above
Oceanside Beach Resort.

Opposite: Dug Desjardins
"The epitome of the New England surfer. Artist extraordinaire," says cold water lensman Nick LaVecchia.

It's working with your hands and getting something out of the experience that's more than just a surfboard – something that will stick with you for a long time."

Grain HQ is on a small farm, close to a small town on the Maine coastline. Outside the wood-slatted barn, chickens roam and peck, cows graze the fields, there are sheep and pigs. It's an idyllic setting that perfectly reflects the organic feel of the finished product. "It used to be a winery," explains Mike. "It was a big space when we moved in, kind of intimidating, but it turned out to be the perfect place. We're about eight miles from the beach. York is a neat little town, it's got a summer beach community, but a lot of the area is pretty rural, a lot of open land and wooded land, little farms. We just happened to find this great building for rent." Mike grew up in New Jersey but spent a lot of time in Vermont. Snowboarding became his passion and his employment, followed by spells as a boat builder, sail maker and captain. His life was boats and powder carves. "When I finally got into surfing, which was only about ten years ago, it was something that took over. It became what I wanted to spend all my free time doing. I was living in Vermont at the time, which is only about three hours from where we are at the coast, but my brother Nick and I got tired of driving up and down every time there were waves. One day we went, 'Fuck it, lets just move down there. See what we can do, even if it's just for the summer.' We moved here, didn't really have any work, but I just started thinking about wooden surfboards. Because I was into wooden boats, it seemed like a natural thing for me to do. I built a board for myself for fun; it got me thinking about building another one better. Then a friend ordered a board, my sister ordered a board. It kind of went on and on." But Grain is no one-man show. While Mike was toiling in his basement with early designs, another New Jersey transplant,

Less haste
Snow lies deep on the ground as off shores groom the incoming lines. More speed.

Brad Anderson, was working on his own wooden craft nearby. "Brad read about me because I had a little story in the local newspaper," says Mike. "He rang me up and said, 'Hey, can I come and visit,' and went on from there." Eventually Brad and Mike saw a common goal, and a business partnership was forged in wood shavings. Today Grain has seven people working full- and part-time, including five on the shop floor. It might be easy to think that just because this workshop sits on farm in a rural county, out in New England, away from the industrial heartlands, that this is merely one of surfing's evolutionary blind alleys. But Grain is reflecting the current Zeitgeist: the realisation that the products of our lifestyle are ultimately the offspring of the petrochemical production line. Grain's entrepreneurial venture embraces the theories of Blake and, in bringing them up to the cutting-edge of board design, proves that, far from being a material from the annals of surf history, wood could be an important part of its future.

Grain has integrated seamlessly into the local community. Only the occasional famous face in the line-up hints at something out of the ordinary – that and the wooden exotica on show. Recently, there was Rastovich riding an Alaia, Keith Malloy on a Paipo. "The local surf scene, there might be twenty or thirty guys that surf year round," explains Mike. "There are spots around there that are like a peak or a point where you have to sit in one spot and those places get pretty crowded, especially in the summertime. In the winter you're likely to know pretty much everybody out there. There's enough variety in the coastline that there's plenty of room to spread out. At the same time we're careful not to over-promote the area." The coastline north of Boston is a complex and diverse playground. Open farmland, coves and headlands where the possibilities seem endless. "You start getting into New Hampshire and Maine; just look on a map:

Above
Lined up as snow falls. Maine.

Opposite top
Mike LaVecchia in the warmth of the workshop.

Opposite middle
Lined up as snow falls. Grain.

Opposite bottom
Grain co-owner Brad Anderson. "We're just bringing it back to the roots of where wood surfboard construction left off but using new techniques that can produce some of the most advanced shapes ever made."

the coastline is so jagged, there's so many places to go and explore," says Mike. Having braved the Vermont winters for twenty years, Mike is philosophical about the bite of the Maine cold. "I guess it's all relative," he says. "The winters were much colder and snowier than here. We do get nor'easters and we'll get storms coming through, and they might dump some snow – you might get a couple of feet at a time – but the ocean keeps things more temperate. You can have a sixty-degree day (15°C) in the middle of winter or, alternatively, you may have a week of ten degrees (−12°C) – really nasty weather. It's a rugged place to be but, when the beach places are boarded up and quiet, it's a whole different scene than the summer bustle, it's really peaceful. We're all still enjoying the beach and it's beautiful."

Living the surfer lifestyle has always been something of a tightrope act. The lure of the beach and the pull of the coastline tempered by the anchor of work and the need to fill a wage packet; so many aspects of modern life impact on the search for the utopian saltwater dream. Waveriders have, for generations, struggled to square that dilemma. Countless individuals have bailed for their dream destination, figuring they'll make it all up as they go, only to find the shine of their perceived paradise somehow tarnished after an initial honeymoon period. Others have come up with ingenious ways to satisfy the many demands that life places on us as surfers. For Tyler Breuer, NYC solves many aspects of the grand surfers' equation. "You know, ultimately, you're in New York City," he explains

CICERO DEGUZMAN JR

Tyler Breuer
The overpass at the corner of
Varick & Laight, Manhattan, NY.

Opposite top
New York; yin yang; city surfer.

Opposite middle
Blue note.

Opposite bottom
Twin peaks.

with a smile. "It's great. You can go for a surf and forty-five minutes later you can be in the city. You can be at a gallery, you can be at a show, you can be at a nice restaurant. You can be doing something really cool and interesting. You surf, but you also do other things. Surfers aren't just surfers, there's more depth to it. I can imagine if you go to San Clemente and you meet a surfer, sometimes that might be all there is to him. In New York they might be bankers, actors, or play all these other roles." For him the New York scene is a diverse and interesting social soup for surfers to paddle out in. "I love the fact that I can sit in the line-up and strike up a conversation with someone and hang out with them and find out they're a big-wig artist or a film-maker or a plumber; you never know who you're gonna meet in the line-up. It's always really exciting and cool. It's given me access to a lot of places I wouldn't have had access to if I didn't surf."

In some locales surfing has almost become the norm. Like Parmenter's lament, 'Everybody surfs.' Yet, in this city, being a waverider still has something magical attached to it. "There's still a uniqueness about surfing in New York," explains Tyler. "There are still people who can't believe that there are surfers in the City. There's something fun about that – you feel special. Growing up, I loved the fact that I was the only surfer. When you're a teenager, you're trying to identify yourself and you're wearing all these different roles; some kids become hoods and some kids become jocks; you're trying to label yourself. It gave me an identity when a lot of kids were struggling for theirs. I could say, 'I'm not a jock, I'm not a nerd, I'm a surfer,' and that helped define me. It helped define my goals and what I wanted out of life. It helped a lot in grounding me at a time when I probably could have been a lot more confused. I still have that: say I'm at a posh dinner with some bigwigs, I can always say, 'hey I'm a surfer.' You can play the surfer card. That helps you stay grounded. "

There is an eerie silence, a complete lack of any auditory stimulation that leaves the brain feeling strangely numb. The only intrusion emanates from a passing shadow, the squeak of footsteps in the deep snow. Looking along the shoreline, there is a lack of movement, a sanitary cleanliness that has erased all hues, transforming the coastal backdrop into a monochrome diorama. The dawn of a new decade has been ushered in by a string of winter storms sweeping along the US eastern shore. The Northeast is beamed to TV screens across the globe. Seventy inches of snow seems staggering in newsprint; it has more impact when you open your door to it. Deep blankets lie snug across the whole region, bringing everyday life to a halt. Even Washington DC is paralysed. However, while government may be halted, nothing will keep the area's determined surfers from the water. For Johnny Knapp, winter in New York is something else altogether. "Surfing in the winter is a way different experience," he says. "I'm still trying to come up with the right way to explain it; I feel like there should be a different name for it sometimes." In the grip of conditions like these, you can see why normal surfing parlance just doesn't seem to sum up the encounter. How can a glassy morning session in Santa Teresa, Costa Rica compare with wading through knee-high drifts encased in five mils of neoprene? Is it all just surfing? It's like trying to compare hooking into a perfect Malibu wall with dropping down a Mavericks bomb. Maybe we simply need more words, just as the Eskimo have for snow. "In the wintertime, there's a whole process to it, where you're really dialled into everything," explains Johnny. "If you're of the mindset that, 'Aw this sucks, it's cold out,' you might as well not leave your house. You have to be totally stoked that it's snowing and freezing out, and about what you're doing, because if you're not, you might as well not bother."

Witnessing the changing of the seasons is one of the great joys of living in the Northeast. "It's crazy the extremes that we go through," says Tyler Breuer. "In the winter you can be surfing and it's twenty degrees (–7°C) and the water temp is probably about thirty-six degrees (2°C) with blizzards, nor'easters and big storms, lots of wind – it's crazy. Then, in summer, it's boardshorts, it's hot and your wax is melting off your board. I think the people who surf year-round here can be a bit resentful of those who just surf in the summer. You always hear, 'I can't wait for September and October,' or, 'I can't wait for winter, when the crowds are gone.'" For Tyler, there's a different feeling in the line-up when the mercury falls. "I definitely think in the summer you see people get a little bit more aggressive in the water; there's more aggro, more of an attitude. In winter, I think people share a bit more of a common stoke because you're out there and it's cold, there's snow and you definitely feel more of a bond to the other surfers. There's more camaraderie, for sure."

The winter surfing experience can offer great rewards and, for Tyler, the more you have to fight for something, the more you appreciate and savour it. Winter surfing means having to put much more in. "I love it because I'm not focused on performance, I'm not focused on surfing well, I'm just focused on getting in the water and enjoying it," he says. "I know I surf less frequently in the winter because the waves have to be good to go in. In the summer, you'll ride anything because it's easy. There's definitely more savouring the experience and enjoying the smaller things about it. I love that feeling after a surf, getting changed in the snow, getting in my car, not feeling my feet, not feeling my hands, driving to work and my core is freezing, but then I get a good egg sandwich and I get a hot coffee; you can't help but feel amazing. I leave the water much more stoked in the winter than I do in the summer, it's much more gratifying."

Opposite top
Cold charge.

Opposite bottom
Snow birds.

NICK LAVECCHIA

TOMMY COLLA

There's an affinity that binds together those waveriders who endure the big freeze. A shared appreciation bred from common ground. Tyler agrees. "There's something that connects all cold-water surfers, I feel. When you grow up and know what it's like to surf in the snow. I spend a lot of time travelling and my focus is on places that are more cold than normal, not really seeking out the warm-water spots. The waves are just as good in these places, but less crowded. You've already grown up surfing it, so you don't mind, and I've met some really great people along the way."

There are many souls whose journey leads away from the icy fringes of home to seek solace in the warm waters of sunnier climes: Florida, Hawaii, Australia, So Cal, the Caribbean. Many never return to the chilblains and the frosted windows, the icy wetsuits and the numb fingers. They kick back on their verandas and watch the sun set on yet another golden day. But for the few, there is a connection that can never be broken. A gravity that draws them back to the autumn gold, makes them yearn for that first winter swell and that neoprene-shrouded heaven. "I missed the change of seasons the most," says Andrew Gessler. After relocating to California, he was moved to return home. "I missed surfing in a five mil with boots and gloves – I don't know why. I missed that brain freeze. I missed the adrenaline rush of surfing big dredging barrels in the most frigid temperatures. I'm truly happy surfing in the wintertime here. It weeds out a lot of life's frustrations. The cold may be brutal, but there's something about it that we love. I guess it's ingrained in our hearts."

Iceland

TIM NUNN

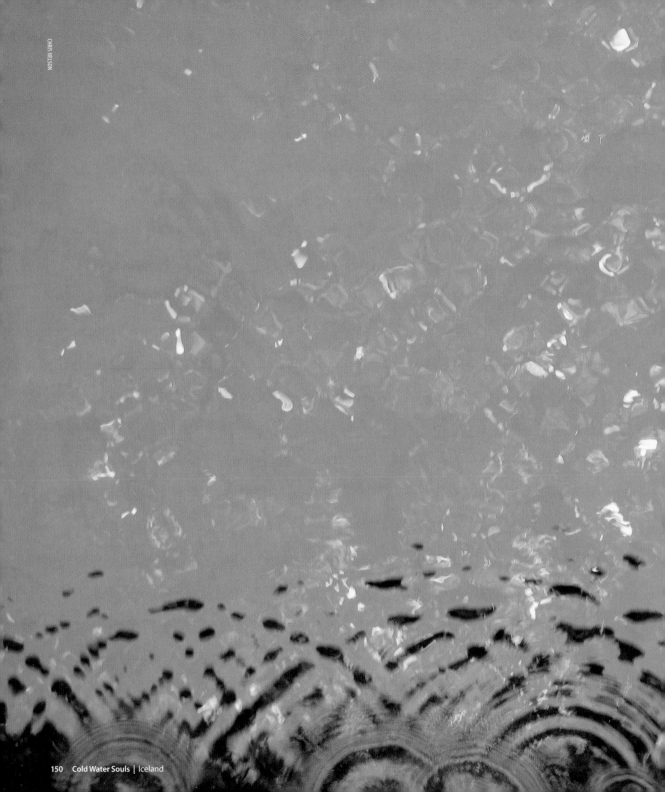

B ut why should *I* have to pay? I didn't damage the car!" Leaning on the counter at the hire returns desk at Reykjavik airport at five thirty am, I was becoming increasingly frustrated. Icelandic roads can be treacherous, the pitfalls are legendary but we had carefully negotiated the sheet ice, the sheer drops, the drifting snow, the torrential downpours. Yes the interior had a liberal dusting of black sand, and yes the boot was a little damp from our towel wrapped neoprene, but on the whole we'd kept to our side of that Karmic pact you make with a shiny new hire car – you make sure we get back in one piece and we'll make sure you do. Only this time the rental didn't quite survive with all appendages intact. "Look, it's not our fault that bits flew off the car. How well can it have been made if bits can just fall off it." The previous day had flipped from fresh breeze with a dusting of white, to raging maelstrom that saw lamp posts bending like straw, us holding onto buildings to avoid rolling down the high street like desiccated tumbleweed in a cheap western and me counting my blessings that we hadn't been out on a trawler when the front moved in. "You'd figure a car designed to tolerate speeds over a hundred miles an hour could stand up to a little Icelandic weather. I mean the filler cap? How does that just blow off?" The car hire guy just looked at me, a look that said, 'In Iceland the weather can be so bad that it will take any bits off your car that aren't welded on. And, stupid tourist, will do if you don't park facing into the wind.' Then his eyes glassed over as he murmured "Company policy, we've already taken the money from your deposit."

A taste of sulphur rides on the wisps of heavy mist that drift across the dark barren landscape; bleached peaks of far-off summits fade from view. The foreground is fractured and broken, the surface a crumpled canvas riven with deep channels and sheer faces. Black rock is rippled and contorted, still caught in the agony of its birth, when it strained every sinew to escape the smothering blanket of the Earth's crust and fight its way into the light, the quicksilver of its glowing fluidity frozen into twisted leaden matt. Far away, on the margin, a blue ocean folds into white, tantalizingly out of reach. Between the corrugated dust of the track and the shimmering ocean lies an unremitting, unforgiving lava field. No road traverses its broken skin, no track winds through this serrated

pasture. The only visitor is the ethereal drizzle that drifts ever onward, stooping occasionally to crown the moss and lichen. The Reykjanes Peninsula defies the raging North Atlantic in its youthful enthusiasm, still angular and abrasive against the onslaught of time and tide. Aside from the glistening moss that clings to windward features, the only soft texture is the vast sweep of dunes that run down to the black arc of Sandvik beach. Here, a surfer crouches on the summit of the damp ridge, watching. He scans the two-kilometre curve, the foil for the waters that rise and fall in the impact zone. At the northern edge, bodies are being dumped onto the ebony sand. The khaki-clad carcasses stack up in rows, slumped at awkward angles, all arms and elbows. Voices rise and fall; the lilt of a lazy Californian

Continental rift
The little church is caught in a cruel embrace between frozen waters and fractured fault lines.

drawl is audible over the background crescendo, as figures appear carrying more bodies to lay alongside their comrades. "Dummies," says a voice nearby. The surfer turns with a start towards the source, a small guy in a baseball cap. He nods acknowledgement. "We have to weight them just right so they float like real bodies," he says. Hollywood has come to town: Clint Eastwood, tanks, landing craft and all. Iceland becomes Iwo Jima. The watcher remains for a while, switching his attention between the surreal sight of a box van unloading casualties of war and the unpromising waves, until the pins and needles signal it is time to return to his car – one more spot to check.

Iceland is growing. Not the kind of growth any mere economic downturn may influence or a change in fiscal policy can hold back. For this is a new land, an island of fiery volcanoes, petulant geysers and steaming springs. Its physical mass increases with every eruption, extrusions emanating from deep within the Earth. It may be a cliché, but it really is a land of fire and ice. This island of a hundred thousand square kilometres – larger than Ireland but smaller than Cuba – lies directly on the Mid-Atlantic Ridge, a rift in the planet's crust where the Eurasian plate and its North American counterpart are moving steadily apart. Iceland may have close political affiliations with its European cousins, but it is geographically isolated. Surrounded by the North Atlantic, it sits at a latitude higher than Anchorage, Alaska. Its most northerly tip brushes the very fringe of the Arctic Circle, making Iceland's capital Reykjavik the northernmost major conurbation in the world. The coastal waters are kept free from pack ice by the calming influence of the last tendrils of the Gulf Stream. During the frigid depths of winter, daylight is limited to a mere sliver, when four hours of brightness break through the grip of night. Temperatures can be punishing, with sustained periods in the minus teens. Malevolent winds haunt the streets and roam the highland plains. Tarmac glistens with sheet ice and metal-studded snow tyres hum as each passing 4WD negotiates the treacherous roads. In the hinterland, many routes are impassable to all but the most rugged vehicles, while ploughs take on the thankless task of holding back the ever-drifting snow. On clear nights, the aurora borealis illuminates the heavens, dancing hues and shades splashed across the dark skies, as incoming solar radiation bombards the upper atmosphere. As the balance of the seasons shifts, the summer brings almost constant daylight, a near blinding onslaught that harries sleep and distorts the onward motion of time. Rivers rise with swirling chocolate melt waters, while high glaciers shine like beacons in the August sun. In the shadows of conical peaks, strange architectural apparitions shimmer ghostly beneath veils of white steam. Chrome pipes hiss and umbilical tubes plunge below the blackened earth, hunting the geothermal energy beneath the crust, reaping the country's clean harvest of electricity.

This is a Viking land, a place untouched by human hands until the ninth century, a place where harsh times mixed with good. The distant

Darkness falls
Snow dances on the streets of Reykjavik.

SCOTT WICKING

rumble of the Second World War brought change. In the context of this conflict, the geographical position of this young, often overlooked country leant it key importance as a staging post for the Allies, a stopping-off point for transatlantic flights. Keflavik Airport was established by the spring of 1943, as first British and then US troops took up station here. As the Cold War intensified, the base became a vital NATO outpost, changing the economy and the status of this small nation. Iceland invested its newfound wealth in the capture and export of the mighty cod. Then, in the 1990s, as the fiscal brakes came off and capital flowed into this hothouse economy, the small island nation offered itself up as a big fish in banking and technology. The financial crisis of 2008 took a heavy toll and Iceland was suddenly left on the rocks. The people took to the streets.

Iceland's landscape is characterized by low coastal pastures, backed by high central peaks and valleys. The coastline is a complex series of jagged lava reefs and dark boulder points, punctuated by black sand beaches. The northerly location brings fickle and changeable weather; swell arrives courtesy of depressions spinning off the eastern seaboard of the American landmass, which traverse the Atlantic on an eastward journey. Winter seas are frigid and fierce, while autumn and spring deliver consistent swells. In the lee of the southwest peninsula, nestled out of the line of fire in the shelter of safe water, sits the capital. Reykjavik is a contradictory assortment of brightly coloured tin houses, modern high street boutiques and a cathedral that appears to have risen organically from beneath the ground, bleached basalt columns erupting to a lofty spire crowning the city. On dark afternoons, coffee shops cast a warm glow onto the frost-edged pavements, pulling at the passer-by with background beats and the smell of fresh Java.

Today, Reykjavik is bright and sunny, but any

Top
A modern take on old traditions.

Upper middle: Geyser
Thermal power fuels both the national grid and the tourism industry.

Lower middle
Pipe line.

Bottom
Volcanic crater, frozen lake.

Above
Point of inception.

vestiges of warmth delivered by these golden rays are swept away by a wind that scythes between the buildings. Across from the harbour rise the hills, bright summits cloaked in white. Jon Teitur Sigmundsson is fighting to be heard against the background growl, as the espresso machine builds to a roar. Coffee in Iceland is good; it has attained a status bordering on national obsession. Café chalkboards offer a vast array of blends and specials, with spices or the warming hit of Tabasco as additional options. Perhaps the dark, claustrophobic winters breed this dependency; other regions of the globe at such high latitudes could lean towards a propensity for alcoholism but, in Iceland, the cost of such a habit is somewhat prohibitive. Jon casts his mind back to the origins of the Icelandic surf scene, the cryo-

genesis of local waveriding. He doesn't have to travel that far. "It started out with the snowboard scene; I don't know how many of us there were, maybe seven," he explains. "There was a small skate scene, too. We also used to windsurf a lot. Two of my friends were selling equipment from their garage, and one of the brands they sold started making snowboards, so they got this idea of starting a snowboard shop." They opened 'The Missing Link' on the high street in Reykjavik. Bringing together all tribes under one roof, it has remained the hub of the board-riding scene in Iceland. "I worked for them from the beginning, from the garage years. We were into all board sports, so, after running the shop for two or three years, we thought it was ridiculous that there wasn't surfing. We'd seen the waves when we

Jon Teitur Sigmundsson
Four corners.

SCOTT WICKING

were windsurfing but we'd never thought about trying to actually surf them. One of the shop owners, Heida Birgisdottir, had a cousin in the States who had a surf shop. We sent him an email and got one back saying, 'send your specs and I'll send you some boards'. We sent our weight and height and stuff like that, what kind of surf – like a questionnaire – and three weeks later we had four boards. Two of us had suits from our windsurf days; we found two other crappy suits and, from then on, we would go out all over trying to find some waves." OJ Simpson was about to walk free from a California court, *Braveheart* was cleaning up at the Oscars, while, at the Pipeline Masters, Kelly Slater and Rob Machado were high five-ing in the line-up, as the Florida kid stormed to his third world title. It was 1995 and, as the Dream Tour began to crystalize, with the Quiksilver G-land Pro opening the door on a new era in competitive surfing, in Iceland the very first local surfers were wading out into the frigid waters of the North Atlantic.

Jon and the Missing Link crew of Heida, Johann Oskar Borgthorsson and Runar Omarsson began to scour the coastline for suitable spots. As the pioneering generation, they had no one to ask for advice. Without mentors, everything has to be trial and error. How do you learn the technique? How to pop or duck-dive? What are the characteristics of a good wave? How do you know if there will be waves or not? How can you spot a rip current? For true pioneers it can be a hard path to tread. They would load up, take to the coast and try to find waves, hoping that proficiency would follow.

The sheer, clean water gently washes over the front of the board, its white nose raised towards the horizon, where an endless train of low grey cloud shunts by. The surfer sits and watches the shifting textures brush the smooth ocean surface; dappled patterns fan out across the bay, riding on the pulsing offshore winds that buffet his back and whistle past his claustrophobic hood. A crumbling cascade of white water crashes over the end of the point, the indicator that a set is incoming. He lazily slips down his board and gently reaches forward with his right arm, watching his fingers dip into the clear waters, feeling the resistance in his cupped hand, and he draws backwards, the board rising into forward momentum. He paddles out towards the horizon, casual, coiled. He can see the lines now, already rising, manes of white, feathering high off the face of the first wave. Turning, he pushes out his chest and strokes towards the shore; as the board rises from behind, nose angled down, his hands find the rails. The board hangs in the lip for the merest instant, then begins to drive down the face; with that slight feeling of weightlessness, he is on his feet, board planing straight down into the trough; he hesitates momentarily, before bending his knees, leaning onto rubber clad toes, the rail biting into the wave, as the edge carves into the slicing arc of a bottom turn, arm stroking the face. He aims the nose for the shoulder, instinctively knowing that it will have risen into the vertical summit of a curling lip by the time he arrives, laying down a gauging cut-back. Out on the face again he is trimming, gaining speed; he rises and falls, gliding over crystal waters, racing down the line. Legs aching, he prones out, dropping to his stomach in the collapsing white water and belly-boards in. Towelling down at the salt-caked Pontiac, he casts his eyes back over the empty waves, peeling endlessly down the point. That's why he came, despite the long nights and harsh climate, that's why he came. He smiles, pulling on his khakis, then shoves his board in the back seat. He glances at his watch and sighs. Tyres spinning, kicking up a cloud of black dust, he is heading back to the base, back to the rules and back to the world. These waves were an open secret amongst those Americans who served and surfed. Stories passed around, photos of empty breaks, disbelief, quiet smug smiles. They'd been scoring waves in Iceland for decades. There weren't many, but they came for one reason. Quiet perfection.

Right
Tucked up under a cold Icelandic lip New Jersey's Mike Gleason looks perfectly at home.

SCOTT WICKING

Left
Lone surfer.

Jon and his friends heard of the US surfers through a snowboarding friend from the Keflavik NATO airbase. "An American we knew saw we had surfboards and told us there were guys from the base surfing at a place called Sandvik," explains Jon. "This turned out to be a really good beach break, really safe, in a small bay, not a lot of current, so we started going there all the time." In the early days, before they had mastered the art of duck-diving, they would walk along the cliff and jump in out back to avoid a pounding from the white water. Through their visits to Sandvik, they gradually got to know the servicemen. "We met some other guys from the base who were surfing already and we started going with them," says Jon. "Through them we heard about more spots. We were going all the time, when it wasn't weather for snowboarding, so it became a perfect summer sport for us. We used to take the boards with us everywhere. We'd to go to Snæfellsnes to snowboard on the glacier and we'd have the surfboards along, so afterwards we could try and go where we saw waves breaking."

The embryonic Missing Link crew enjoyed sharing the waves with the more experienced Americans. Sandvik became their spot, and they would head for the peninsula at every opportunity. They were also aware that some of their new mentors were venturing away to more secluded secret breaks. These were solo missions, stealth operations. "I don't know how far back the guys on the base have been surfing here, but it is quite a while," explains Jon. "When we were going out surfing with them, there were only about four guys. There was already this competitive scene between the American surfers – who got how many waves, who got this good day, preferably not surfing with one another. There were plenty of waves for everybody; it seemed that as their scene got smaller, they wanted it completely to themselves. We heard stories of one guy who'd just surf alone; he wouldn't go surfing with the others. This was within a community of only four guys, so we didn't really understand it." It was hard for the locals to comprehend the need for solitude that drove the Americans to seek out isolated waves. In the flush of a new and exciting venture, the locals saw surfing as a social event, a stoke best shared with friends. For servicemen who spent their days within the rigid confines of the military establishment, surfing was an escape. They no longer had to be part of a team, waveriding freed them from the structure and order of their working day. While busy peaks have a natural hierarchy, a pecking order, there are no ranks in a deserted line-up; carving up an empty point break is the ultimate act of freedom. For a world-weary Joe, brought up hassling for waves out at Lowers, the pull of a classic day at a secluded reef would be impossible to resist. Landing a posting to a place where the native surfing population could travel in one car was a golden opportunity. "The NATO guys told us stories of way back, and that the surf was the reason why most of these guys applied to come to Iceland and be stationed here, because there was this incredible beach break which for them was not even a ten-minute drive from the base."

As to when the very first waveriders arrived on Iceland, Jon is unsure. One thing that is pretty clear is that the first person to surf here was almost certainly a GI. "I think the Americans surfed here almost as long as there has been a base," he explains. There have been web stories and photos over the years, postings from ex-servicemen describing days riding waves on the land of fire and ice. However, in the ethereal universe of the world wide web, nothing is etched in stone. Hostings lapse, people's focus changes, the spotlight of interest moves on and, so, sites are lost. Faint digital footprints are all too easily swept over in a white-out of new code, like waves breaking on a shore.

The stark blockhouse stands high against the horizon, crowning the headland, proud corners harsh against the weathered boulders. Rooted firmly in the dark volcanic rock, it keeps a desolate watch. Outside, the ocean heaves and moves in chaotic turbulence but, within the bay, the waters are smooth, save for the furrowed rows of dark lines that travel shoreward. The harbour sits further inside the protective folds of the cape, fortified behind battlements of black stone. Trawlers line the wharf, bleeding slowly into the rainbow-hued waters. Battle-scarred hulls bear testament to a hard life fighting off the onslaught of the elements. Not a soul stirs, save for a lone herring gull that skulks lazily among the stacks of empty pots lining the quayside. Out from the harbour, through the rusting chains, concrete blocks, pyramids of sand and long-abandoned machinery, a small cluster of cars is parked in a tiny gravel clearing. They have a familiarity that resonates with any surfer, the tell-tale signs that would tip off any searcher: stickers, flat racks, the shimmer of a silver board bag through steamed-up windows. Ingolfur Olsen looks out. Two surfers are paddling back up the point towards the empty line-up, as crystal walls race through. Ingo starts to fidget and shuffle as the adrenaline of excitement and anticipation starts to kick in. But there is no rush, no crowds to beat. The tide is perfect, the winds are light and the swell is solid. Time to savour the scene, drink in the essence.

Ingo Olsen is at the vanguard of modern Icelandic surfing. His enthusiasm and infectious stoke have seen him guide visiting searchers like Dan Malloy and Dane Reynolds to where the waves are happening. Although he was not part of the original crew, he is certainly one of the pioneers, helping to push the boundaries out to new spots and new regions. "There was no real board culture before the Missing Link," says Ingo. "No one was selling snowboard gear, then

Ingolfur Olsen

"December gets light around eleven and is pitch black at five," says Ingo. "A lot of time you spend in the water you can't see shit waiting for the wave because the surf is perfect but it's got dark. I don't mind the cold and if I get good waves with no crowds, I don't really care. We have six millimetre suits, and after one and half hours you can't feel your feet anymore. That seems to be the thing with surfing: you surf until you can't feel your feet anymore, then you get out and it feels like you're walking on a piece of meat. I always knew what surfing was, even from when I was young, but I never thought I'd be surfing in Iceland."

TIM NUNN

SCOTT WICKING

SCOTT WICKING

it kicked off and became really popular because we had a lot of snow. We got more people snowboarding and skateboarding, and the ones that ran the store, they picked up surfing and introduced it to us, the young people." Ingo was part of the second wave, inspired by the stories of the four pioneers. But it was really a case of sink or swim for the new recruits. "Maybe the other guys got some pointers from the people on the base, but it was hard to learn how to surf here, when you don't know anything about the sport. When we started, it could be sketchy; we didn't know anything. We didn't know a good wave from a bad wave, we didn't know anything about currents, we just went, 'Hey, a wave, let's go out'."

By the age of sixteen, Ingo was a sponsored snowboarder. With his myopic focus on travelling and contests, the ocean was the furthest thing from his thoughts. However, once he had tried surfing, the call of the Atlantic became more and more powerful, drawing him away from the hills and out into the water. "I simply found I had more fun surfing," he explains. "So, I gradually started surfing more than snowboarding. I guess I was about eighteen." So from cutting-edge snowboarding, with sponsors logos and high-end design, Ingo found himself scrabbling in the white water on make-do-and-mend equipment that was scrounged or loaned. "I started out in a really ugly and small wetsuit that I borrowed; it was black and pink and peppermint green. I had wool socks, plastic bags and sneakers and a boogie board with no fins. I was always the youngest in the group; my other friends where a couple of years older than me or more. They went to the States and got boards. They started surfing and I was following them around on the boogie board. Maybe once in a while I got to try a board out. Then, my Mum went to Scotland, and I got her to buy me a board, my first surfboard! Here it's hard; you don't have anyone to give you lessons. We kind of have to learn it

ourselves. My first wetsuit was horrible – like an old dive suit with the zipper across the shoulders so it was super stiff – but I was so happy when I got my first wetsuit. This was probably '97 or '98. There were maybe seven or ten people surfing at the time – not much different to now."

With the growth in snowboarding, people were heading for the hills, but a sudden shift in weather patterns brought about a concurrent adjustment in lifestyle patterns for some of the young boarders. Iceland's surf scene received an unexpected kick-start from climate change. "Seven years ago, there was loads of snow, and snowboarding was booming," explains Ingo. "Then, one season, there wasn't any snow at all, which followed for two or three years." The lack of snow made some of the board-riding crew look at the embryonic surf community and want in. "Surfers here are outdoor people," says Ingo, "and the surf culture is really close to the snowboard culture. That's pretty much where the scene came from. Plus, there have always been girl surfers too, because, if you go surfing, your friends want to come as well." Even with more bodies in the water, numbers were still close to a dozen. Iceland was a cold, quiet outpost slipping by under the surfing radar.

The bookshop is bright and airy. The magazine rack runs the depth of the store, a kaleidoscope of colours and images; the sharp, glossy collage dazzles and confuses. The air is heavy with the smell of fresh paper and new ink, diffused by the fanning of pages, as solitary figures leaf through periodicals, eyes scanning the zoetrope of illustrations. Jon Teitur Sigmundsson aims for the shop's sports section and spots the familiar masthead of *Surfer Magazine* immediately. The tag line promises surfing from the 'Four Corners' and his eyes settle on the word he's been waiting for: Iceland. "First and foremost for us it was crazy cool," explains

The promise of shelter
"I would never want to have
been an Icelander two hundred
years ago, it was way too hardcore.
I suppose even up to the war,
it was really harsh. The second
world war brought jobs,
connections, importing and
exporting." Ingolfur Olsen.

Above
Fight or flight.

CHRIS NELSON

SCOTT WICKING

SCOTT WICKING

Above
Cold promises lure travelling waveriders. Toby Atkins reaps the rewards.

Opposite top
Sky surfing.

Opposite middle
Tinna Sigurdardottir.

Opposite bottom
Apparitions in steam.

Jon. "We were in the surfing world all of a sudden, still an unknown factor, but we were a factor." It was 1997 and *Surfer* mag arrived in Iceland, not just on the shelves – it had been available for a while by then – but actually in the water. A crew of pros and leading lensmen alighted at Keflavik airport and ventured into the unknown. "It was amazing," says Jon. "There was actually a team of them. There was Donavon Frankenreiter and Wingnut, photographers, but also they had a guy just doing charts, and he had the whole island with maps of the ocean floor and he was in contact with weather stations – it was really professional. They were clued in about where to find the best surf. We found out about a lot more places from them and started to think about surfing the way these guys were doing it."

This was a steep learning curve, but the knowledge proved invaluable. "My father used to service fish-finding equipment and radars for the boats," explains Jon. "He knew about the ocean and he showed me a website you could go to for wave information about swell direction, potential height and also the weather. Pretty early on we found out about this; it was meant for ships and boats. Of course, we have a huge fishing industry here, and everybody knows about the waves and how to stay away from them. But we found out we could actually use that for getting *into* the waves. Then, when these guys came with all their charts and forecasts and maps of the ocean floor, we saw it first hand. Still today, we mostly use the local forecast the same as fifteen years ago. It's pretty accurate; we can rely on it." For the small local scene, the schooling they gained from the visitors was an epiphany. They coupled this knowledge with a real swell-prediction site, based not on stars and ratings but designed as an indispensable tool for men whose lives and livelihoods depended on the open ocean. They learnt what it meant, the correlation between weather, waves and bathymetry. This was the start of their rites of passage into the world of the surfer.

The *Surfer* article proved to be a turning point in many ways. Not just in terms of the way the local crew felt about themselves, but also how they fitted into the surfing world. They were on the radar – not a huge blip, but a blip none the less. As Jon explains, suddenly people were calling *them*. "We started getting requests almost immediately through our contacts from the shop. It was a bit sporadic; sometimes people would come here testing some extreme wetsuit. People wanted to know about the surf. I think we were also still gaining a bit from the NATO base, because of the rumours from there. Over the years, maybe you have fifty people from the base who have spent time in the water here; they are still spreading the word."

For the pioneers, surf knowledge seemed to come in great evolutionary jumps, like a distance learning package from the University of Surfing. US servicemen contributed locations and the first leg-up; *Surfer Magazine* brought knowledge on bathymetry and swell prediction. The next step came from the other side of the globe. "Georg Hilmarsson," says Jon. "He and his brother Ollie had been living in Australia on and off. He had an Icelandic father and Australian mum, so they had grown up surfing in Australia. But then, they moved to Iceland and Georg hooked up with the local surf scene. That was a really big, big step for us – to get someone who was not just so much better, but someone who

stayed here for the whole season. Not like the guys from the base, because they used to be here for a period of time and then go. To have a good surfer that we surfed with all the time – that took it up a notch." The impetus and motivation that a waveriding peer like Georg provided inspired everyone to raise their game. Having someone to emulate not only improved the way the local crew surfed, it also changed what they surfed. "As a result of Georg's influence, we got new boards, more advanced equipment," explains Jon. "That was probably in 2000 that Georg came. We were already starting to do some tricks on our boards but they were like seven-foot-four fun boards, really good for beginners, but he helped us progress a lot to the next level."

A small cluster of Toyota Hilux and Land Cruisers are corralled together in a huddle. This group of huge, heavily modified 4WDs have an almost otherworldly appearance: swollen and super-sized; they are covered with a fine mist of dirt, having just made their way back down the mountain from roaming across the huge, fractured glaciers. "We had a good day today, nobody got lost; we came back with everyone," says the blond-haired tour guide, crouched next to the huge wheel. A compressor whirrs in the background, as the monstrous tyre slowly inflates. Traversing the ice, tyres are run virtually flat to widen their footprint and increase grip. As a result, they need to be fixed onto the rims to stop them ripping off at low pressures. "Yesterday there were 600 people up on the glacier looking for two lost tourists," he explains. "They were part of a snowmobile tour, when one of the machines got separated in a blizzard; they didn't find them until three am." Glaciers are a hazardous environment in which to operate. To illustrate his point, the tour guide starts on a series of tales, most of which don't end well for those involved. "People take their off-roaders up there, but you

Opposite top
Mercurial black-top flows through the Reykjanes lava field.

Opposite bottom
Inhospitable conditions do little to curb the enthusiasm of the commited.

Kristján Pétur Sæmundsson
"There are twenty to thirty regular surfers, fifteen to twenty that do it all year long. There are probably three more guys our age and a couple of guys younger than us – not much more."

Opposite top
Concentric circles.

Opposite middle
Even in this inhospitable land the seed of something special managed to take root and push through.

Opposite bottom
Steinar Þór Bachmann.

have to be aware of the risks and stick together. Last week a boy and his mother fell into a twenty-metre crevasse; they only walked a few feet from the car. Only one of them survived." He returns to the hissing tyre, as the Land Cruiser slowly rises from its crouch.

Kristján Pétur Sæmundsson has the ultimate surf mobile. With huge wheels, balloon tyres and flared arches, the truck has a slightly steroidal appearance but will handle the worst terrain with the minimum fuss. "Tyres go from thirty-three inch diameter up to about fifty-seven. 'Regular' vehicles get between thirty-three and thirty-eight-inch tyres, like this one has thirty-five, and with that you can get pretty much anywhere," explains Kristján. "There's a lot of places to go but you never go anywhere alone. That's kind of the rule with these. Normal tyre pressure with these is thirty pounds or so, and we're dropping it down to five or six for the snow – that's pretty much flat. We've taken this car up to the top of several glaciers." This is a serious, go-anywhere kind of truck, just the sort of thing you'd want to be in to explore this country's true potential. Kristján started surfing at the beach at Þorlákshofn, a huge strait of black volcanic sand, backed by a ridge of dark dunes. Protected by the long boulder point, it's perfect for beginners. "A few of us started going there. The other guys didn't keep going, but we hung on," he explains. "We knew some of the other surfers through snowboarding, as it's kind of a mixed scene: everyone who surfs snowboards." With access to the breaks difficult, boards expensive and no easy route in, there is not a constant flow of grommets coming through. Kristján is one of the youngest on the scene at twenty-one. "I'm in my first year at university studying psychology. I started surfing about April 2008, I think. I got into it because of Steinar." He nods towards his friend, who leans on the other side of the silver 4WD. Steinar Þór Bachmann is a twenty-two-

year-old student of environmental engineering. Like most of the local crew, he doesn't wear branded gear but, to a surfer, he is still clearly identifiable as kin. His traditional fisherman's jumper, knitted by his mother, seems to be essential wear. "Surfing was always a big dream for me as a kid," he explains, "but I never had a chance to try it until I went on a trip to South Africa. I met up with some people down there and just surfed for three months. I just went in the sea and got pounded but I picked it up and loved it. After a while, I took some surf instructor qualifications. Then, the following summer, I went to Cornwall for the season and worked teaching people to surf." When Steinar returned home from South Africa, not only did he bring the stoke for waveriding, he also brought two boards – precious commodities in a land with no surf shops. "I tried it," Kristján explains, "I loved it, so I borrowed a board that our friend had for sale, but, as soon as I got home, I called him and said I'd buy it. I was hooked."

Despite the locals surfing for over fifteen years, waveriding hasn't exploded in Iceland as it has in so many places around the globe. We live in an era when surfing is easy, accessible, when everything is there on a plate. Elsewhere in Europe surfing hasn't so much boomed, as gone full nuclear. However, on this frosted isle you still have to forge your own way. New faces still have a hard time; you have to put the work in. It's still about the commitment of surfing rather than the lifestyle. "It's a hard place to start off, here in Iceland," says Steinar. "It's getting easier; when we started we weren't really sure where to surf. It's just this last year that people could actually rent gear and get lessons, before that you were on your own. It's quite hard to start if you don't know how or where. Especially if you don't know anyone." As Steinar explains, even the lure of surf schooling hasn't brought more into the fold. "I've taught a few lessons, not many. It's more like an adventure day. I think of the people who've had lessons; I don't think any of them have got into surfing. It's more like if you go rafting, you don't necessarily start rafting afterwards, it's more of a one-day experience. People still don't really know there are waves here in Iceland. We don't have a university surf club or anything. There's probably only fifteen to twenty that do it all year long, probably three more guys our age and a couple of guys younger than us. Not much more."

The winch creaks under the strain as a stack of white plastic crates rises from below deck, swinging around towards the quayside. The forklifts move in synchronicity. The trawler *Steinunn* is being unloaded, the success or failure of this week's voyage broadcast by the bright digital screen above the huge metallic scales. Pollock, haddock and ling: glassy eyes unblinking from beneath the ice. Next, the ugly, razor-mouthed monkfish, evil and menacing even in death. Then they are whisked onwards, ever onwards in a race against time, through the dark recesses of the warehouse, bound for England and glamorous Grimsby. Empty crates replace the full, an endless cycle, as the ship prepares to take to the ocean once more. Time is money. Further down the quay, a row of rusty whaling vessels wait, like relics from a bygone era, a time when the ocean ran red and gulls peeled and circled in swarms, swooping to feed on the cast-offs from sei, fin and minke. But these are no museum exhibits, these dark silhouettes still ply their soulless trade in a world where whale oil and baleen are long-since outmoded commodities – a stubborn throwback that defies modern logic and mores. Tied nearby, in an uncomfortable juxtaposition, are the whale-watching boats who draw in the tourists of today, so essential for Iceland's fiscal rehabilitation.

Opposite above left
Ex-trawlerman and Saegreifinn owner, Kjartan Haldorsson. "If you were big and strong enough you worked the nets. If not you were put to work in the galley – that's how I became a cook."

Opposite above right
Repatriate Georg Hilmarsson: sea change.

Opposite bottom
North Atlantic gold.

Gartar Berg Gretarsson is taking a lunch break in the harbourside *Saegreifinn*, a canteen-style restaurant of trestle tables and wipe-down covers, where tourists sit elbow to elbow with fishermen. The walls are a collage of oceanic images: mountainous seas, taller than the tallest masts, bearing down on foam-drenched ships. Iceland is an extreme place with extreme conditions. Gartar, an ex-trawlerman, now runs a special course for fishermen in sea survival. Traditionally, those who worked the sea never learnt to swim – for them, prolonging the inevitable was a futile effort – but, today, in Reykjavik, every ocean-going man and woman is versed in the art of survival: if you don't pass the course, you can't go to sea. "Force eleven is so strong it will just blow the sea flat; it's just white out there," explains Gartar. "Then, your biggest enemy is the wind. We were once on the western side of the island in twelve- to fifteen-metre swell – that's a height of over fifty feet. In those conditions you need to be on full power as you go up the waves, then no power down the other side. Twelve hours going into the swell; all the rails on the boat were gone. We were within three miles of shore; it took us six hours to reach safety." Many around the table have those deeply furrowed brows and crow's feet that come from outdoor life in an unforgiving environment, faces chiselled from harsh experience. "I think that all trawlermen have had a moment when they thought they weren't going to make it," he says, pausing, before picking up his glass and drinking.

Outside Grindavik stands a memorial. It is a simple statue with a powerful message: a wife, daughter and son await the fisherman who will never return. For generations, the sea has been respected, feared even. No one ever entered its embrace voluntarily. Iceland's surfing pioneers encountered a whole gamut of reactions. People who stumbled across the waveriders were often

TIM NUNN

Timmy Turner
Cold water searcher heading for the snowy line-up.

amazed; onlookers would gather from villages to watch. But there were also times when reactions were not quite so positive, perhaps not the outright hostility and sporadic acts of localism enacted by the fishermen of Nova Scotia but, "there were occasions when people were outraged," explains Jon Teitur Sigmundsson. In this dangerous environment, where people often plied their trade on a knife edge, the surfers' frivolous play could seem arrogant and naive. "Once we showed up to check out the surf by the harbour at Grindavik. It doesn't go off very often but they get big surf there, and, when we arrived, there was a crowd gathered. We thought, 'Oh, who's in the water?' We thought our friends must already be in there having a crazy nice time." However, they quickly realised that there was no surfing today; the ocean was in full fury. The huddled figures by the ocean's edge were relatives from the town, watching on in dread as a small boat tried to weave its way through the monstrous white water to safety. "These were mean, mean conditions, crazy, crazy surf," explains Jon. "The boat was about two hundred metres from the safe shore. From a surfer's point of view, on a calm day, you wouldn't really think it was that far. If you lost your board, you'd just swim to shore, body surf a few. But here, there were two guys struggling to survive on this boat. The families were there, people from the harbour, friends, even the rescue force was there. It was a crazy scene. People were crying." As the skipper fought to avert disaster and bring his boat and crew into harbour, Jon realised why traditional Icelandic attitudes sometimes struggle to understand surfing. "I remember this moment very well; it put me in contact with our history. They had a rule back in the day that a father, a son and a cousin were not allowed to be on the same boat. Because, if it goes down, then you have two families left with nobody to take care of them. And yet, we were there to surf and have fun. It made me realise that was why, sometimes, when we are out in bad weather, they'd wonder what we are doing," he explains. "People thought playing in the sea is not something you do. Yeah, you have a little play date at the beach, but you don't play in the water – it's dangerous. The sea around Iceland is something you survive for a few minutes. It's a very foreign idea to play with the dangerous surf."

One could paint a summer scene of idyllic life here, when the driftwood fire of a beach camp smoulders in the midnight sun, as neoprene-clad figures saunter in through the foam, driven from the waves by hunger and the promise of a cool beer. Tomorrow, they will ride up to the glacier, build a kicker, enjoy the snow park. However, life here is a double-edged sword. Winters can be brutal, the surf capricious and the winds punishing. Just getting around is a serious undertaking. Ice sheets lay a deadly sheen across the blacktop. The main roads through the heartlands are raised strips of tarmac edged by sharp drop-offs into the unforgiving clutches of the lava fields. Here, huge, jagged boulders the size of family sedans litter the landscape. The crumpled carcass of a nearly new Opel is mounted on a plinth in a lay-by like a giant moose head, the mangled remains of the hatchback offered up as a warning to the unwary driver. "The roads are pretty unforgiving," says Ingo. "They are narrow, slippery, and the wind

Valdimar Thorlacius
Iceland's first shaper hand crafts only a limited number of his Unique Surfboards.

is a big issue, especially with a big truck. Surfing in Iceland means many of the spots are inaccessible. It's not so bad down south, because many of the breaks are near the roads." This doesn't help, if you are against the clock on a short winter's day, racing the falling sun. 'Window surfing', as Ingo describes it. When conditions combine you have to be able to go. "You get plenty of swell, maybe for three days, but the conditions are actually only good for maybe four hours," he explains. "If you want to be an Icelandic surfer, you need a job where you can bail out when you need to." Even if conditions look like coming together, getting to the breaks can be a mission. "Iceland is not as small as everyone likes to think," explains Jon. "The nearest place to surf is about forty minutes from the capital. Some places much further. You don't just pop out of the capital for a six-hour drive for maybe/maybe surf. Sometimes I get a call from Georg and he says 'It's going off!', so we drive through the mountains, and the sun is setting, and we drive down to this beach, and it's breaking, and we get maybe an hour, and you share a beer and you drive back; it's a full day." For Jon, this is one of the reasons surfing in the country hasn't expanded like in other places. Here, on Iceland, you take the difficulties of surfing elsewhere and multiply them to the nth degree.

The essence of surfing in Iceland is that it possesses a purity of spirit that harks back to an era long gone, one where the hassles of crowds and competition are absent, one completely devoid of the pressures of commercialism. It is all about the experience. For Jon it's more than a sport, more than just the physical act of riding a wave. "Sitting in the water here, with your hood on, a six-millimetre suit, your nose running, and it's a beautiful day: the sky is clear, the light is very dynamic, especially if you are surfing in the fall. Surfing is about the fact there's a pulse of energy travelling across the whole

Top
High clouds, morning light.

Upper middle
Whaling fleet: outmoded but still out hunting.

Lower middle
Volcanoes frame a snow-dusted lava field.

Bottom
This is a land born of fire, sculpted by Vikings.

Home

"We were always ordering surf videos, then we started to travel to new places: France, New Zealand, Australia, California. It was like being a kid in a candy store, finally you were there and there's all these boards and you're flicking through different wetsuits, different wax, it's like going to Mecca or something. But there's a buddy system here in Iceland, I know all the guys and it's all about having a good time. If you can catch a wave, but the guy who almost never catches a wave could get it, you just leave it for him. It's really friendly. For me that was the shitty side of surfing: when you were abroad and there were guys who were ruling the water – you had no chance of catching a wave. It was more a lesson on dealing with territorialism and the bullshit we never knew about here. To have this great land, and these great waves, and this whole scene and story of surfing – and yet people would be fighting for each wave? For me that was really strange." Jon Teitur Sigmundsson.

Atlantic and it breaks beautifully on this rock in the ocean; it's not just about getting some three-sixty or some trick. If you're surfing that barrel, you were actually there when it broke at the end of its journey – that's a beautiful experience."

Today all the US surf magazines have carried their Iceland stories, the European media, too. Top pros have flown in and sampled the waves on offer. *Castles in the Sky*, with Dan Malloy, Timmy Curren and Dane Reynolds, showed the harsh potential of this land. Tropical searcher turned northern light, Timmy Turner, has been here for his *Cold Thoughts* film, camping on the edge of the glacier, brewing up with melted ice. But the locals are yet to see many visitors. These brutal conditions have produced a very social crew where crowds are still an alien concept. "We never had this in the surf scene," explains Jon. "We always wanted more people to come. We never worried that it's becoming too crowded." In the expanding global surf market, where we trade in a limited resource, perhaps more visitors or crowded Icelandic peaks are inevitable. This is despite the harsh realities that no photo can capture: the shocking jolt that comes with that first duck-dive in subzero temperatures, which even the most modern neoprene cannot ward off, or the chill that cuts through the huddled pack when an icy wind blows off the highlands. Visitors would do well to remember that this is a Viking land, one forged in the fires of the earth's fury. And while the environment and the locals may currently be hopsitable, it would be unwise to cross the line, ignore the rules or breach the boundaries. It is but a thin crust separating cool times from hell fires.

Top
"Runar Omarsson and Heida Birgisdottir of The Missing Link are behind Nikita. They started out with the shop, which was the centre of the whole board community in Iceland, now they are a hugely successful snowboard brand." Jon Teitur Sigmundsson.

Middle
Snowfall in Reykjavik: an earthly aurora.

Bottom
Empty peaks tempt the explorer.

Opposite
To the glacier's end.

Scotland

TIM NUNN

T yson! Sit!" I turned, startled by the sudden shout. A huge bearlike creature had materialised by my side, its icy stare fixing me dead in the eye. I froze, one leg into my contorted neoprene. On the far side of the Rottweiler a figure in a hooded sweatshirt and baseball cap emerged, my attention immediately drawn to the handgun protruding from his waistband. Not something I'd expected to see on the deserted north coast of Scotland on a sunny autumnal day in the late 1980's. Coming from a country which, at the time, had virtually no gun culture, it was not a sight I'd ever actually seen before. "Just thought I'd come down and give you the once over," he said, matter-of-factly. I was half naked on a cold, empty shoreline with an armed man and a salivating sidekick that obeyed his every command. I had no idea who this guy was but none of the possibilities running through my mind were good. "I see you're going surfing." Dry mouthed, I nodded, although those empty, glassy lefts seemed a long way off now. "We've been watching you through the binoculars." We? I thought, as all possible scenarios suddenly worsened. "Her Majesty is in residence," he said, a flick of the head indicating the silhouetted ramparts overlooking the bay. Relief flowed as the backdrop came into context: Mey Castle, the favoured retreat of the Queen Mother. I presumed the Royal Protection Squad officer was about to escort me efficiently off the Queen's land, but instead he wished me a good surf and sauntered back towards the castle. I looked down. Tyson hadn't broken eye contact. I waited to see who'd make the first move. "Tyson, come!" and with that he was gone. Sitting out in the empty line-up, I had the distinct feeling of being watched.

Cold Water Souls | Scotland

CHRISTMAS 1978

Farmhouse Cottage
Silkie Styx,
Thurso East,
THURSO, CAITHNESS

Dear Northwest.

Excuse the writing, I've just got out of the water.

The past 3-4 weeks have given almost constant perfection from 6-12 ft. and one memorable howling north-westerly that gave us 15 ft outside the house and at a guess, 30-40 ft. TUBES, breaking on a rock, 7 fathoms deep at low tide, right out in the middle of the bay. You wouldn't believe it if you asked Chris Tony and Dave how unlucky they were. But it's Autum now, the swells are pumping and it can only get bigger. Last Sunday I found a new reef breaking 30 yards from a harbour wall and peeling left for 50-100 yds over very bumpy rock, but perfect and all to myself of course. I'm building boards for a few friends who I'm getting stoked into it. I've finished 2 and I've got 2 more waiting to be glossed. I've just finished shaping myself an 8ft pintail winger, to get into the big sets just a second earlier cos theres no hanging about in my backyard break, it's take off and G-O-O-O like shit off a shovel. Very hollow and very fast its been likened to Porthleven but its got to be better, anyway, its more consistent, it works whenever theres a swell from the north to the westerly direction.

I was down in Cornwall a month ago for a week with the 3 Glasgow lads and Any Bennett from Edinburgh (I've just checked out of the window and it's still pumping 6 ft. winding walls, no sections and I mean NO sections). When I got back from Newquay (the mecca of slop), it was 1 ft gloss outside the house and I was expecting a big swell bummer. At 1o'clock it was 2 ft. at 4 o'clock it was 6 ft as I paddled out every set was a few inches bigger than the last one, so by 7 or 8 o'clock that night it was 10-12 ft and spitting and I was surfing on the beach in 4-6ft lefts by the promenade lights, since then we've had 4 or 5 swells, all of them at least 6ft.. Now the clocks have gone back. I can forget weekday surfing but it looks as though there'll usually be a wave at the weekend, I think. Even if it's blown out, theres always that harbour reef break left, it faces north-east (tee hee!!) (Chortle, Chortle etc.) I'll send you some photos of the last huge swell, when they get developed, there's no surfers on them cos we were out surfing and no one was around with a good enough camera to record the very pleasant things that were happening in the ocean.

Till X'mas.

Mucho waves and happiness.

PAT & MICK

HELP!

1 or 2 SURFERS WANTED TO SHARE PERFECT RIVERMOUTH BREAK 6-12 ft. GLASSY PEELING USUALLY OFFSHORE AT THIS TIME OF YEAR
LOCATION: NORTHERN SCOTLAND   ACCOMMODATION. DOSSING SPACE IN COTTAGE
                                                    OVERLOOKING BREAK.

EXPERIENCE OF SIMILAR SITUATION ESSENTIAL AS WAVE IS VERY FAST AND VERY HEAVY. REMUNERATION. BRAIN LOOSENING HOLLOW RIGHTS AND A PERMANENT ACHING TO SURF HERE AGAIN. CHARACTER. MUST APPRECIATE PEACEFUL SURROUNDINGS WITH VERY LAID BACK INHABITANTS. SIMILAR WAVES OF COMPARATIVE PERFECTION WITHIN EASY REACH IN EITHER DIRECTION.

15

The Vikings were warned to avoid Scotland. Though they settled the outlying islands of the Orkneys and Hebrides, ancient chronicles describe the medieval mainland as an inhospitable and unwelcoming country, offering rewards only to the brave. It warns that those who venture there may pay with their lives. Vikings did come to mainland Scotland, and the peaty moorlands were stained red from ferocious battles that raged through the centuries. Names like Skirza, Wick and Thurso stand as testament to the settlements that were once established around the fringes of the land, and a distinct Nordic lilt lingers in the thick, rich accent spoken by the Brochers. The Scots have always proven to be a tough and uncompromising tribe; even the march of the mighty Roman Legions was halted at the border and they built Hadrian's Wall to keep the marauding Celts out. Today, the northern lands of this proud nation may be a less murderous destination, but it can still be a bleak and foreboding place.

Scotland is a country of high mountains cleaved by deep valleys, urban lowland plains giving way to soaring peaks, where golden eagles circle and strutting stags roam. It is a place where whisky-brown streams run with bull salmon, while butterflies flit between blossoming heather and blood red orchids. The summer sun rules over the moorlands, as pheasants and grouse skim the verdant hedgeways and dodge the oncoming traffic. In the winter, the highlands are cruel and savage places, where even the most seasoned Himalayan climber would be risking all pushing for the white jagged summit. Winds whip up a white-out and the main arterial blacktop can be lost in an instant, stranding foolish travellers who await the rescue of the plough. There are winter playgrounds here: a multicoloured mozaic of random skiers zig-zagging down leeward slopes to waiting lifts. During the dark winter

TIM NUNN

CHRIS NELSON

DEMI TAYLOR

DEMI TAYLOR

Top: Winter gold
Thurso town.

Upper middle: Peak of winter
Caithness flagstone still brings rich rewards.

Lower middle
Cold comfort.

Bottom
Nuclear flower.

TIM NUNN

Above
Crystal voyager.

temperatures, can drop into the minus twenties on high ground, while even the lowlands can feel the cutting edge of the northerly fronts that blow out of the Arctic. The aurora makes a rare appearance, dancing green, blue and purple hues on a few clear cold nights. In the northern highlands, the twin counties of Caithness and Sutherland relax their grip on the mountains and lie down to rest by the ocean. Small parcels of pasture are broken by occasional massed ranks of pines or wounded by the scars of peat cuttings; the browns and reds of heather fill in the rest like a child's lazy shading between the features. While these counties may seem alike at first glance, these sibling lands differ in subtle, yet very distinct ways. Caithness is fringed with a series of flat, flagstone reefs – angled pavements upon which the anger of the north Atlantic is vented in regular outbursts. These valuable sedimentary deposits provided the county with a precious income during the nineteenth century; the quarried rocks borne from the harbours of Scrabster, Castletown and Ham now line streets and sidewalks from London to Buenos Aires. Neighbouring Sutherland is also fringed by an undulating coastline, but this one is peppered with pristine golden beaches and reeling rivermouths. Marram-topped dunes and shallow cliffs line these bays and peat-stained rivers bleed into the cold, blue ocean. Seals chase salmon in

the inlets, while basking sharks cruise the shores under the summer sun. The June solstice on the north shore sees the sun barely skim beneath the horizon before climbing again to extinguish the short, dusky night almost before it has begun. In winter, the cloak of darkness shrouds the land for all but a few precious hours, while the wind can whip the rain and snow into a horizontal frenzy. Swirling low pressure systems roll off Nova Scotia, and depressions born in the seas off Greenland make their angry way through the North Atlantic, skirting Iceland and setting their steely gaze on northern Norway. Outside the tranquil summer, the jet stream turns this storm track into a conveyor belt of tempests; consistent swells line up to bombard the reefs of Caithness and the beaches of Sutherland, from huge westerlies through to groomed northerly corduroy. Through the winter, six millimetres of neoprene is the norm, as water temperatures drop to four or five degrees, even with the warming vestiges of a fading Gulf Stream. It takes a certain kind of person, a certain personality and a certain sense of humour to relish the extremities of the seasons here, where latitudes are on a par with Juneau to the west and Stavanger to the east.

Spread a map of Britain on the floor, unfurl the crisp folds, iron it flat with outstretched palms. It is a physically impossibility to trace a line longer than that between the surfing heartlands of Cornwall in the southwest of England and the immediate area around the town of Thurso, the most northerly on the British mainland. Despite this space, despite the physical, social and cultural distance between these two points, this close-knit community has developed into the epicentre of Scottish waveriding. There are more surf shops in Newquay than there are surfers in Thurso, yet it is this fiercely Scottish town that has played host to the UK's most prestigious surf contest, one that has drawn waveriders from across the globe.

Thurso lies at the very end of the A9, a road that winds its way from Edinburgh through the Highlands and Inverness to the heart of the north coast's only town. To the west, a ribbon of tarmac links tiny villages of slabstone cottages that dot the hundred and twenty miles of coastline. In town, orderly lines of stone terraces form neat furrows on the western side of Thurso River, while, towards the seafront, granite fishermen's cottages crouch against the onslaught of the elements; the names in the thirteenth-century church graveyard are weathered by wind and salt. Pebbledash maisonettes sprouted in growth rings around the town as it expanded in the 1950s. Schools, banks, chemists, petrol stations and a supermarket: this is a well of resources that draws in those from satellite villages. Gleaming shop windows crowd the claustrophobic, pedestrianized main street. Winters can be bleak. The cold is that of isolation, not the bright white romantic cold of snow-capped mountains, après ski and hot chocolates, but the grey, frigid, biting cold of back aches and clenched jaws. A short drive west sits the round metallic dome of Dounreay Nuclear Plant, home to the UK's first atomic reactor. Its construction in the mid fifties saw the population mushroom through an influx of workers, from engineers to physicists. Although

AL MACKINNON

Chris Noble

One-time Middle Cottage artist in residence, still at home on even the biggest days at the reef. Originally from Fraserburgh, Chris is a stabilizing force in an expanding line-up: part enforcer of the rules, part peace-keeper, full-time charger. Above at Thurso, left at Brims Ness.

New realm
Where angels fear to tread.

the site has ceased energy production, it is still a major employer in the area for those versed in the dark arts of decommissioning. There are many places around the UK where a nuclear plant would not be a welcome neighbour; Thurso is not one of those places.

Driving out of town on the Castletown Road, Bob Treeby sees the road climb slightly to his right while, straight on, a small country lane, ruler straight, heads into the fields. With a flick of the wrists, the hum of the tyres is transformed into a rumble, as he leaves the coast road behind. There are battlements to the left running parallel behind a gaggle of buildings, smoke rises in pulses from some hidden fire. Ahead, the track takes a ninety-degree turn; Bob slows and, looking left, sees a huge lip reeling in the gap between cottages and farm. There is no smoke, just the rising plume of spray as the swell unloads on the reef ahead. Bob slows the car, eyes transfixed. Squeaking to a halt in the muddy yard, a huge vista is laid open: to the left of his vantage point the river, then the town; to his right a headland curves away and away into infinity. The swell rolls into the bay, almost invisible out in the deep water, like a mighty leviathan cruising below the surface, hardly a bow wake to be seen. The flat flagstone shore gently angles below the peat-stained waters, slippery seaweed blankets the exposed rock and a swaying tangle of jaundiced kelp dances in the shallows. Out back a single hump begins to rise, moving inexorably towards shore, growing in height and girth. Like a great predator breaking cover, it seems to rise onto muscular haunches, feathering as it stands tall and stretches out, arms wide. Suddenly it lunges, arching into a crystalline chasm that pitches and spins away down the fringes of the reef, chasing a walling wave that runs ever onwards towards the rivermouth. A finely oiled right hand barrel, it thunders like an advancing storm before collapsing into an exhausted surge of white water that spills through the kelp, coursing into fizzing rock pools. Already a second feathering peak is rising, breaking the surface. The auburn flow of the river meets the cold blue ocean, draped across the shoulder of the advancing wave, drawing across its open face like a tousled fringe. Bob Treeby's journey from his home in New Zealand has brought him here. Where many can only see a muddy farmyard in Scotland, Bob can see clear perfection.

The beach at Dunnet Bay is over three miles of smooth compact surface. In the late sixties and early seventies it was the hub for a growing Sand Yachting Club run by the Dounreay staff. With the sun burning overhead and a light offshore, the sea takes on a Caribbean hue. Photos of their beachside gatherings could easily have been mistaken for snaps of their ex-pat peers sipping beer on a beach in Bermuda – jumpers aside. Unlike many locals raised with a

healthy suspicion of the sea, Grant Coghill always had a love of water. Born and raised in Thurso, he took up a job at the Dounreay plant after graduation. "We used to paddle down Thurso River from Halkirk, about six miles, then we started to try and surf canoe, but using proper long canoes. I remember one time at Dunnet Bay, coming in on a wave, going down the face and, because of the long nose, the front went straight into the sand. When the wave pitched over, the whole thing snapped in the middle and I was left with two halves. It was then I realized that maybe this wasn't such a good idea."

It was into this embryonic beach culture of the early seventies that Bob Treeby materialized. The sight of a car driving around town with surfboards on the roof caused something of a stir with Grant and his canoe crew, and it wasn't long before Grant manufactured an introduction. "Bob never mentioned if it was the waves that brought him here or the work," says Grant. "But

Left: **Nuclear legacy**
Signs forewarn of the hazards associated with one of the region's better waves – Sandside.

Opposite top left:
Crisp winter's morn
Alex Sutherland checks one of the Caithness slabs.

Opposite top right
Perspective.

Opposite bottom
Northern exposure.

I suspect that given he had a good supply of boards and access to more, plus I remember a 'primitive' caravanette, then I think he had a fair idea he would get a surf here as well. He'd come to work as a contract draughtsman in the Central Design Office at the plant, so we said, 'Come on Bob, show us how it's done.' So the surf trips started, mostly to Dunnet, and he would teach us how to catch a wave and go a long it a wee bit. Knowing what I know now about surfing, we were nowhere near any sort of standard. We were just doing what most surf school kids can do, but, at that time, there was nobody else surfing up here." So, however tentatively, the first Thurso crew was up and riding – Grant, Ron Gallagher and George Grant. "There was never any question of surfing over rocks; reefs were considered dangerous things that would split your head open, so we surfed the many beaches all along the north coast: Farr, Strathy, Melvich, Sandside, Thurso Beach and Dunnet. We didn't spend our whole time scouring the coast for surf, it was more that, if there was a wave, we'd go; if there wasn't, we'd do something else."

Bob turned out to be something of an enigmatic surfer. Grant recalls that he didn't actually know where Bob went to catch his own waves. "He was probably pretty good, but we never saw him surf. He would either come with us to Dunnet and show us what to do, or he would go do his own thing. Where that was…" Treeby became the epicentre, the inspiration, the font and the source. The earliest surf culture flowed from Bob in the form of magazines and advice. He was also the only way to get boards, shaped by a mate of his down south called 'Mike'. "My first board was like a mini-mal, with a very upturned, rounded nose, two glassed-in fins, square at the back," laughs Grant. "It caught everything, simple as could be. My wetsuit was another story – a GUL diver's two-piece with a crotch strap, six millimetres thick. It had very little flexibility

and was actually not very warm, as water poured in every time a wave hit. Worse still, it had a towelling lining which made it great when you first put it on but it took a week to dry out!" Ron Gallagher and George Grant both ordered new boards from Bob's mate. "I spoke to Mike's wife, an arty sort, about what I could have in the way of artwork to personalize my board," says George. "We settled on a Tweety Pie, the cartoon character. I can't remember how the boards were delivered but we got them and, shock horror, alongside my new board was another, identical surfboard with Sylvester on it! That was about the limit of Ron Gallagher's attempt to personalize his board."

What have you got here?" asks the motorcycle cop, giving a cold stare from the hard shoulder. It is a chill, bleak winter's afternoon, shrouded in that special kind of grey light that blankets the sky as storm clouds gather. The driving wind is howling off the North Sea with a biting ferocity. Propped on its stand, the blue metallic Honda 175 ticks as it cools. The folded tubular steel framework is unlike any side car the policeman has seen traversing these Highland highways – it doesn't even have a wheel. And what is this white wing-like object, secured only by the deadly elasticity of multicoloured bungee straps? "It's a surfboard rack," comes the reply in broad Scouse. "A mate of mine made it." The officer turns his harsh stare on the small rider. He is in his early twenties, sporting a dark moustache while a basin helmet tries in vain to suppress a mass of curls. Pat Kieran looks away from the long arm of the law towards his bike. He isn't surprised he's been stopped, in fact he knew it was inevitable from the moment the white police Norton came into view on the dual carriageway. The officer raises his eyebrows, blows out a lungful of air and passes his judgement. "Alright then son, off you go." Pat springs onto the little Honda, kick starts

the engine and weaves off into the mercy of the cross wind before the motorcycle cop has a chance to change his mind.

"I deserved to get pulled over; that thing was bloody lethal back then," says Pat, smiling as he takes a sip of his Dark Island Stout. Pat places the letter he wrote to the northwest surf club back on the table. Sitting illuminated in the light of the peat fire, it's hard to imagine he hasn't always inhabited these northernmost fringes of the British mainland. "Pat and Mick, that's what they called me. Scouse humour. I was born and raised in Liverpool," says Pat, "but I left there in 1976 to come up here to work at Dounreay." As an electrical engineering student a lengthy work placement was an essential part of the course and, being a keen surfer, Pat knew exactly where he wanted to be – southwest England. "I'd spent a couple of summers surfing down near Westward Ho!, so that was my first choice of placement. But I didn't get my first choice, or my second choice. It was my third choice, Dounreay, that came up, so I thought, 'Why not, bit of adventure!' I'd seen this article in a magazine – before 'Wavelength' existed, more a type-written newsletter – and there was a really grainy picture, I think it was of Farr Beach. There was a right-hander breaking off the cliffs, and the article was called 'Land of The Midnight Sun'. It was about surfing through the night, and I thought, 'That sounds really romantic – I'll give that a go.'" Bob Treeby was already long gone from Thurso, but his legacy was the tiny nucleus of a surf crew and an article that would convince a young Pat Kieran that the North Shore wasn't too much of a short straw.

So, in the summer of 1976, Pat packed his bags, loaded up his motorbike and started the long drive north into the unknown. "God Almighty, it was five hundred miles away. It's a long, long way. I take it for granted now – I do it in a day, but back then… I came through so much

JOHN NUNN

Pat Kieran

"When we first surfed Brims Ness, the fishermen weren't that happy that we played there, where they made a living. Not that we were in the way, they just thought it was a bit weird – strange that we were playing in their workspace. I used to get frustrated with people; you'd tell them about the surf, but I've noticed a lot of people don't believe in something unless they've seen it on the telly. It wasn't until after the European Championships in '81, really that's where it took a quantum leap. And then another leap after the British Nationals in '89. Then the same again in '93 after the Europeans and after the first O'Neill. Locally, we were surfing Thurso and, because there was only a handful of us surfing and not someone in the water every day like there is now, you'd say to people, 'Ah it's world class surf up here,' and they'd say, 'You can't surf here, you've got to go to Cornwall to surf.' You'd say, 'There's people coming from all over the world to surf here,' and they'd go, 'Nah…'"

weather: I went through sun, wind, rain and hail, all in one journey. I remember stopping just north of Glasgow to warm myself up because my hands were just frozen. I put my gloved hands on the engine and couldn't feel anything, so I took my gloves off and put my hands on the engine casing and I could still only just get my hands warm. It was so cold the engine wasn't really warming up enough." Pat arrived for a long hot summer that is spoken of in wistful tones to this day. "I came up here for six months and that summer was fantastic – the weather was just brilliant. I seem to remember being in the water every night." For most in the UK the summer of '76 means one thing: a heatwave that's seared onto the national psyche. For Pat that summer was the beginning of a lifelong love affair with a region and its waves – a summer that would change the course of his life forever.

Two ladies are sitting on the bench outside the bakery. They meet here every week at eleven, but today they have company. The shivering Hawaiian rustles a pastry from within the grasp of a paper bag, beanie pulled down tight against the mithering grey, sandals no defence against the cold. Strains of damp Portuguese rise as two Brazilians shuffle down the high street. Despite the April rain, all hotels and boarding houses are full. The World Tour is in town for the O'Neill Cold Water Classic. New Zealanders, Canadians, Mexicans and Californians have all made the long pilgrimage for their chance at points and a berth on the 'CT. Heats are beamed across the planet by live webcast, as globetrotting athletes do battle man on man. The right-hand barrels that peel at the rivermouth in Thurso are visible from anywhere along the seafront; they are impossible to ignore, they draw the eye even though they are framed by dark, looming battlements and sponsors flags. It is still unclear who was the first to venture into the line-up here, this small competitive take-off

zone where the sea is chilled by the peaty riverwater. By the early seventies there were certainly a few hardy surfers venturing north to sample nearby bays and rivermouths, but the wave at Thurso East was yet to be recognized as one of the world's greats. It remained virginal in its blatant isolation until an undefined moment, a point in time between Alby Falzon's discovery of Uluwatu and Peter Troy's first wave at Nias, when it finally moved into the realm of the surfed. Charging on a fat, rockerless single fin, was Bob Treeby the pioneer of those machine-like hollow rights? "We never knew where Bob went to surf," says Grant Coghill, "so nobody can really tell who was the first to surf Thurso East." Certainly Grant went out on a small swell and came back with the bruises to prove it, a few other Scottish surfers too, and Welsh waverider Paul Gill was here in '75. "During my first six-month stay, I surfed Thurso East once," says Pat Kieran. "Myself and a couple of the local guys had looked at it – we'd heard of folk that had surfed it before – but we just thought no, it looked crazy; we were used to surfing beach breaks. But it didn't look difficult to surf, so eventually we thought, we've gotta give it a go. I can't remember who I surfed it with the first time but I remember just sitting on the shoulder going 'Ohhh!' It was like nothing I'd ever surfed before. I thought, there's no point just sitting out here for a couple of hours, I might as well go for it. I got absolutely rinsed loads of times before I could actually manage it. It was just such a perfect wave, fantastic. Like nothing I'd ever surfed before or since. I went away Christmas '76 and then I finished my course in '77 but I was determined to come back."

There has never been a huge affinity between the Scots and the water. The sea, yes, for they are famed the world over for their seafaring skills, but, unlike the ancient Hawaiians and Polynesians, they never

The 'Summer Breeze' collection
"Boards I shaped for friends of mine. I got the chance to ride each one of them, which was cool."
Kevin Rankin.

saw the ocean as a place for frivolity, even in recent times. It's hardly surprising really; in summer the sea retains a distinct chill to it that's not exactly conducive to swimming. "I remember I was once out surfing in Sandside Bay, and someone called the police because they found my clothes on the beach and they thought someone was committing suicide," says Thurso local Chris Gregory. "That's the first thing that they thought, not that someone would have gone for a swim or anything, more likely they were ending it all." Among the first waves to be ridden in Scotland were those off the beaches of Aberdeen in 1966, when four friends, including Alexander Mathers, rode hollow wooden boards,

locally made, from blueprints they'd acquired. A couple of years later, a young Andy Bennetts returned from a trip to Cornwall and started surfing Pease Bay on the eastern shore near Edinburgh. North of Aberdeen, a truly hard-core crew of Fraserburgh locals had begun to take on the waves at The Broch, spearheaded by Willie Tait. By the early seventies, groups were making forays onto the north coast and an embryonic Scottish Surfing Federation was establishing itself, fed by the growth around the developing scenes in Pease Bay, Aberdeen and Fraserburgh. "The surfers from Edinburgh had started coming up here, guys like Andy Bennetts and Billy Batten," says Grant Coghill. "We formed an alliance, a common bond. They had a qualifying event towards the Scottish Open, and they held some of the heats up here. It was tiny, wee slop at Farr Beach. They were all sat out back waiting for the bigger waves, and I was on the inside, picking off the smaller ones and I ended up winning, so that got me an entry into the Scottish Championships."

PAT KIERNAN

Kevin Rankin lifts the tail of the surfboard blank, closes one eye and peers down the bottom contour of his new waveriding vehicle. The nose rests on one of the wooden stands in Pat Kieran's shaping bay. Pat's shaping bay resides in the attic of a barn attached to Pat's cottage, and Pat's cottage sits on the edge of Thurso. It's the tail end of the seventies, a decade big on flares but small on health and safety. A fresh snowfall of foam dust covers a rich seam of amber resin stalagmites that have grown around the base of the stands. "I'm gonna call it the 'Rocket Fish'," says Kevin, pleased with his shaping attempt. He gathers together his collection of calipers, surforms, rulers, templates and routers. Standing at the other end of the bay, Pat Kieran is the most northerly board shaper on the planet, though his self-taught approach might be considered a little more 'organic' than his friend's. "Hang on a minute," says Kevin, arms full of tools, "do you even use a ruler or anything to mark out your blanks?" "Yeah, of course," replies Pat, a little offended that his technical prowess would be challenged. Reaching down, he produces a piece of driftwood with some pencil marks scratched into it. There is a pregnant pause before Kevin, armed with a setsquare and a look of disbelief, dissolves into hysterical laughter, followed closely by Pat. There's a pause for breath, Pat raises a finger for silence. "Oh, I bumped into a guy the other day and he says, 'You that bloke that shapes them surfboards out at Thurso East?' I said, 'Yeah,' and he replies, 'Could you shape me a shed?'" The sound of sobbing and crying fills

TIM NUNN

TIM NUNN

TIM NUNN

Top: Silkie Styx

Upper middle: Andrew Cotton
Slotted at the reef.

Lower middle: Morning light
Castletown Road.

Bottom: The new yardstick
Long-range forecasts have changed the dynamic.

the barn as the two friends double up. In a close-knit community this far from… well, anywhere, it's the craic and the camaraderie that keeps everyone going through the dark winters. Outside, laughter catches on the wind and is transformed into a lament, a wailing that drifts over the battlements of nearby Thurso castle, like the rising hue and cry of the long departed, mourning the loss of loved ones fallen to Nordic raiders over a thousand years before.

Kevin Rankin first started surfing the North Shore in 1976, ploughing up the A9 into the eye of the storm. "We'd be travelling north with surfboards on the car through sleet and snow," explains Kevin, "while others would be driving south with skis on their cars!" His first voyage into this new territory was with friends Ian McKay and Frank Paul – "another couple of soul searchers". It didn't take long for the new boys to attract attention. "We got flagged down by a local guy, Ron Gallagher, who was already surfing up

there. One trip and we were hooked! I've surfed all over the planet and enjoyed many different adventures, but I have to say nothing comes close to the spirit of Thurso. There's that certain 'Celtic Magic' that works its way inside you and never leaves. The people, the countryside, the atmosphere and, of course, the waves." By 1979, Kevin was living in a cottage that looked down over Brims Ness, an isolated point to the west of Thurso. Brims is a huge slab of flat rock that arrows out into the North Atlantic. Swell arrives and lunges onto the reef here from a huge drop-off into deep water. Even on a day when all the beaches are sleeping, there can be rideable waves at Brims. The Vikings named it well, for it translates to 'Surf Point'. "I lived with a guy called Sandy Lamont just a kilometre from the famous point; you could see it break from the cottage window," says Kevin. "In summer, the farmer would often give me a lift down around nine at night on the back of his tractor and I would sit out in the break alone, sometimes 'til midnight.

The Big Drop
"The swell was building all week. I spent an amazing couple of days at Melvich rivermouth, surfing some of the longest fun waves I ever rode. The right off the river was peeling for ever. You'd take off on a 6 foot face, ride all the way to the beach and kick out in ankle deep water – that's if your legs didn't give out first! Thurso this day was over the top, my heart was pumping looking into those huge barrels as I paddled out. The bigger sets were easy double decker bus size! Not another living soul out, just me and my stupidity! I was riding an 5'10' MR twinnie which I finally smashed into a million pieces on a wave of little consequence other than the fact that it could have killed me."
Kevin Rankin.

A MALTMAN

Some of the most peaceful, content moments I ever felt in life were sitting there, waiting for the next wave to arrive out of a mirror of glass and orange-red sky, dissolving into the dusk as the sun set late into the night. Indescribable joy! What made it more special was that I was the only one there in that moment. You don't move to a place like Brims Ness to find company. Perhaps it's about finding yourself. Whatever it was or is, it still haunts me to this day." Many people came and went through the north shore surf community; the living can be hard and the temperatures can be harder. Today Kevin has been lured to the altogether warmer climes of Australia. "Sometimes I used to surf Thurso East for a bit of company," says Kevin. "Pat Kieran was by then in residence on the break, living at Thurso East cottages. We had so many classic times there."

The hamlet overlooking the break hosted a series of tenant surfers, each the epicentre of an era. Pat Kieran spent the late seventies in Farmhouse Cottage, a decade later Neil Harris resided within the chilly walls of Middle Cottage, pushing boundaries, charging harder. Chris Noble followed; quietly spoken but chiselled from Scottish granite, he has shown there are still new lines to be drawn on this ancient Celtic wave. Each has painted the canvas with a style defined by the times – single fin lines, open face carves, deep throat barrel rides. The four houses are part of the estate of Lord Thurso, local Member of Parliament, next-door neighbour – his castle stands along-side. "Thurso East was a great place to live," says Pat. "It was a great community, still is. It's still got that hippy sort of feeling about it." Pat's house was open house – the place for visiting surfers to crash. "I'd get mates coming up to stay with me and folk coming up just for the weekend. I never locked the door. I had the place for about three or four years and I never locked the door once. When I moved out, I picked up the key to hand it back to

the landlord and it left this big key-shaped hole in the dust." Even when Pat was away, the hospitality continued. "I think I was in Liverpool seeing my mother, and I came back to a note on the kitchen table from Nigel Semmens and a couple of other guys from Cornwall. They'd legged it up here, surfed for about four hours, slept in my place. Didn't ask – didn't need to. Surfed in the morning, then went back down south and left a note. Fantastic, just come up for a long weekend." As 2009 draws to a close, Alex Sutherland resides here, wetsuits drying on flagstone hearth, keeping the 'open door, kettle on' spirit alive.

"With the Fijians, Australians or South Africans, I just saw them in the water and there were so few surfers, everyone you saw was new." Pat had a veritable United Nations of Surf sleeping on his floor through the late seventies. His motto at that time: why go off around the world, when the world comes to you? When you don't have a surf community on your doorstep, you open yourself up to other surfers, others imbibed with the culture of surf. "I remember surfing big classic Thurso East by myself sometimes – ten- to twelve-feet surf, scary. That's why I wrote that letter. I thought I could do with a bit of company here. I'd give anybody my floor, because you do that and you meet some great people and you've got some great memories. You learn a lot from other people, if you just open yourself up to them." Pat looks back at the idea that you'd have to try to encourage people to come surf world-class waves and laughs. "Today, at Thurso East, I'd say there's hardly a good wave that goes unsurfed now. There's always someone in the water if there's a swell, every day of the week. You certainly couldn't say that back then. There would be hardly a decent wave that was surfed thirty years ago. Those that were surfed were surfed by me and a handful of other guys. It was just amazing having this wave for just you and a couple of lads." Pat's role as surfer in residence

didn't just extend to hospitality to visiting surfers. As with Bob before him, Dounreay was his nine to five but, outside this time, he provided the boards for the locals he could entice into the water. The barn attached to the cottage became a shaping bay, his spare room was for glassing. In ancient Celtic lore, the Selkie was a female seal that comes ashore and transforms into a beautiful maiden to take a lover for a night. Pat's 'Selkie Styx Surfboards' carried the Thurso crew out into the line-ups. "I built about a dozen boards there," says Pat. "If you go up in the bedroom, you can still see surfboard-shaped resin marks on the floor. God knows how I got away with it. They should have thrown me out. I took the shaped blanks into the spare bedroom so I could get a bit of temperature to do the resin and fibreglass. I built them just for the cost of building them. I did single fins, a couple of twin fins, and I built a Stinger. Jackie, a girl I was going out with at the time, used to do the artwork for me, things like dragons. I loved shaping boards. They used to run craft fairs in the town hall. I went in there one day and shaped a board from scratch, so people could watch me do it. This would have been about 1978 or '79; I wouldn't get away with it now."

The music builds to a crescendo, 'O Fortuna' from *Carmina Burana*, almost hypnotic as chanting voices rise and fall. The surfer ducks into a barrel – Shaun Tomson almost noseriding on his short pintail as he cruises by in a slow-motion crystal cavern at Off-The-Wall. A bronzed babe on a beach sits up and looks on adoringly as the surfer walks by. "Old Spice." The surfer splashes something on his chiselled jaws. "The mark of a man," states the deep voice. Commercial break over, back to the 'Morecombe & Wise Christmas Special'. In Britain of the early eighties, that Old Spice commercial, with its promise of sun, sea, sand and sex, was the only hint surf culture to wash across the mainstream subconscious. This was an era dominated by Mrs Thatcher, economic recession, high unemployment and social unrest. Industries were collapsing wholesale, bands like The Jam issued a call to arms to an angry and politicized youth movement. Scotland felt a long way from London, cut adrift in a sea of rising capitalism. While city traders shopped for Testarossas, and Brixton burned, surf culture seemed to be the antithesis of everyday life in Thatcher's Britain.

If the teachers on playground duty strain their eyes, they might just spot the puffs of smoke emanating from behind the bike sheds. The source of the signals, a fifteen-year-old schoolgirl, is having a sneaky dinnertime cigarette. Peering through a window she spots a pile of strange-looking objects stacked at the back of a garage – her curiosity is tweaked. She puts her hands up to the glass to shield her eyes and looks again. "I saw all these completely out of it, bizarre surfboards with fantastic designs like huge dragons across them and big fish with scales," says Sheila Finlayson. Next thing, Sheila is rousing the troops. "I got all the girls that had been skiing and I said, 'I found these surfboards, has anybody got a wetsuit? Shall we give it a go?'" Recruits came quickly; now all the budding crew needed was someone to show them the ropes. "Mr Culley was quite a young maths teacher," says Sheila. "He said, 'I don't know how to surf.' But I said, 'Well we've all seen the Old Spice advert, how hard can it be? I've seen waves like that. Shall we have a crack at it?' So we persuaded him to take us. We used these old boards, which turned out to be Pat Kieran's – somehow they'd ended up in the school."

With the school minibus secured, the band of would-be surfers headed for the beach. OK, maybe not the beach. "We went immediately to Brims Ness," says Sheila, "because that's where the waves were that looked like the Old Spice advert." Brims is now the alternate WQS contest site, epic Backdoor-like barrels break at this isolated spot. "We started at The Point first. We went, 'That's a nice big wave. That's got a big tubie thing, let's have a crack at that. Ahhh, shit, that's quite difficult.' We weren't very successful really but, because we were young we didn't break, but we basically got pummelled. Then we tried Thurso East, and that was no good so, we kind of sussed out that we needed smaller, gentler waves. We started going out west and using the yellow mini-bus probably every weekend and maybe once or twice a week, and we'd go to the nearest place that had waves. After about three months, we all started standing up – with a very unique style. We'd go out west, often to Farr Bay, that's where I remember going the most, because it is such a nice shallow, gentle beach. And Torrisdale, lots of good surf at Torrisdale." A lack of equipment wasn't going to hold the girls back in their new venture. "We started out without gloves or hats or socks," explains Sheila. "Our wetsuits didn't even fit. We had verucca socks and washing up gloves to try and see if that would keep the cold out – very gorgeous. It worked a bit – worked better than nothing." Looking back from an era dominated by law suits and Risk Assessments, a young teacher, with no surf experience, taking a group of fifteen-year-old girls out to a beach and then letting them float off into one of the world's most notorious stretches of sea may seem incredible. However, it was only their uncompromising drive, guts and sheer determination that got them past mere playground bravado and out into the water. "We were basically teaching ourselves, it was great. There was Debbie and Sarah Cox, Barbara, Carol Wilson and Alison Ross. Aileen Kiddie used to take us as well. Then a few boys started turning up, but we thought it was a girl's sport. When we went to Cornwall we got such a shock. We thought, 'It's so effeminate down here – where are the girls?'"

Brims Ness Bowl
"I said 'Well we've all seen the Old Spice advert, how hard can it be?' said Sheila Finlayson. "We went immediately to Brims Ness, because that's where the waves were that looked like the advert. We started at The Point first. We went that's a nice big wave. That's got a big tubie thing, lets have a crack at that. Ahhh, shit, that's quite difficult." First surfed by Pat Kieran, Brims has been a contest venue for the Cold Water Classic WQS.

That chance discovery in 1981 has given Sheila a life-long love of surfing, a passion that has taken her around the globe to places like Indonesia, Australia, New Zealand, South America and California. Today she still manages to get in the water every week, sometimes two or three times. "We entered some contests just for fun. If there was a contest, it was good because lots of people came, and you got to meet them. Like these guys from Fraserburgh, like Ian Masson; the Kirkintilloch boys were all good surfers. Eventually, after a couple of years I managed to win the Scottish Champs. I think it's nine or ten titles now," she says almost embarrassed. "I do enjoy competing, and it encourages me to surf a little bit better." She even surfed at the World Masters in Taranaki, NZ. Today Sheila passes on that surfing stoke to local grommets. Whether it's taking them along on a run out to the beaches, allowing them to store boards in her shed near the break or offering words of advice and encouragement, Sheila sees surfing as something

that could be a real positive for the local disenchanted youth. "There's lots of kids kicking about a bit bored, loads of… I don't know, aggression – lots of adrenaline-seeking tendencies," she says. "All they need to do is get in the water, that'll give them plenty. They don't really access it. I think that's a shame. If this was down in Cornwall, it'd be mobbed. I know that some other people feel differently and want to protect their waves, but I'm personally supportive of getting more youngsters into the water. I think I had so much fun with it that it'd be nice to share that with other kids."

In Cornwall everyone surfs. Go and visit a doctor and they'll probably start a little banter by asking how the waves are. The police officer that pulls you over for speeding surfs, the postman, the baker. Surfing is mainstream. It used to be a select club, a bond, something the few discussed among the many. There is now a surf shop in every town and nearly every coastal village. In Thurso surfing is still something that the mainstream don't understand. Up here it's still a counter culture, just a small tight crew. Even the Cold Water Classic surf contest hasn't really broken the ice. Alistair Coghill is at the vanguard of the next generation, still a grommet but having already made the progression into the line-up at the reef. "I suppose in Cornwall you can just rent a board and go in at Fistral with hundreds of others," says Ali. "Where as up here, it's just, 'The sea is bad, you don't go in the sea.' Up here there's no one and nothing to get you started. It's not an option unless you *really* want to get into it. There's only a few people who actually put in the effort." Surfing in the north of Scotland has access problems – as in how do you gain access to the waves? After all, wetsuits are £200, boards £300, plus boots and gloves, and it's not like there's a glut of second-hand gear going spare here. That's before you factor in actually getting to some beginner-friendly waves. Luckily for Ali, father Grant had a little previous with the waves around Thurso. "We went fishing a lot and my Dad told me about how he used to go diving and stuff," says Ali. "One day we saw a guy surfing Point of Ness, and I said, 'Who's that!' and my Dad said, 'It's Andy Bain'. I got in touch with him, and he took me out to Dunnet Beach on a foamie. He sorted me out with a wetsuit and a board, and I went from there I suppose. I really wanted to get into it. I think I missed the first winter but every winter after that I was on it. After Andy Bain gave us lessons, my Dad took me out and pretty much taught me. Then we were surfing better waves at Dunnet, and then we went to waves like Melvich and we surfed together. We used to have the trailer and we'd have these two huge boards, like a seven-feet ten-inch and six-feet ten-inch. A two-hour surf would take four hours – getting into wetsuits, loading up the trailer, having a checklist, 'Wetsuit – check, rash vest – check,' and there was a picnic: kind of an all day kind of thing. Now I get to surf waves at Thurso East. A lot of credit goes to Andy Bain but most goes to my Dad."

Left
Cold, clear and crystal.

A. MACKINNON

Melvich
The beaches of Sutherland
offer empty peaks and rivermouth
sandbars. Rights going unridden.

The parking area above the fabled right-hander isn't so much a car park as a muck-splashed farmer's yard, wet and muddy year-round. In the winter it's cold, bitterly cold. To the left stands a corrugated barn, to the rear, Pat's old cottage and in front, a short drop down to the reef and a long, slippery low-tide walk out to the water's edge. A rideable wave brings a line of cars, campers and pick-ups. Surfers hop around open doors, pulling on boots, trying to avoid the mire. The farmer's tractor tiptoes through, a golden bale hoisted high over its rusty bulk. Andy Bain leans against the front of his white VW combi, watching the sets break and reel along the reef. He's waiting for the tide to push in, for perfect conditions. Bainers isn't the kind of guy you'd miss easily, a man mountain with long flowing hair, he'd look equally at home standing on the front line with the massed ranks of William Wallace's troops at the Battle of Stirling Bridge. Pat Kieran sparked something here, lit a candle that illuminated a great beauty, a gemstone of reflected light that enchants all who gaze upon it. If Pat provided the candle, Andy has become the torch-bearer – a Thurso lad brought up in this harsh northern town, embracing a lifestyle born on the beaches of Malibu, melded with the Highland experience. "I grew up with great waves," says Andy, "but the disadvantage being this far north would be the atmosphere; there was no surf culture, so you couldn't go out to like a surfy bar, you never had surf shops. Once you got out of the water it was back to normality, back to Thatcherism. That's why surfing was good up here, you could escape from everything – once you got off the land it was brilliant. But once you got back in… There wasn't that Cornwall-type thing, the buzz. I spent three seasons in Cornwall working as a chef and surfing – it was absolutely fantastic, surfing in a shortie in the summer, going in the Watering Hole on the beach at Perranporth at night and having a drink. You blended in with the crowd, where as up here people don't understand surfing, you're always battling against that element, you know. Still, to this day."

Andy was a product of the North Shore Surf Club, a couple of surfers and a few parents who brought young groms into waveriding and helped them find their feet. "Back then there was about ten to a dozen of us. Normally, if there was surf in the evenings, there'd be about six of us out. We'd just go out and have fun. There was the older generation like Neil Harris, John Broch and Ross Ireland, and the Castletown surfers, and we were kind of the next generation." Surf for the groms meant the relatively small waves of Thurso beach, but, eventually, the pack ventured out onto the Shit Pipe, a quality right-hand reef across the channel from Thurso East. Somewhat overshadowed by it's larger sibling, it has become a proving ground, a rite of passage. "You progressed onto the Shit Pipe," says Andy, "and then we went to the beaches out west for a couple of seasons. We never even knew anything about Brims for about two years. One day me and my friend were down by the beach having fish and chips and Neil Harris came up and said, 'Do you want to go for a surf?' and it was absolutely like a mill pond. We thought, 'He's stoned,' but we went, 'Yeah, alright.' He took us to Brims and we surfed the Bowl. It was overhead; for us it was pretty hardcore. Soon after that we were out at Thurso East." Harris was a hard charger who moved north for the waves in the late eighties, moved into the Thurso cottages, returned south a few years later.

Few graduates of the surf school have remained in the line-up. Some have moved away, most gave up surfing. Andy explains, "I get a lot of bad image because I'm the one shouting at the surfers who come up, but a lot of my friends stopped; I'm the only one of my generation left surfing. I feel – I don't know if it's a burden – but I feel I'm carrying the flag for Thurso East. I'm quite a chilled-out person but, if someone's being an idiot in the water, you can't help but go off at them, you know. I mean, half the guys these days are surfing places and there's fifty on a little peak and they're having to fight for waves, and when they come here, they still have that mindset. I'm like, 'Look, you've just had a set wave and now you're paddling past everyone; use the line-up and then everyone gets waves.' Over the last four or five years it's certainly got busier. People will adapt."

Pat hoists down a board from the wall of his cottage near Dounreay. It is a twin fin, thick with boxy rails, shaped in the barn, glassed in the bedroom, ridden on the wave. Pat Kieran is the common thread woven through the fabric of surf culture here in the extreme northeast of Scotland. First surfer in residence, he shaped boards for those who wanted to take to the sea, the same boards found by Sheila Finlayson. He encouraged grommets through the Surf Club, donating his time, sharing his stoke, giving lessons and lifts to the beach. The fabric and history here would have been of a different weave if Pat had gained his first choice and headed to the waves of Devon instead of Caithness. "Once I'd been here and surfed this wave, it really was exactly like – I described it at the time – it was like an elastic band. The further I got away from Caithness and that wave, to be honest, the tighter that band got, the more determined I was to get back."

A burnt orange fire licks the blue-black horizon. An overnight sprinkling of snow has dusted the landscape, spilling a fine layer of crystals that glint and glisten in the first rays of the rising sun. The drab Land Rover bumps its way down the farm track before crunching to a halt in a frozen puddle. The distant Orkneys, those dark Neolithic isles,

recline offshore, red cliffs offset, blue ocean clear and sharp. Smooth flagstones stacked into regimented walls, lined battalions backed by the sharpness of rusting barbs, the field crisp underfoot leads to the cliff top. The savage peak unloads in three feet of water, three surfers paddle around the heaving lip, as the wave spits its salty breath into the channel. Mistakes here are costly, pitching the rider into waist-deep water, leaving the surfer marooned on the flat slab, as the fluid around drains away, tugging at feet, stranded knee deep under the towering onslaught of a looming lip – nowhere to go, no water to duck dive, just the savage reef's impenetrable skin. No rolling white water here, no gentle faces to cruise and glide, just the harsh angles of the pitching barrels, the steepness and precariousness of the tube-ride. The most risk, yet the biggest reward. The north shore of Scotland has become defined by a single wave, known throughout the world. It is the only cold-water location in which this has happened. It took the crowding of Thurso East to push the locals to push the envelope, but now it is the indigenous tribe that treads beyond old boundaries. Just as Thurso East was once dismissed as a mere phantom, best left to the realm of mind-surfing, now hidden slabs and reefs have crossed the threshold into the rideable. New names are spoken in hushed tones. The hunt is on. Clothes piled on the shore by icy puddles, here they share the lefts, just three friends, taking turns to charge.

Northeast England

SCOTT WICKING

Your first custom steed is a thing of magic. And here was mine, light beneath my hands, Hollywood-smile-white against the coffee coloured waters. It glided effortlessly over the wall of advancing foam as I waded out into the frigid ocean. I knew its dimensions – I had written them on the crumpled order form, memorised them while the foam-covered shaper offered up wisdom. Until that moment I'd existed on a diet of lightly battered, mostly unsuitable, second hand sticks, but there weren't really enough boards around in the North East of the late '80's to be choosy. Now here was my brand new Nor-Easter, made in England, for England, coconut waxed and tropical scented heading out into the embrace of a malevolent North Sea. Each duck-dive drove an icy shockwave through my temple, but sitting out back, looking down at the fresh spray job, a warm glow melted through the cold. And it definitely seemed to glide better for its reverse-vee bottom, I thought. "Like Tom Curren's *Black Beauty*", that's what I'd asked for.

Twenty minutes later I was standing in the snow-covered car park, broken leash gripped in a neoprene fist. One wave ridden, one glorious open face, 'Curren-esque' I deluded myself, before the ignominy of the end section closeout. I was looking at a black tarmac square where my car had rested – waiting faithfully with the promise of a towel, a heater and a brimming flask. There was but one conclusion - my girlfriend had taken off, bored of watching dark silhouettes bobbing in a dark sea while wipers squeaked away falling flakes. I stamped my numb feet, hoping the percussion could raise some warmth or quell my frustration. I understood then that not everything is built to go the distance, but more than twenty years down the line, I still have that Nor-Easter, that magic board.

It lies across the landscape like a giant sleeping beast. Twisted pipes like great metallic bowels, huge chimneys issuing orange flames that roar into the evening sky, wailing like a pack of angry wolves. Bright, white marshmallows of steam billow from stacks adorned with pulsing red illuminations. A backdrop embossed with scenes from *Blade Runner*, visions of Armageddon. It is a brave new world: a world of plastics and oils and alloys and atomic power. Here is its genesis. Here lie the sprawling chemical plants, the spewing blast furnace and the foreboding nuclear reactor. Built on the banks of the river, fed by the river, whose waters are used and abused in return. A tanker cruises past towards the sea, bulbous bow riding high to reveal a belly of oxide red as it shovels water in front, a leviathan muscling out into the ocean's highways. The rusty buoy rolls with the swell, tiny below the towering hulk. Wrapping lines round the end of the sea wall, wheeling on their axis as they change direction, pivoting into the huge, dark rivermouth. Almost unseen in the shadow of the tanker, a tiny black figure is paddling, steady headway, arms taking long lazy strokes as the surfer rounds the fizzing white water, the air a heady ether of aftershave-sweet ozone. A lone figure watches from a bank of sharp boulders, an inhospitable platform at the base of the sea wall, waiting to stub numb toes and puncture clumsily placed resin. But beyond and out back, the first wave is breaking; a pack of dark silhouettes scrambles over the shoulder, a brown face, steep and angry, furrowed brow. The pitching lip detonates in the shallows, its steep frame reeling into a tubular right-hander, spinning down the cobble point. The pack scrabbles over the next as the lip begins to feather, then a solitary shape turns and starts to drop, angling down the face, pursued by the thick curtain, a trailing arm leaves a white jet-stream across the wave face as the lip gains, before the figure is gone, lost behind the fringe. Onward races the wave,

hugging the shallow contours of the point, bending round the deep channel before drawing and exhaling a salty breath, spitting the surfer into the channel, arms held aloft, mind lost in the moment. Momentum drains away and the form compresses headlong into a plunging dive; a moment of sheer joy wrapped in cold hard drizzle and the drifting intimation of sulphur.

England's Northeastern shore is a complex patchwork of landscapes, crafted by the graft of hands and the hands of time. This is a stretch of coastline drenched in history, steeped in the blood of Romans, Celts, Vikings, Normans and Saxons, fringed by and shaped by the North Sea; the shoreline sculpted by mighty glaciers and fettled by ocean currents. The summer solstice burns long: dawn cracks the horizon by five am and the evening's last rays blaze a fiery red around eleven. Mercury peaks in the high twenties during tourist season, while the short days of winter's dark can be blanketed under a fine dusting of white. Britain's eastern shore looks out over the frigid hunting ground of the North Sea. Wars raged and whole industries were built here around the twin pillars of the mighty cod and all

Below
The North is divided by great rivers, united by immense industry.

Above
A fresh dusting of white powder covers the early February landscape.

powerful black gold, our insatiable appetites fuelling the enthusiasm with which the sea was mined for these precious natural resources. It was thought the fish and the oil would last forever; we now know this was a pipedream. The fishing industry is all but gone, and less oil flows year on year as reserves begin to drain away. The ocean here can be a wild cauldron. It is a stretch of water that misses the gentle warming touch of the Gulf Stream, it has a cold heart that runs deep. Low-pressure systems that spin off the eastern seaboard of Canada race across the Atlantic towards Iceland, before passing above northern Scotland. These spiralling depressions channel groundswell generated in the Arctic Circle towards England's eastern shore, long distance, lined and groomed. The resulting collision of corduroy and coastline

creates a goofy footer's paradise, for the waiting beaches, points and flat sedimentary reefs offer predominantly left-breaking fare.

The North is more than just a sign that straddles the M1, it is more than just the forgotten sibling in the North-South divide; it is an identity built with hands and graft and labour. The North was coal mines, steel making, textiles and dark satanic mills; it was the social cohesion of working men's clubs and unions and belonging and community. It may have been grim up north, but it was a grim that you belonged to. There may have been no such thing as 'society' in the south, but here it was inclusive, it was collective. The waters of time may have washed in a new social movement, but there is still a

TIM NUNN

Forged in the North Sea
Heavy industrial walls rise up.

bedrock in the North that is not so easy to erode. The ancient kingdom of Northumberland crowns the coastline, a wild region of open shores and empty expanses of golden sand, watched by ghostly keeps and dark monasteries. Small villages huddle down, away from the wind's onslaught, while towering dunes cushion the high tide line of curving bays. The water shimmers in cold cobalt, seals and porpoises skim through the clear, circling offshore islands where white lighthouses cling precariously among nesting seabirds. This swathe of green collides with one of Britain's great industrial heartlands, where wealth was built on foundations of toil and sweat. Three great cities cleaved by three great rivers: Newcastle by the Tyne, Sunderland by the Wear and Middlesborough, the Tees. It is here that great ports arose, where colliers were laden with dark, dusty cargo, where the *Mauretania* was forged and where iron was wrought in fires as hot as Phlegethon. The building blocks of an Empire were assembled here and delivered by sea to the four corners the globe. Today, old sites gleam with new industries and new technologies; car production lines spark under robot arms, aseptic computer plants replicate circuit boards and the ominous clean-burn promise of a nuclear future stands silhouetted against the ocean. City centres have regenerated into quayside bars, while malls and chain store have drained away the heart of commerce. Leaving the suburbs, heading south, brown waters run up against high cliffs, green farms and fishing towns: Whitby, with its ancient harbour or the Victorian resorts of Saltburn-by-the-Sea and Scarborough, with their seafront promenades and grand hotels. Between Alnwick in Northumberland and Bridlington in Yorkshire lies one hundred and forty miles of coastline. Over two-and-a-half million people call this coastline home; people divided by four rivers, five professional football teams and six dialects, but united by one mighty force: a collective respect for the all-powerful ocean.

DEMI TAYLOR

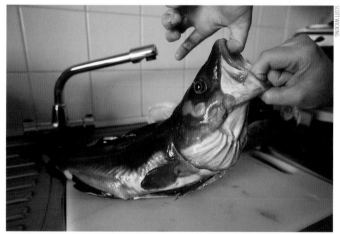

SCOTT WICKING

TIM NUNN

In a country where eccentricity has flourished, it is no surprise to learn that there have been brave souls wave-sliding in England since the 19th century. All manner of craft were tried and tested, but it was not until the 1920s that any kind of scene developed. Belly boards gained popularity at resorts around Cornwall and Devon in the southwest. Long before the days of neoprene and balsa, the whitewater was alive with bathing caps, speeding plywood and broad grins. By 1941, Pip Staffieri was riding a hollow homemade board in Newquay, a spark that helped ignite surfing in Europe. In the late fifties, in Jersey, there was a burgeoning scene, a surf club was formed and the beach lifestyle exploded in popularity. By 1965, the UK's first surf company, Bilbo, was formed in Newquay by Bill Bailey and Bob Head, making boards and threads. Gul Wetsuits started soon after, and Newquay became the hub of European surfing. But the British fascination with waveriding began long before this, an interest spawned by the voyages of one Captain J Cook.

Britain is a small island, yet one that rose to become the most powerful nation on the planet, controlling over a quarter of the world's territory. But how did it manage to exert such control? How did Britain build its mighty Empire? It did so through its mastery of the ocean in the name of science, land, wealth and God; through the exploits of men like James Cook. Yet, in 1744, Cook was marooned, trapped behind the dark wood, hidden within the smoky light of a haberdashery, entombed in the heart of a fishing village by a stream on the Yorkshire coast. Ambling to work down steep cobbles towards the harbour, his peripheral vision was channelled through narrow rain-soaked streets; shaded by red tiled roofs and dark crumbling cliffs, out away over the ocean. Eighteen months was as much as he could take, drinking in the opportunity of the broad horizon, before moving down the coast to the harbour town of Whitby,

TIM NUNN

a bustling port crammed with tall masts, the air bruised and blue with the clang of anchors, the flapping of rigging and the creaking of wood boughs. Here Cook began a new life as a merchant navy apprentice working for the Walkers, a local shipping family. Their stock and trade was transporting coal from Tyneside to London aboard their fleet of colliers. These vessels were shallow of draft and flat-bottomed, designed to be grounded at high tide on flat local reefs, loaded while the sea receded, then refloated as the waters returned. It was aboard these vessels that Cook learned astronomy, trigonometry, mathematics, chart reading and the navigational skills required of a sea captain. He would remember his time aboard these vessels well, for when he was asked to lead his first expedition around the world, his vessel of choice was the *Earl of Pembroke*, a collier bark, Whitby-built and shallow-keeled. It was renamed *Endeavour* and its voyages would become legend. Cook's converted colliers would take him to new lands, deep into the South Pacific, to New Zealand and Australia, Canada and Alaska, Indonesia and, finally, to Hawaii, where he would witness surfing but not live to tell of this strange new discovery.

Saltburn-by-the-Sea was once a sleepy beachside hamlet, where fishermen launched their boats off the beach, braving the waves at the cobblestone break known as Penny's Hole. The Victorian resort town grew atop the cliffs overlooking the sea in 1861. Rows of terraces were built, named after precious gemstones. This was an era when the seaside became a place to visit, where you could walk and even to take to the water. The magnificent hotel boasted not just sea views but also its own private railway platform, while the promenade was linked to the pier below by the water-powered funicular railway. It was Victorian grandeur fit for a visiting monarch; just as well since Edward VII was known to 'visit' his mistress here. Surfing first arrived just over a century later, when the 'big three' launched into the waters in 1964. John Roughton, John Smith and Ian Davies were inspired by a newspaper article about the sport and, looking out at the ocean on their doorstep, decided to give it a try. Board availability was extremely limited: there were a handful of emerging board builders in Cornwall, but their products were not only expensive, they were over four hundred and twenty miles away in Newquay – nearly a twelve-hour journey in the pre-motorway era. So, like many surfing pioneers through the ages, John Smith decided to build his own board with the raw materials at hand. With polystyrene foam and determination, he set about crafting the first boards. Then a breakthrough came, when a source at the nearby ICI plant at Redcar provided him with 'A' grade polyurethane foam and the means to take his R&D to the next level. Clad in crude diving suits and a steely will, they would take to the sandbanks that built up alongside Saltburn pier whenever the swells rolled in. Tim Gladders and others began to form the nucleus of a surf club and a waveriding community was born. Like the local sedimentary stone, its history was laid down in fine layers of stories, photographs, tall tales, broken boards and trips planned, building a scene that would become the bedrock for the region's waveriding heritage.

The tide is pushing and the waves are small but clean. Saltburn Pier rises tall above the line-up, tiptoeing out beyond the line of white water. Gary Rogers stands by the sea wall and at the heart of the local scene here. The car park buzzes with activity: day trippers returning from seafront walks, classic car owners enjoy a break from their wind-in-the-hair blast, and surfers pulling on thick layers of still-damp neoprene. The sea is dark, heavy with fine sediment that bestows the hues of chilled brown ale upon the winter waves. Spoiled snow lingers in ugly patches around the roadside and on the grassy cliff. "I came here about '77 for a contest. There

was really good surf; that's when I fell in love with the place," says Gary, pushing hands deep into pockets for the lingering vestiges of warmth. "I was a member of Sol-Y-Mar Surf Club, which was a national club run by Bez Newton. It was the second biggest surf club in the country, with about a hundred and fifty members. I was part of the northwest team. It wasn't until the summer of '82 that I moved up here. We came to live in Darlington – which is about thirty miles away – so I came surfing here. The summer of '82 was good surf, the autumn was fantastic, the best surf I've ever had. I actually gave up playing rugby because the surf was so good. I spent all my time, all my weekends coming over here surfing."

Gary Rogers first saw surfers aged eleven at Caswell Bay in Wales. He was so fascinated that he sat and watched, enthrawled by the display of wave sliding. At fourteen, when the family moved to Pembrokeshire, Gary had his first real contact with surfing through the local surf club, borrowing a board down the beach. "That Bilbo was kept in the surf club hut," explains Gary, "and three of us used to take it in turns. Then, in 1974, I bought a 7'6 single fin Bing at the beach from a visiting surfer for £25. The following year my

SCOTT WICKING

brothers, Malcolm, Mark and Jeff, we all went up to Swansea looking for boards. It was an eighty-mile train journey. We got all the local papers, looked for boards in ads in the back. We walked, got on the bus and managed to get two. The only place that sold wax was a music shop in Swansea – you wouldn't get people going eighty miles on the train these days to get wax. Bit of a mission."

With a VW split-screen van the world is your oyster. From California to Cornwall, it is the classic surf mobile, the ubiquitous people's wagon: rugged, reliable and simple, with room for boards and a bed. With combi loaded, Gary would drive down from Darlington to Saltburn, park up by the beach and stay for the weekend. Other times he would jump on the train with his board, surf for three or four hours, then head back. "When we had our split-screen van, quite often you'd get ten or twelve VWs down here on a Friday night," says Gary. "We'd all camp over and stay in our vans; we'd have BBQs and fires on the beach. There'd be twenty or thirty people; it was a good social scene." By 1986, Gary had relocated to the beach. The first year in the northeast was a shock after growing up surfing in Wales, where the Atlantic's waters draw warm comfort from the passing Gulf Stream. "I'd bought a four-millimetre winter deluxe Australian wetsuit from Ma Simes, it was a Piping Hot. It was boiling when I lived in Wales; came up here and I realised I needed a thicker wetsuit, a five-millimetre. Snugg and Second Skin, they became the wetsuits of choice, they were warm and made to measure. I think I surfed for the first five years without a hood, which was silly because it's given me surfer's ear. Generally round here it's five to six degrees in the water, end of January to mid March. One year we went down to three degrees. That was a hard winter, we had a lot of easterlies. It was about minus twelve with the wind chill and the ice stayed frozen on the cliffs for the whole time."

SCOTT WICKING

Top
Shite hawk crown,
Captain James Cook.

Bottom
An instruction in Gothic settings:
through the cold, damp archway
towards Whitby Abbey.

"We started the mobile surf shop because I was bringing a few boards up from Roger Cooper in Wales and Nick Noble was selling wetsuits, so we decided to get a van. We did have a look at getting a shop in the town but we thought it wouldn't work there. So, in 1986, it became the mobile surf shop." In rural communities and outposts, the mobile shop was a tradition; even banks rolled in on set days in order for people to balance their books and draw out their cash for the week. On the seafront the mobile surf shop plied its trade for the two months of summer season, parked up by Saltburn pier, renting out boards and selling basics. The following year they extended to three months, June to August, then to September, then to October starting in May. "We'd got a Luton box van that we'd leave up the top of the cliff and sometimes we went up to Tynemouth and Scarborough. At the time there were no surf shops on the east coast." Sensing that it might be time to expand the business into a bigger, better, more permanent base, Nick and Gary undertook some market research to help sure up the belief of the local bank manager, as well as bolster their own gut instincts. They soon had a list of over one hundred and fifty names – surfers who came from within the Saltburn scene, the Whitby crew, the Hartlepool crew, as well as those drawn to the coast from nearby cities such as Leeds, Durham and York. "We built the shop in 1990 and Saltburn Surf Shop was trading by '91." By '94 there were around two hundred and forty names on the list. "We always had a special bond with the Whitby crew," says Gary. "We'd often have little contests and sometimes they'd win and sometimes we'd win. There was a bit more rivalry with the Scarborough crew. They've run a contest there since the seventies, and we'd all go down and take part. But, after the contest was finished, we'd all go out drinking on the night and have a good laugh together."

It was the mid seventies when surfing came to Whitby. Phil Marshall and Andrew Bradley were surfing in the long hot summer of '76. Jo Botham had tried skimboarding, body surfing and belly boarding on holidays in Newquay, but the fact that older brother Nick was one of the first guys on the surf scene meant Jo was reluctant to follow. But in February of '81, curiosity led to a few white-water waves on the beach at Whitby, under the shadow of Captain Cook's statue, and another surfing soul had been claimed. Jo's baptism was that classic scenario of make-do-and-mend, of one board shared between three eager groms shoehorned into ill-fitting wetsuits, stoke easing the biting chill of wind and water. "I remember walking home up Argyll Road," says Jo; "and suddenly realising that I'd lost a flip flop somewhere and

I hadn't even realised it had come off my foot. We had no gloves or anything. It was like anaesthetic in your lower leg; you couldn't feel your feet until about four hours after. At least I had a wetsuit, even if it was too big and leaked, I think Greenie started out in jeans and a rugby shirt." For grommets on this early scene, there was no instant fix when it came to equipment. It was the harsh world of supply and demand – and supply was strictly limited. "I was only 14 and you couldn't just go to somewhere like Saltburn unless you could blag a lift – Saltburn's under twenty miles but it seemed a long way away, going there was like a surf trip," he explains. "As for boards, you had to wait for one to be vacated by someone higher up the pecking order. That was the only way you could acquire one; there were no surf shops. And there were only eight

Jo Botham

"The East Coast Open in Scarborough became a social gathering of the clans," says Jo Botham. "There'd be a film, maybe at the Cricketers. We'd see people dressed as surfers, wearing shirts and thongs. In Whitby there were skinheads and greasers. We'd also go up to Tynemouth for contests, that would be the only reason, no one considered there'd be waves worth travelling for up there. There was no crowd pressure."

SCOTT WICKING

TIM NUNN

surfers at the time." As in most fledgling surf communities, boards were a precious resource to be recycled religiously and worshipped unconditionally. "There was an Atlantic Surfboards single fin, which was a really weird-shaped board but quite progressive for its day. It was 6'0 or 6'1 that Greenie brought back from Cornwall. It was a great board; at least four or five other people owned it including myself. It was known as the 'No Nose' – not because of the design, but because Greenie had smashed the nose out of it and it was taped up. Ding repair wasn't really high on the agenda in those days."

It's 1985. The time-weathered scar stretches from under the towering cliff's bitter shadow, a long angled triangle of sedimentary rock grasping for the sunlight. This flat reef tapers out towards the brown waters, barnacle-studded, harsh on cold soles. Out on the tip a peak is rearing, rising, dark and menacing. This is a weighty wave, hollow and powerful. To paddle out here means taking up the gauntlet, facing down a challenge. The Point is a serious undertaking. A select band of searchers have been surfing here for a couple of years, charging the vertical drops and hollow walls on equipment that hasn't quite evolved to a level where it can pitch in and help. The shelving coastline catches the swell in a number of spots on this stretch. Close by, the lines collide with a tapering edge, a fringe of scar that angles below the impenetrable brown hues of the North Sea. They had watched this unridden hollow beast rifle down the scar in ruler-edged perfection, a cylindrical racetrack speeding, almost unending and there was one question that had been playing on their minds. "Do you think that's rideable?" asked Jo Botham to Greenie and Sedge. On this day they decided to find out. "Tuesday 16 April, 1985," says Jo, leaning on the huge metallic surface, deep in the heart of the family bakers. "We had two sessions. We'd originally gone down to surf the Point, but we decided to give this wave a go instead. I think I paddled for the first wave and went over the falls. Obviously we knew nothing then about the best take-off spot or anything. I'm not sure who rode the first wave, whether it was Greenie or Sedge. Greenie kept a diary that year – coincidentally the only year he kept one. We called it 'The Cove' and had it completely to ourselves, just the Whitby crew, until 27 October the same year. That's when the first person from outside our crew paddled out. There are only two words in Greenie's diary for that day: 'Cove R.I.P.'"

By the mid eighties the embryonic Whitby crew consisted of Alistair 'Brock' Brocklehurst, Paul 'Greenie' Green, Michael 'Sedge' Sedgewick, Howard, Jo Botham, Andrew 'Brad' Bradley, Phil Marshall, John 'Lanky' Hill and Andrew 'Harry' Harrison and they had begun to push out to explore the local breaks. In order to compete in local surf competitions you needed insurance through the BSA and, in order to get the insurance, you had to prove you belonged to a bona fide surf club. And so, Whitby's own official surf club was born. "You needed a letterhead, so one evening in the pub we were having a discussion as to what the club could be called," says Jo. "Lanky came up with lots of good suggestions, like the Strongshore Boardriders; everybody was going, 'Naarrr!' Eventually Lanky just threw his hands in the air and went, 'Ah man, you might as well just call it the Wibbly Wobbly Surf Club!' and everyone went, 'Yes, that's the one!' It was always written with the Ws as two pairs of boobs. That was our logo." Nineteen eighty five was a seminal year in surfing. It was the year Curren and Occy slugged it out toe to toe in the line-up: Occy all goofy-foot gouges and powerful, sweeping turns; Curren the nimble, flowing stylist, a master tactician. Their heats at the OP Pro and at Bells were pro surfing at its zenith. On the east coast of England, however, there was little news from the competition circuit and little interest. Surfing wasn't about what happened in contests, it wasn't about what you wore, it was about what went on in the North Sea. "Then you were just a surfer; we all were part of the same clan," says Jo. "There weren't all these sub groups you have now. Like today, people start in splintered factions: a surf punk, a surf hippy, some are professional athletes and others look at it as just a pastime – like golf." Here the crew spent long autumn evenings surfing the reef, losing fins, charging their newly found private playground, learning its moods and revelling in the isolation. It was a time of secret signals, a mafia-like code of silence, a shared knowledge between the few. 'How was Sandsend today?' accompanied by a knowing tap or scratch of the nose. A hidden spot could be talked about openly without spilling the beans.

"After a while the Saltburn guys never saw us," says Andrew Harrison. "They'd say, 'Where did you get in?' and we'd say, 'Aw we were just down at Whitby,' and they'd say, 'We came down and we never saw anybody, and we'd say, 'Ah, we were in earlier.' We used to touch our nose. It was a secret sign." Harry leans back against the railing that runs along the western side of the harbour. Behind, the jagged black silhouette of Whitby Abbey stands imposing against the skyline, dominating the view. Weathered steps draw the eye down to the sandbank below East Cliff, where the Russian schooner *Demeter* grounded, driven in from the eye of a raging storm, captain lashed dead to the wheel. It was from this deserted vessel that Dracula disembarked, bringing the shadow of death to this town. Bram Stoker penned his magnum opus while resident in the Royal Hotel here, imbibing the heavy, heady gothic atmosphere that spills through the town like a North Sea fog. Today, the bi-annual Whitby Goth weekends see the streets full of dark spectres, shrouded with black flags. The Dracula connection has put Whitby on the map – more so than Cook, more than ship building or *Heartbeat*. Or surfing.

With the eighties waning, the Cove gave the Whitby scene a fulcrum, a thrilling focal point, the buzz that comes with discovering a world-class wave on your doorstep. "The irony is we had been looking at the Cove for ages but nobody wanted to surf it because it just looked too fast," says Harry. "We'd go to surf the Point and it works on the same swell; you'd look at it rifling and think 'no way, it's just un-makeable'. Where as the Point looks more makeable but, in fact, it's the heavier wave." Being away at college when it was first ridden, Harry returned to a quiet storm of expectancy. "Greenie was saying 'You gotta surf this wave.' I remember paddling out there with him; I was on a Hot Stuff 5' 6" twin I'd bought down in Cornwall. Where as at other waves you'd get to your feet, get a bit of a face ride and then close out, this thing just kept on going, and going and going and going. It was just us Whitby guys. We used to go and find people to go surfing with – we'd say, 'Don't tell anyone.'" There were occasions when other surfers would come and check nearby reefs, but the guys surfing the Cove would duck down off their boards and hide amongst the kelp. It was six months before anyone twigged. "We were out one day surfing and a car drove down with surfboards on the top," recalls Harry. "I think it was Nick Markl or Tilley from Saltburn, and they paddled out. We'd never seen another face there apart from the crew. We went, 'Fuck!' They paddled out and went, 'Hey, what's it like?' Well, we had to say to them then, 'cause if you don't say anything, you know they're just gonna blab it out. So we said, 'Look, we've been surfing this for ages, it's absolutely awesome; keep your fuckin' mouth shut.' But, you know, it's like the pin prick in the football, you know it's gonna go down eventually. To be fair, most of the guys were pretty good, they realised how good it was. Just every now and again another face would turn up, then another face, and another face."

SCOTT WICKING

Andrew Harrison, Freespirit
"The cold is the cold. But you forget about it. As soon as you're in the water it's gone – as long as you have a good suit."

The ballad of the Cove is a tale carved into light brown ironstone, a classic tragedy of paradise found and paradise lost. The complex blend of Jurassic rocks, a perfectly angled platform, took millions of years to form, weather and wear into this incredible reef. The erosion of the secret happened a whole lot quicker. "At the Cove, 1995, something like that, we had guys coming up from Wales to surf there," explains Jo Botham. "Personally, I didn't see that that might open the floodgates. I think we thought that it was so fickle and you had to be really on it, it was never going to get that crowded. Nobody foresaw the impact of the Internet, and how people in Cornwall could go, 'Oh, in two days time the Cove should be working.' Suddenly you get two busloads arriving. With more than six people, it's crowded; get a few from Saltburn, a few from Whitby, a few from Scarborough, a few from Tynemouth, a few more from Cornwall and Wales – it's busy." Add to the mix the people who had heard of this legend and just wanted to be in the line-up. Drawn from across the country, the surfers came, fed by photographs, videos and magazine articles, the drip of information onto the web and the magic of swell prediction sites. The vibe became more dog-eat-dog; it doesn't take long for you to stop counting bodies in the line-up when you reach twenty; after all, drive four hours, you gotta rack up the waves to make it count, right? "We surfed it, we named it, it was our wave, a Whitby wave," explains Jo. "You don't own it, that's ridiculous, but you certainly feel a bond to it." It's a theme that's both universal and controversial, that of ownership, locality, respect and rites of passage. Although the regulars are still largely drawn from the northeast area, many of the Whitby crew are only enticed back for classic swells and magic days. "It is a shame that there isn't still a core crew of Whitby surfers at the Cove because, at the end of the day, it's still the best wave on this coastline, but, if it's not a fun session, it doesn't matter how good the wave is."

The christening of a surf break comes with responsibility; it's the giving of a name to piece of surfing folklore, adding to the tomes of surf history. It's an honour that falls to those who discover a break or pioneer a new spot. The resulting monikers are many and their reasons varied. Mavericks was named after a dog, Pampa Point after an advertising hoarding, Morocco's iconic Anchor Point after the factory that used to sit at the head of the break. Lance's Right was named after Lance Knight, the first person to surf it in 1991, while a rival faction now calls the reef 'HT's'. Some have names that exaggerate prowess, while others joyously mislead. After all, if you name your secret spot after its locale, it will not aid the ongoing preservation of mystique. "We called it the Cove in an ironic way," says Jo, "because it isn't one." Localism never existed in the northeast; there was never any need. There was secrecy, subterfuge, a healthy dose of deception and an underlying belief in the rules of the line-up. Some feel the lessons of the Cove have been painfully learnt, and that their few remaining secret spots need to be protected before they too are lost. Non-locals who stray onto these waves will find themselves ordered from the line-up. A line has been drawn. It is a reluctant form of localism, a last ditch stand to preserve something in danger of being lost forever.

Andrew Harrison got into surfing through an unconventional route. "Glue sniffing," he says in typical deadpan humour. "You think I'm kidding. I got caught; I was knocking around with the wrong crowd." Harry's mum had a simple cure. "She got me a board and a wetsuit and it was the best thing she's ever done for me," he says. "Absolutely fantastic, changed my life. So I went out with Greenie; he'd bought an old Atlantic Surfboard single fin, I had a Tris twin fin that I bought from Saltburn Surf Shop and a Gul wetsuit that was fuckin' freezing. Everybody had started about the same time – Jo Botham, Sedge, Lanky – it just all seemed to happen."

Cover up
Secrecy, subterfuge, a healthy dose of deception and an underlying belief in the rules of the line-up are what guard this coastline. That and the fact that when it turns on, this playground does not suffer fools gladly.

As the eighties stumbled to a close in the northeast, things were brewing in the surf scene. Nick and Gary were starting up in Saltburn and, in Whitby, Harry and Sedge had a plan: Freespirit Surfboards. "I guess we started Freespirit after we came back from Australia, about 1990," explains Harry. "Sedge had already done a couple of boards before, but I'd never done any. So we got a power planer and foam from Seabase in Newquay. Then we got a barn. It was a typical surfboard factory: toxic substances everywhere, out in the middle of nowhere, some farmer who doesn't give a shit what you're doing in his barn as long as he's getting some money for it. We both did everything: I did my boards and Sedge did his. I think neither of us wanted to relinquish the glory. I was rough and ready and Sedge was Mr

Perfect." Whitby now had its own shapers and Freespirit boards trickled out into the line-ups of the northeast. But, at the start of the nineties, the surfing community here was still only small, and the barn industry struggled. "That went on for about two years, maybe. We were doing Freespirit and we were both working for builders, but gradually it became we weren't making enough money out of the boards. Eventually we packed it in, shut the factory down – that was it. I probably did about twenty or thirty boards, all local, word of mouth. We didn't advertise or anything. It was a time when there wasn't a lot out there. We couldn't just shape them to stick on a rack, though a few shops took some: stuck a few in Saltburn, a few in Secret Spot in Scarborough. It was a great experience, but you can't make

money out of shaping boards. You couldn't then and I don't know how they make money now."

Despite a faltering start in the surf industry, Harry went on to set up Zero Gravity in Whitby, the town's first surf shop. "I was working at a builder's, and looking to get a job as a fireman at Fylingdales, so I could have time off to go and do a bit of surfing and shaping and maybe have a surf shop. It's not that I thought the scene was big enough, I just thought that's what I'll do. I had no idea – you don't. I think Secret Spot had been open and they were doing well. It wasn't as a response to them, it was more thinking, 'What am I going to do with my life?' I mean it was Whitby. Saltburn, Scarborough – yes. You've got all the Teesside lot go to Saltburn, all the people that go from inland go straight down to Scarborough, and then you've got Whitby in the middle which only got a few rogue elements travelling here. I thought I'd do it as an aside to doing a proper job, but a proper job never came. I did fifteen years, but I came to the conclusion you never make money out of surfers. People who want to buy a nice top yes, but surfers? We want to spend our money on surfing."

During the eighties, the northeast was a grey place. The winters were cold but the economic climate was frigid. In Tynemouth and on Teesside, industry was dying. Mrs Thatcher had broken up and privatized a ship-building industry that employed 86,000 workers. It was the beginning of the end of boat construction in one of its traditional strongholds. The year-long miners strike ended with a coal industry on its knees; pit closures followed in wave after wave. Unemployment topped three million; over ten per cent of the workforce were without a job. It was evident, even from the line-up, that an ethos of profit maximization ruled the boardroom, as water companies being prepared for privatization pumped raw sewage

CHRIS NELSON

DEMI TAYLOR

SCOTT WICKING

Top
Nor Easter.

Middle
In the mouth of the Tees the water fizzes with intoxicating scents while the banks, home to ICI, a steel works and nuclear power plant, steam with industry.

Bottom
Alistair 'Brock' Brocklehurst. "For wetsuits everybody who could scrape the pennies together went to Second Skin in Devon; they were considered the best," says Jo Botham. "Either by mail order or by going down and getting measured up. We all considered you had to have a suit that fitted well in order to stay in the water for long enough. To my mind the weak component was always the boots and gloves. They were always rubbish compared to the wetsuits, which were good. You ended up with diving boots or washing up gloves."

straight into the sea. This was pre-SAS, before the country developed an environmental conscience and the feel-good spin of PR-cleansed actions kicked in. Shorelines were littered with sanitary towels and condoms, some beaches saw faeces washing up on the sand, while surfers leaving the water with skid marks on the bottom of their boards were not unheard of. This toxic, shit-slicked North Sea coastline was the grim reality for many of the crew at the time and a long way from the California dream.

Tynemouth surfers would often head south to Saltburn and the reefs. "I don't remember there being Tynemouth surfers at the Cove until we got back from Oz in about '88," explains Jo Botham. "Nigel Veitch used to come down and surf there. He was alright to surf with, because, although he was like God – he was just way in another league from anybody else – he was by no means a wave hog. He would sit outside and take the Macker wave nobody else was going to take in any case

and sit in the barrel for a couple of hundred yards. He was an awesome surfer, awesome." Surfing is a rich tapestry, interwoven with the lives of characters that defied the norm, who found the surfing family and were made welcome. There have been extroverts, introverts, enigmas, legends and casualties along the way. Nigel Veitch was a character that probably encapsulated all of the above. There was no career pathway to follow, there was no surfing infrastructure or support, but Veitch was a natural talent. He had come to surfing as a sixteen-year-old; within two years he was British Champion. In 1986 he packed up his boards and took off on the world professional surfing tour. It was an era before today's 'Dream Tour' – exclusive domain of the top 44; it was a time when qualifying rounds meant those hungry enough to paddle out could try their hand at getting into the main event. With sponsorship from the local brewery, the non-drinker headed off to take a foundation course in being a professional surfer. The '86 tour included the likes

Rock pooling
With only primitive water treatment facilities, unwanted items flushed down the toilet from sanitary towels to condoms were washed wholesale onto the beaches with incoming tides. Northeast 1989.

The Nigel Veitch dichotomy
The brewery-sponsored, non-drinking, pro-surfer from the non-surfing northeast of England.

of Tom Curren, Tom Carroll, Mark Occhilupo, Gary Elkerton, Martin Potter, Damien Hardman, Shaun Tomson, Derek Ho, Barton Lynch and Mark Richards – ten names that between them would amass fifteen world titles. That's a steep learning curve for the boy from Tyneside.

"For the first couple of years I hardly ever saw him," explains big wave charger and son of Newcastle, Gabe Davies, "because he was out on the tour. He was an incredible surfer, he paved the way for British surfers. He was one of the first pro's really. There was no one out there on the world stage. Carwyn came after him and so on. It ended up we just went surfing with him. He took us to various places, up to Scotland and round the coast. We were about fourteen or fifteen. We surfed some huge waves in Scotland. We were always asking him a thousand questions about Hawaii. The photos of him at Pipeline; I'd never seen a British surfer in a photo on a wave that big. So we used to say, 'What do you do, do you duck dive or do you bale out?' and he used to say, 'In Britain you never, ever have to bail out, simple as that.' Once we were out on the left at Brims Ness (in Scotland) and we paddled out and it was big. This huge set came through and caught us inside. I looked across to see where Veitch was, and he threw his board, and I just went, 'Oh my God!' It was twice as big as he thought it would be. He threw his board away, and I threw mine, and we just dived."

"Veitch had a fascination about the police but was unable to join because of the height restriction," explains Jesse Davies. Until the 1990s regulations meant an applicant had to be over 5ft 10 to even be considered. "He was very anti-drugs, drank once a year and did not smoke, but he was still the wildest bloke you could imagine. He once attempted to paddle out in twenty-foot Brims Ness. The rip wouldn't let him and Paul Russell certified him as mad from

ALEX WILLIAMS

Above
Across the broad surfing canvas, lines have been painted by extroverts, introverts, enigmas, legends and casualties. Nigel Veitch encapsulated all of the above.

that day on. Veitch just completely ripped. He could fit into eye-shaped back-hand barrels like no one else I have ever seen. He charged Black Middens (in the mouth of the River Tyne) alone on a massive day, snapped his board, then paddled out on a shorter one. It was in the middle of winter and it was the closest he had come to drowning. At the Cove one day he was in the tube for so long everyone had stopped watching because there was no way he could have made it.

Left
Longsands, Tynemouth.

Opposite: Jesse Davies
The Tynemouth local regularly
charges some of the most
challenging conditions thrown
up by the North Sea and is one of
the region's most accomplished
yet unassuming surfers. "Dealing
with the cold you have to do
what ever it takes to make things
more comfortable. Spending
post surf time in a bath or by
lying by a radiator helps. The flat
spells can be hard to deal with…
waves come and go. Sudden big
swells are a shocker. My brother
Gabe came back from Hawaii one
winter and overnight we had the
largest clean swell I have seen.
Waves were breaking in places we
had never seen them breaking.
Gabe had a bit of a surprise. Even
after plenty of surfing in Hawaii
it was not so easy with a full
6mm suit and howling winds.
My youngest brother Owain was
out and scored some screamers
before snapping his board."

Several seconds later out popped Veitch to the complete astonishment of those who witnessed it. He was a great tube rider who had excellent timing and acute wave appreciation."

For Veitch, the first year on the Tour was always going to be a platform, a settling-in period, a time to get dialled into the challenges mentally and physically; learn how to surf competitively at the top level, how to cope with the travel, the time zones, the arrangements. But after a year on the tour, having built up debts and lost the backing of Newcastle Breweries, Veitch did not have the finances to continue. And yet, for that year, he was living the dream. Before his suicide, Veitch had settled into a new role, soul surfing the Celtic fringes and quietly showing the way to the region's grommets. He followed in the tradition of many British icons – the struggle against the odds and ultimately a heroic failure to achieve – yet it was the legacy that he left that was his ultimate achievement. Veitch died in April 1990 in his mid twenties. Gabe and Jesse Davies

paddled out and scattered his ashes at Hartley Reef, one of his favourite surf spots. "Veitch was one of the first ASP professionals," says Jesse. "He charged in Hawaii, turning many heads. The man had more balls than any surfer I have come across; he was one in a million. He battled against the odds to fulfil his dream of being a professional surfer." Whenever a group of surfers from the northeast sit in pub and talk of days gone by, of great waves ridden and classic sessions seen, it isn't long before the name Nigel Veitch is spoken, and a new vein of stories is mined.

The scents of fish and chips, marine diesel and burnt, caramelized candyfloss drifts by like weather fronts. Squabbling herring gulls bicker in ear-piercing tones over discarded scraps, living up to their well-earned epithet, 'Shite Hawks'. The seafront throngs with families clustered in tight pods, weaving as they lick melting yellow streaks of ice cream from their fingers. The harbour is quiet except

for the deep burblings of a speedboat cruising up to the dockside, returning trippers who are smiling through damp fringes. Scarborough is a Victorian resort that lies twenty minutes south of Whitby, at the end of a meandering drive through green fields corralled by dry-stone walls, purple-tinged heathland and regimented battalions of conifers. It's a town built on the steep, overlooking two large bays. At low tide North Bay is a huge expanse of open sand, where dogs manically zig-zag and fishermen dig for bait, while at high the sea collides with the huge curving sea wall, sending fans of white water high into the air. It has an old-school feel, conservative, like a well-tailored tweed jacket. By comparison South Bay seems a little brash and intense. It sparkles with noisy amusement arcades, seafood stalls and cafés, packed in tight between the harbour and the faded grandeur of the old spa. It's all a little frayed beneath the bright surface, but well-loved, like a dazzling set of antique paste. Standing proud on the headland between, perched atop crumbling cliffs, sits the medieval fortress of Scarborough Castle. The fractured edifice, once splashed red by feuding Roundheads and Cavaliers during the English Civil War, again came under fire as recently as the Great War, when huge iron-clad German warships bombarded its lofty position, raining shells on the town. Today, Scarborough is all about creating that quintessentially English scene of deckchairs on the sand, fish and chips wrapped in paper and drizzly Bank Holiday traffic jams. Famous around the world for its medieval fair, it is less well known as the thriving hub of the Yorkshire surf scene.

Roger Povey grew up by the sea; early summer days were spent in the outdoor swimming pool and playing in big swells. A brief flirtation with surfing in his late teens didn't stick, but when he reconnected with his old flame in his late twenties, the timing was right. It was a time when surfing was confined to a few diehards. This wasn't an image-dominated scene, it was all about the glide. "You were almost considered uncool if you were a surfer," says Roger, perched on the arm of the leather sofa, grey hair cropped spikey short these days. "Surfers were just anyone who liked going surfing. It was never an image thing, you were never cool because you were a surfer." Surfing in Scarborough first took off in the '60s. Tony Hogan owned an ice cream shop and together with Tim Popel was an early pioneer. "There was a second scene came along in the early seventies with Dave Bell," explains Roger. "Another guy called Big Dave who lived in Leeds and used to travel over every weekend and sleep in his van and go surfing. Then there was Eric, Gringo and Pete Britton, who still surfs. Crabby and Del Boy came along mid to late eighties. Then there was a young crew who at that time were about twelve to sixteen: the likes of Mark Dickinson, who is still in the industry making surfboards, and Jamie Lawrence."

For a surf community to thrive, the scene needed a focal point, a hub and hang-out. Saltburn Surf Shop had just opened up the coast; Roger saw an opportunity and Secret Spot was born, perhaps the world's smallest surf shop. "There were about fifteen of us," explains Roger. "Everybody came to the opening. The shop was tiny, ten foot by ten foot, I don't know how but we had all fifteen people in it." The shelves were stocked with Billabong and Quiksilver clothing; a few locally produced surfboards gleamed under fresh resin coats: Freespirit from Whitby and Nor-Easter from Hartlepool. "Mick Lesley and Audrey of Nor-Easter were making boards and had just opened their shop in Hartlepool," explains Roger. "The thing about running a surf shop in Scarborough was people would always say, 'There's no surf in Scarborough', it's the thing with the whole east coast, and I'd say, 'Well what destroys your sea wall every year?'" Roger had grand plans. "I hoped that there would be a meagre living in it – which there was, a meagre living." When Roger's lease was due for renewal, local surfer Paul 'Tommo' Tomlinson offered to go in with Roger on a bigger shop. "We found premises at Pavilion Terrace, where the shop still sits. It made a huge difference to open a big store. That was 1992." Scarborough occupies an easily accessible position at the end of the A64; traffic from cities and towns like Leeds, York, Manchester, Sheffield and Doncaster is funnelled to the coast here. These transport links had helped drive the resort's boom, now they helped feed the exponential growth of the surf scene. Roger no longer runs the shop, having passed the reins to Tommo; today he waits for the best conditions to get into the water. In Scarborough the line-ups keep swelling under the weight of a thriving, active surf community that could rival those in Britain's traditional surfing strongholds of Wales and the southwest. There are film nights, contests, a wetsuit test centre and a flourishing grommet scene. "From the late '80s recession and the four day week, when I had three days off to run my newly opened shop, there were fifteen hardcore surfers, to now when there can be one hundred to two hundred surfers in the water, the growth has been pretty amazing."

The snow is drifting on the moors, spindrift dancing over dry-stone walls, respecting no boundary it flows like a silky life form, hugging the ground as it creates intricate dunes and angled, sharp-edged drifts. The ploughs have yet to re-open the Pickering Road over the high ground, past the Fylingdales base where ghost of the giant early warning 'golf balls' still linger, past the mighty Hole of Horcum glacial cwm, which resembles an Alpine backcountry bowl on this February morning. The coast road is open but there is little traffic. The few cars that scuttle past have the tells: fins visible through back windows, the reflective shine of stacked board

Top
Dunstanburgh Castle.

Upper middle
Up above the streets and houses.

Lower middle
Lobster Tails.

Bottom
Scarborough.

bags. The surf is pumping. But the weather is immaterial. "It's the climate that makes the waves and keeps the crowds down," explains Gary Rogers, hat pulled down, collar upturned against the biting breeze. "We don't get surf as regularly as the west coast, so when it's good you've gotta make the most of it. If it's minus three and the waves are pumping, you go in. I remember when I moved up here, there was snow in June – it didn't lay but it was summer and it was actually snowing. I know the Cornish come up and they say, 'It's not that cold,' but they only come for a day or two and then they're away again. But it's the wind, that's the thing, it doesn't blow around you. The wind actually blows through you."

"It's the cold that makes the scene without a doubt," says Roger Povey. "People don't just jump in and out of the surf scene. You surf because you love surfing, you definitely don't surf because you think it's a cool thing to do. Just to put a six millimetre wetsuit on and venture out into the freezing North Sea, and get battered by cold water waves, you've got to want to do it – otherwise you're just punishing yourself. Some people think of surfing as something you do in the summer, where as for east coast surfers, it's something you do in the winter. The days may be shorter, the water may be colder, but that's when we get the better swells. It's the old story – if you start surfing in April, you might not make it

Below
Northumberland.

THE GILL

SCOTT WICKING

Bif
February's North Sea explorations.

through to next Christmas; if you start surfing in November, you'll still be doing it in ten years' time." The scene that has developed here on the fringes of the North Sea has a unique genetic fingerprint, a genome that has evolved through interaction with this harsh environment. Like a wind-cropped tree exposed to the elements, it has been carved by the gales, the rain and the drifting snow. This coastline breeds a drive and a commitment in those who join. Swells arrive suddenly and with size. It can go from flat to ten feet overnight. It makes for a hard charging mentality; what's lost in paddle fitness is made up for in application. The North may not get quantity, but the quality of waves can make up for the lack of days.

Jo Botham gained an appreciation of the weight of these cold dark waters, from spells away, surfing in Devon and Cornwall. "It's a lot harder here. I always thought that from when I was down in the southwest for a few years that the water was a lot softer down there. Here it hits you with a lot more velocity somehow. I don't know if it's actually denser, but it certainly feels it. There's also that isolation and not having other people to watch all the time, like in some places where they have someone with a huge natural talent. I'm not trying to belittle the Whitby surfers… but where did Veitch's talent come from? I don't know, but I'm sure that's what kindled more people in Tynemouth to be better, and they've produced a lot of pretty good surfers – like Gabe Davies and Sam Lamiroy. There needs to be that spark to ignite it. But as for surfing in the cold, that WAS surfing for me. I didn't know any different. I guess having a wave as good as the Cove on our doorstep felt like some sort of compensation for the hardships. Maybe, in a way, that's why some of us feel more aggrieved than we would when it's crowded with people who don't put up with living here all the time, they just come in and cherry pick on the best days."

As for the aforementioned reef, there are still those epic sessions when the crew score it without the crowds, when swells slip through beneath the Internet's ever-watchful 'Eye of Sauron'. "There are still days when you get it with us and the Saltburn crew out, Frazer and Robbie Hildreth, and it's a really, really good vibe, no hassle," says Harry. "There's a good craic, everyone's hooting each other into waves. It does make you laugh sometimes, 'cos you're walking out on the scar and some guy from Cornwall comes up and says 'Alright, have you surfed this place before?'... and you're going 'Fuck off!'" says Harry with an ironic smile. "To be fair, though, I'm quite nice, 'cos there's no point in having aggro in the water. There's no point being bitter – old and bitter, it's just one of those things."

Jo Botham still surfs the Cove when the swell demands. There are days that stand out, waves ridden that still crystalize into moments of sheer magic. "Who can remember their best sessions? Those sessions seem so perfect they probably didn't even happen, they're probably just figments of my imagination. I remember one session when I'd been a bit down, as I didn't seem to be getting into it, and I got a wave. I got into a small barrel and the moon was just rising. And getting this barrel as it was just getting dark, then coming out onto the reef as the moon was reflecting on the water lying on the scar, I thought, 'This is why I still surf.' Mind you," he says with a wry smile, "I probably dreamt that as well."

Lone peak
Just rewards for the cold water
searcher; this is no place for sheep.

Hokkaido

TARO TAMAI

KI SURF BOARDS

We are standing on the corner looking at a street map but seeing nothing. This goes against the grain, against my base instinct to just wander and explore. But to be honest, after ten days out in the quiet wilds, Sapporo is a bewildering environment and hunger has taken hold. The moon has risen high above the skyline, yet it is the sunburst billboards that illuminate the street, imbedded speakers broadcasting fast-track jingles and jaunty product slogans. The world is streaming past in an endless flow of glistening traffic and dark suits. "Are you lost?" asks a voice. We look up from the folds to see a young local: styled hair, designer glasses, smooth jacket. "We're trying to find an ATM." He looks down at his phone and starts typing, then smiles. "OK, follow me," he says and takes off against the flow. We trail in his jet stream, heads revolving like owls trying to absorb the sights, sounds and smells as we glide. In the pedestrianised arcades, groups of street dancers are gathered like moths around naked light bulbs, their perfect synchronicity mirrored in the reflective shop windows.

We turn out of the glow, into an alley, past tiny doors embedded in a dark wall, only red flags identify them as cosy, inviting restaurants. Would we have blindly followed a stranger into an alley in London, New York or any other large urban conurbation? Yet here there is an altogether different atmosphere that permeates, even in this gloomy cut through. We cross the road and are delivered into a bright auditorium. "Here you are," says our guide with a nod and a smile. "Have a good stay in Japan," he says, nodding again. We all shake hands, he turns and is gone, back into the flow of razor sharp suits and unfeasibly short skirts.

The police officer pushes his glasses up the bridge of his nose with his forefinger and surveys the two figures standing in front of him. Noboru Tagawa jumps up and down on the spot to keep warm, as the chill begins to seep through his damp wetsuit; Kasagi Hajime glances repeatedly over the cop's dark epaulette as the next set peaks and peels along the sandbar. The officer shakes his head and continues scribbling on his flip pad. 'How many times are we going to have to drag these two out of the water?' he wonders. "Ok, sign this," he says, handing over the ballpoint to the shivering surfer. Noboru scribbles his name and passes the now damp paperwork back. The officer snaps his pad closed and turns on his heel, kicking sand off his immaculate leather shoes as he heads back towards his car. "I'm coming back again tomorrow," shouts one of the neoprene-clad figures, as the officer climbs into the driver's seat of the Nissan Cedric patrol car and starts the engine. It's 1978 and a quiet revolution has begun on this northern isle.

"Every time I went into the water back then, the police would come and kick me back onto the beach," says Noboru, taking a sip of his black coffee. "They would write me a ticket for responsibility, because there was no one else there. It's like a statement to say I won't do it again. But after writing it I would always tell them 'I will be coming back tomorrow!'" This was a game of cat and mouse that would go on for the next three or four years. In Hawaii, Shaun Tomson was redefining the art of barrel riding at Off-The-Wall, and Rabbit was attempting to Bust Down The Door at Sunset and Pipe. On Hokkaido, Noboru was just trying to avoid being busted by the law for the simple act of surfing.

Cold, empty temptations
Storms front inviting peaks.

KASAGI HAJIME

Japan was born from the waves as molten rock violently extruded from the Pacific 'ring of fire', creating an offshore archipelago that, in part, buffers the huge Asian land mass from the great ocean. There are 6852 islands within Japan, Hokkaido being the northernmost and largest prefecture. It is the second biggest island, with a population of over five and a half million spread out over an area just smaller than Ireland. The majority of Hokkaido sits at latitudes to the north of Vladivostok, enduring winters that can test the hardiest constitution. The provincial capital, Sapporo, is a bustling metropolis of nearly two million; the country's fifth largest urban conurbation. It provides a dazzling sensory collage that satisfies every preconception of urban Japan. Traffic, shopping, crowds, street dancing and the intense work ethic of a twenty-four-seven society are set against a background noise of Pachinko halls and rafts of neon billboards that sing out competing advertising slogans. Yet within thirty minutes of its centre, you can be transported to wide valleys where shrines wait in shady woodlands and herons stalk shimmering paddy fields.

Summertime means sunny days immune from the sweltering humidity that weighs heavily on the main island and Tokyo in particular. The countryside is swathed in a lush green of forest and bamboo; misty mornings linger, while regular typhoon swells illuminate the Pacific coastline. Winter sees the whole island transformed into an almost featureless amalgam of monochrome hues, as deathly winds slice in from the Siberian plains with the clinical sharpness of a Samurai's cold *Katana* blade. White landscapes contrast grey skies, while temperatures plummet towards minus twenty and up to five metres of snow smothers the whole island. Hokkaido has always maintained a slight sense of distance from the main island, in part down to its history and in part to its physical separation. Until the opening of the thirty-three-mile-long Seikan Rail Tunnel in 1988, crossing from Hokkaido to Honshu meant a four-hour ferry ride. In winter the crossing could be rough and, in typhoon season, dangerous: five ferries were lost in 1954. During winter the airport could be closed due to adverse weather and blinding blizzards. However, today the snow-shrouded Jurassic landscape has become Hokkaido's primary resource and biggest draw. The Winter Olympics came to Sapporo in 1972 and showed the word the high-quality terrain on offer here. Look outside the resort of Hirafu and you will find a memorial to those games nestled in woods, reclaimed by nature. The huge, rusting skeletons of Olympic ski jumps stand in stark contrast to all that is shiny, new and modern in the resort.

Naminori, or wave riding, is thought to have arrived during the cultural shockwaves following the Second World War, brought in by American service men stationed outside Tokyo. While a handful of local surfers were surfing the beaches of Shonan and Chiba by the early sixties, the first seeds really sprouted in 1963, when a California-born surfboard shaper called Tak Kawahara visited the region, teaching locals the fundamentals of surfing and board shaping. By 1965 the Nippon Surfing Association had been founded and, by the end of the sixties, Japanese surfers were competing in prestigious events in Hawaii, such as the Makaha International Championships and the World Contest at Bells Beach in Australia. Japan was in the grip of a full-blown surf boom by the late seventies, fuelled by world tour contests bringing star packed line-ups to its shores. On Hokkaido, the beaches remained unoccupied – a blank canvas. By the dawn of the new millennium, it was estimated that Japan was home to three quarters of a million surfers, yet today on Hokkaido, numbers are still relatively low. Those that do take to the waters here are hardy souls indeed.

RICHIE HOPSON

Right
Mist-drenched spring on the
Japan Sea coastline.

Frozen Frame
The bearable lightness of being.

A group stands huddled together in the subzero temperatures; the nearby car sits empty, engine running to keep the heater turning over. Looking out over the sea defences, one of the group points as the dark ocean rises and throws forward into an A-frame peak, walling waves spinning away to the left and right. The land terminates dramatically in vertical, brooding cliffs, the coastline winding its way to the north; boulder sea defences line undulating bays, the dark, rounded stones capped by crisp white snow. The narrow strip of land between cliff and sea is utilized to its maximum potential – a thin ribbon of homes, a car park, warehouses, shops, the coastal road, tunnels, railway line, harbour and a surf check vantage point. Today is a good day. Although the air temperature has dipped to minus ten, there is a head-high clean swell, and the local crew are on it. Looking at a map, the Japan Sea seems too small to be of much use, but, during the winter months, the low pressure systems that swing through to the north or south can deliver excellent surf – the only drawback is that the winter means cold. Not like a chilly day in Santa Cruz kind of cold, but cold like a chilly day in Siberia. The line-ups here are scattered but well known to the locals who, despite the low numbers, closely guard their secret locations. The complex geology of the region and the man-made groynes do not make life easy, but there are reefs, points and rivermouths there for those in the know. On the Pacific Seaboard, life is somewhat easier. The warm summer just happens to coincide with typhoon season, when powerful swirling depressions wreak havoc across the region. One of the side effects of these weather patterns is that they provide Japan with a regular supply of epic surf. Sometimes these typhoon swells can light up beaches and points for days on end, on a weekly basis. For Hokkaido that means waveriding nirvana, while, in the eternal grand scheme, for somewhere else along the Pacific fringe, it means roofs ripped from houses, devastation. During the winter, the eastern seaboard still has surf – after all, that's a big ocean out there – but this coast endures the same freezing conditions as the rest of the island. There are huge stretches where mythical waves break, however, these are all but inaccessible to the outsider. Surfers on Hokkaido know they have it good; they just don't want others to know quite how good.

Taro Tamai is unloading boards from the back of his white, long wheelbase Land Rover; his damp wetsuit drips with fresh memories of glassy Japan Sea waves ridden just as dawn cracked the horizon. He has that slightly dishevelled, serene look of someone who has just surfed away any worries that might have been burdening his mind. Across the valley towers Mount Yotei, the last vestiges of this season's snowfall transformed into golden striations by the alchemy of the evening's fading light. A classic cone-shaped volcano, it dominates the area; it is the backdrop to every photo; the view from every window. Taro lays his boards carefully next to the porch of his modern, Alpine-style wooden house, which nestles between the great Yotei to the east and Mount Annupuri to the west. The Niseko region lies like a giant saddle discarded after a ride; the village of Hirafu sits plum in the middle, one of the world's leading snow resorts. In the past ten years, this part of Niseko has exploded in popularity, with luxury new builds springing up to accommodate those dropping in for a quick fix of fresh lines and tree runs. In springtime, the village is laid bare. Its modern cubist architecture seems somehow to fit with the natural environment: it's all angles, cedar cladding and huge glass-fronted balconies. The buildings are blank canvases, the art is the landscape that surrounds them. Think 'Grand Designs' and grander vistas. Taro was drawn

RICHIE HOPSON

here by the awesome back-country potential of the region, but stayed for the surf. "I've always loved surfing," he says, "but when I came here, I wanted to concentrate on snowboarding, so I would snowboard full time through the winter season. From May onwards, I'd be travelling, taking trips to snowboarding spots. When there was swell in Japan's southern islands, I would jump on a plane to catch the swell. Back then for me to surf meant to surf in shorts – maybe there were palm trees, maybe there weren't, but for me to surf meant in warm water. So I was always primarily a full-time snowboarder, and then, when the season was over, I'd go surfing – that was how it was for the first few years I was in Niseko."

It seems strange to be talking about surfing in the rarefied air of a mountain resort, but Hirafu is only a short hop from the Japan Sea. The ocean has always exerted an uncanny ability to alter the life course of those who feel their career pathways are set, and Taro was not immune to its pull. All it took was one wave. "I was on a fishing trip," he explains, "and we came across this perfect wave – not just a regular beach wave. If you're a surfer, you know what that means – you want to go and surf it. That day I had a little ripped wetsuit in the car, just by coincidence, and my friend had a wetsuit also, so we looked at each other and said 'Let's check that out.'" It took just one duck dive to set the hook. "Before this, surfing meant to surf in the warm, but as soon as I hit the cold water something in me knew this was something

Taro Tamai

"There are some Hokkaido surfers that definitely follow the mainstream, check out the videos and the competition style surfing and I have no negative feeling towards that. But if you go back to the lifestyle and enjoying the surf, the waves, you can enjoy them in different ways other than just showing off with the skills stuff. My crew are more about being in a beautiful place enjoying the scene – how good that day was for them, connecting with friends and just enjoying – more so than just ripping the wave."

WATANABE

RICHIE HOPSON

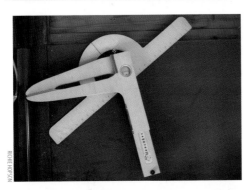

RICHIE HOPSON

RICHIE HOPSON

else – it was a distinctly different feeling. It was something new I never felt before, being in the cold water."

Tamai-san was born into an urban household of a Tokyo that had emerged blinking into the early sixties. However, his upbringing was far from typical. "My family is very active, my grandfather was a hunter and a fisherman – every opportunity he got he would go into the mountains to hunt or fish. My father was also a skier; they would even make me skip school to go to the mountain, go to the river. In the winter there are many ways to go fishing and many places to go but, whenever my dad was available, we would go skiing." For Taro, his adventures skiing deep powder with his father set in play a lifelong obsession. "As long as I can remember it's been a part of my consciousness, when I was at school it was always on my mind." Later in life, Taro's wife ran a restaurant which became an epicentre for free thinkers and outdoor lovers. "There where a lot of musicians, surfers, snowboarders and skiers used to come. I used to look down on the surfers then, because all I knew about surfing was that any time I would go to the ocean, it would be pretty much flat, there was not that much action going on. What I had in mind was surfers in black wetsuits paddling out when it's flat. I thought at that time, which was when I was pretty young, riding the powder was much cooler than surfing. I used to argue with those guys, saying 'Man, skiing's much cooler!'"

By 1991, Taro was a sponsored rider living in Niseko, one of Japan's brightest snowboard stars with a signature model board bearing his name. Snowboarding was booming, but the new focus on tricks, big airs and park riding was not really what Taro had in mind whenever he strapped in. "I really wanted to get a grip on what the snowboard industry was at that time, so I signed with a European company and, instead, I went

all over the world, checking out the scene, surfing and snowboarding." During the mid-nineties, the globe was undergoing a 'triple S' boom, as the sports of surfing, snowboarding and skating were melded together into a neat and easily accessible package. Brands globalized, the Vans Warped Tour brought together bands and boarding, while, in Europe, surfers, skaters and snowboarders competed against each other in the multidiscipline Quik Cup. 'Boardriding' was the buzzword; 'cross-over' was king. Surf in the summer, snowboard in the winter, skate all the time. After all, skating had its roots firmly planted in the boardwalks of the California surf scene. It was the ultimate lifestyle, it was the future. Or was it? Rather than blending influences, the new direction drew on specific elements, drawing the most radical components from each: nineties surfing took the aerials from skating, while snowboarding became about big airs, rails and parks. For Taro, he wanted to bring some of the more soulful elements of waveriding onto the slopes. "The skateboard direction didn't really match my style; it was going in a direction I didn't really want to go in. In '98, I came back and started Gentemstick." The Gentem philosophy involves a complete snow/surf approach of connecting with the mountain, enjoying the flow and feeling at one with your environment. "The concept that I've developed while travelling was that I wanted to ride in a style more like surfing, to connect with nature, not just to ride powder. Using the terrain much like you use a wave: the way you would ride to connect with your surroundings. I wanted to enjoy the environment in that kind of way and, since those kind of boards weren't really available, I had to make my own. That's what it is to me: surfing is to connect with nature – to use the energy and the flow."

The Japan Sea has the translucent green-blue of sand-weathered glass. The dark, jagged cliffs that surround the bay have a fractured abrasiveness that comes when volcanic rock is ripped apart. Two basalt columns stand offshore, a small shrine crowns the grassy summit of the nearest. The winter blanket has only just peeled back to reveal the bedding of sasa bamboo. The sushi bar sits just back from the harbour in the small village, sandwiched between cliffs and sea. Its interior is compact and immaculately clean, the glass counter displays small plates of glistening fish steaks and shellfish. The chef leans over and places a Nigirizushi roll on Taro's plate. The distinctively marbled scarlet flesh of the blue fin's fatty steak is highly prized and highly priced. "This particular fish tastes different to tuna caught later in the year. It was caught locally as it chased mackerel into shallow waters. It has a distinctive taste and a specific story. A good sushi chef can tell you the story of all the fish here. It's like surfing, every wave that breaks has a story, and they are different with every season, every time of the year."

Light is fading fast outside. sitting under the bright neon strip lights of his large open-plan office in downtown Sapporo, Kasagi Hajime cradles a cup of black coffee, while his old friend Noboru Tagawa flicks through images imprinted on thirty-year-old textured Fuji matt paper. Tagawa-san was the very first surfer on Hokkaido, ground zero for wavesliding on this northern isle. "When I was sixteen years old, I went to the United States to study the language and made friends there who lived in Tokyo," he explains. "At that time it was the second boom of surfing in Japan." In the mid seventies, Hawaii was still the focus of the surfing world; images of Gerry Lopez, Mark Richards and Reno Abellira were inspiring waveriders around the globe and, across the Pacific, Japan was no exception. Noboru caught the surfing bug in the US, and the burgeoning surf scene centred around the Japanese capital allowed a way into the waveriding

Top
Snow on the ground, boards on the Mazda: the early Sapporo surf crew set out on a mission.

Upper middle
Hokkaido Surfing Association's first surf contest, the Penguin Cup, 1980.

Lower middle
Summer bonnet: stopping for refreshments.

Bottom
Time out between sessions to warm up – early shoulder-zip Dove wetsuits were the weapon of choice.

lifestyle. "I'd been to Tokyo to buy a surfboard and brought it back to Hokkaido, but I didn't know where I could go to surf. There was no one else here to ask." Apart from the lack of fellow waveriders, Noboru faced another, more immediate obstacle in his new-found life as a surfer. "I didn't have a driving licence. A friend of mine was working at a wholesale jean shop, so, whenever he was going on business, I would jump in his car and go with him. Then, in 1978 maybe, two or three guys who were skiers went to university on the mainland around Tokyo and Osaka, but they dropped out and came back here – with surfboards. Two guys had driving licences, so we started to find new surf spots." In 1979 there came a breakthrough, when the small band of surfers from Sapporo ventured on to the sands of Itanki Beach in the industrial town of Muroran. Today, Itanki has a reputation as an intense spot, graffiti warnings splashed across the sea wall, but what the urban surfers found was a warm welcome from some kindred spirits. "In the Itanki area we met other guys who had come back from the mainland – they were the same age." Itanki Beach soon became the surfing and social hub of the Hokkaido scene. At the same time, Noboru was teaching his friend Kasagi to surf. Hajime-san ran a local coffee shop and the two friends made regular forays to the Pacific whenever the waves were up and work allowed. There was only one real problem. "The cops would find us on the beach and they would say, 'you can't do that'," says Noboru. "Our main concern was to be able to surf and how we could stop the police molesting us. But how could we do that? How could we stop the police from hauling us from the water when we went surfing?"

The answer came to Noboru in a flash of inspiration. "I told Kasagi he should start an association of Hokkaido surfing!" The idea was a simple one – rather than rejecting mainstream society, dropping out and fighting the system, they mobilized into a high-profile organization. Like environmental pressure groups in the west, the surfers of Hokkaido became campaigners promoting the lifestyle. So the Hokkaido Surfing Association was formed. Kasagi leans back in his chair and smiles. "Within one year there were twenty-seven," he says. "These were friends and friends of friends. There were people watching us, who'd come to the beach and ask to join, and numbers rose. Then, we started the competition – which is still going to this day. It's called the Penguin Cup, because of the cold. The way we were doing it was to tie little contests up with local festivals around, Hokkaido. We would do a competition tour, so we were spreading around gaining a reputation and a social status so that the police wouldn't bother us. We said, 'We don't need the cops involved with surfing!'" Not that police attention has completely died away. "It can still happen, even today," says Noboru, jumping in. "Not long ago we went to the east side and the cops came, still."

"The way that we got big was to make branches," explains Hajime-san. "We set up new ones for each location. We went after the gangs. They were signed up to surf for different branches. That was one of the points for joining the festivals in the towns and starting the surf competitions." In the context of waveriding's massive global popularity, the proliferation of the surfing lifestyle within the mainstream and specialist media and the problems of overcrowded line-ups faced today, the concept of actively recruiting surfers may seem like a strange priority. Two decades prior to this, the waves of Malibu were so choked that Mickey Dora and his cohorts were hauling people out of their way in an effort just to get down the line. The irony isn't lost on Hokkaido's pioneers that in order to protect their counter culture, they had to make it seem populist, garland it with a fig leaf of respectability. Bikers were already on the social fringes and the surfers saw an easy vein of bored potential to tap into. Every time Noboru and his crew came across a motorbike gang they would corner the boss and sell the stoke of surfing to them with an evangelical zeal that would shame a New York ad agency. "It was a bit scary having to talk to these gang bosses," says Noboru. "Not all the bikers could swim, but one of them tried surfing and said to all the others, 'Surfing's cool!' so then others tried it, you know. Until that time there was nothing to do around the coastal towns like Muroran or Tomakomai, and people didn't like bikers. But bikers started surfing – surfing is better really – so you could say we were a good movement."

A light pings on and the soft orange-pink glow of a naked bulb reflecting off pine walls spills into the empty hallway. In the corner of the lock-up a tipi of old skis lean together next to an assortment of wooden tennis rackets and a pair of ski boots. To the right of the wooden storage room, two huge shelves are piled high with surfboards, the white foam now sun-faded like pages in a book that have seen many seasons pass yet still have many stories to tell. "Ah, now this was the first board I brought to the island," says Noboru, reaching upwards. His voice echoes from within the confines of the open room, but soon the nose of a board emerges, followed by a face illuminated by a broad smile. "This is a Local Motion board I brought back to Hokkaido. They were very popular back then, Local Motion boards from Hawaii. In 1977 there were no surfboards to be bought here. Then, in '78, a shop called Minami Sport started selling surfboards, so two or three surfboards come in, but only two or three. Me and the guys who came back from Tokyo, we already had surfboards, but there were still not many on the island. I went to the mainland for my wetsuit, it was a diving wetsuit, an O'Neill wetsuit I bought in Tokyo." Noboru disappears back into the lock-up and sounds of exertion again fill the air, before the swallow tail of a twin fin appears through the doorway. "A year later Minami Sport were sponsoring me for skiing, and I told them, 'You should start doing a surfing business'. They had an order with a surfboard company so one by one boards came, and wetsuits. And a friend of mine did the same, bringing boards in, one by one. And wax too. Wax was hard to get, a good one. There was Sex Wax in Tokyo, but the water temperature was different. It was warm water wax, so it was too stiff, too hard." As surfing grew into a worldwide movement, a community, a clan, a way of life, so many of Hokkaido's new surfers followed. "There was a social trend, the surfing thing was trendy around the same time that we started. Since 1977 in Japan, surfing was booming. In 1978 Gerry Lopez visited Niijima (an island close to Tokyo), and I saw him surf there. Until then, fashion and culture was mainly like Ivy League fashion, but after the Vietnam War, the Hippie generation started, like the movie *Easy Rider*. So those from the Hippie generation were coming into Japan with the travelling surfers from around '72. By 1978 it had developed into a fashion, a culture and a lifestyle. We would get together and watch surf movies… Gerry Lopez… *Standing Room Only!*"

Hokkaido was very much split between town and country. The urban areas, like Muroran and the provincial capital Sapporo, were where the majority of surfers lived and worked, but most were office- or labour-bound six days a week. Some of the keenest managed shifts work, but, while Californians, Europeans and Australians around the globe were kicking back and living the dream here in Japan and on Hokkaido in particular, society wasn't ready for those who dropped out, merely to 'drop-in'. "It's hard to be a surf bum here, mainly because it is cold," jokes Noboru. "You need a place to keep warm – if you notice there are no homeless in a cold place! It's easier in California where it is warm. Surfing in a cold place, the mind is quite different, you know. The cold water affects the body – the joints, the neck – there's the heavy wetsuits. Wetsuits weren't that good back in the day, water came in – that made it cold you know. It didn't stop me. I just couldn't stop myself." It wasn't just the meteorological climate that impacted on the growth of the surfing lifestyle, but the economic climate, too. While in Bali, if you had a board, you could get by on just a few bucks a day, on Hokkaido you needed cold hard cash for wetsuits, boots, transport, as well as food to fuel you and accommodation to keep the cold at bay. "The economy on Hokkaido was not strong, because there are no big factories like on the mainland, for example, no car factories," explains Noboru. "So, in the coastal areas you could be fishing or drying seaweed, while inland many people are farmers or involved in agriculture. If they were farmers or fishermen, then they wouldn't have a lot of money, so the quality of their lives would be very different. It wasn't just the lack of equipment, but also the lack of money. So it goes much further than buying equipment; it's more the way they look at things. It's hard to get the money for surfing. Even today, if you go into the surfing business, around the Sapporo area might be alright because we have a large population, but outside this area (it's about one hour to the city of Tomakomai), it's hard to sell surfboards. Everything was different, because the culture and the industry is different here in Hokkaido, you know." However, the early seeds of surfing had been sown and despite the harsh conditions, this hardy perennial began to germinate, like an embryonic plant fighting through the snow to reach the sunlight, and it was beaches like Itanki that became the epicentre of this blossoming scene.

Treasure Chest

After decades of pioneering surf spots, Noboru Tagawa is still pushing at boundaries. During the summer he can be out on the road for weeks in his tricked-out camper van chasing typhoon swells. "We're still trying to find new places to surf, even now. Three or four years ago we started boat trips; after we found an outside reef, so we hired a fisherman's boat to get out to it."

The sun has dropped below the hills, long shadows stretch from the dark factory buildings, over the tarmac, across the dunes and down the beach. It's 1981: the grey days of Reagan in the White House, Thatcher in Downing Street and a Cold War that has turned distinctly icy. But here on Itanki Beach a small band of surfers are savouring a fresh autumn swell, the coconut aroma of surf wax and the feel of salt-crusted hair. A jumble of cars have been cast off at the southern end of the beach road; three dark silhouettes float serenely on the glassy ocean, steadily fading into the burnt pink canvas. Voices rise and fall against the background of spilling white water; a bonfire sends a spray of sparks into the blue-black of the advancing night. A collection of figures laugh, hoot and jostle, as they relive the day's adventure, re-riding waves as they stand around the dancing flames. Candy-coloured boards lie scattered on the ground; one is pushed nose first into the sand, the MR superman logo inverted on a white foam tombstone. Damp wetsuits have collapsed in exhaustion by their towels, black neoprene dusted with a fine velvet of wet sand. Beer caps are popped, the gold star of the Sapporo Brewery glimmers on the dark bottles. The city surfers will soon be making the drive back, but the Muroran locals will linger a little longer, talk story, stoke the fire and fire the stoke for tomorrow's coming swell. "It was like the film *Big Wednesday*", says Kazuhiro Miyatake with a broad smile. "There were about twelve or thirteen of us who were friends. We would come together after surfing, drinking beer on the beach here at Itanki. Now it's very strict: if you drink, you can't drive. But back then it was not so strict – it was not good – but not so strict. So, after surfing, we got together, we barbecued, we drank beer and then we drove home."

Steely silhouettes
Close-knit line-ups against a snowy canvass.

BRIAN NEVINS

BRIAN NEVINS

Muroran is a port city located on the southern Pacific seaboard of Hokkaido. It is home to cement works, steel mills and ship building. Itanki sits on the outer fringe, a sandy haven hemmed in by sea walls and boulder groynes. Open to any passing Pacific swell or classic Typhoon day, the beach is a popular contest venue and the island's best known spot. Kazuhiro sits with his back to the sea, hair still soaked with the memory of afternoon waves. He has a powerful frame and gives off the aura of a pack leader. It is no surprise that today he is a high school teacher and national snowboard coach. He still gets in the water as often as he can. His brother Hisashi has a slighter build but a quick smile. Today he waits for the better days to get his surfing fix. Kasuhiro was the first to take up

surfing while away on the mainland. "I started surfing when I was nineteen years old," he explains with a nod. "I was in the university in Tokyo for three years and, when I returned, there were probably less than ten surfers in Hokkaido, but there were only a few local surfers here, less than two or three. The rest were from Sapporo the city. In Sapporo, they are not surrounded by the waves, so they would often call us and say 'How are the waves today?'" The small local crew took to surfing with a zeal that the winter freeze could not diminish, even when the snowline reached the surging white water. "Now wetsuits are pretty good," says Hisashi, "but at that time we didn't have such good ones, they were seven millimetres thick. In winter the temperature went below zero, so often when it was snowing, our hair was

Above
Cold Air.

Opposite top
The writing's on the wall. Yukki Saito crosses the dark volcanic sand at Itanki Beach

Opposite middle
Minoru Osanai cold filtered post surf.

Opposite bottom
Itanki local Hisashi Miyatake talks waves at his home beach.

frozen." In temperatures this low, getting changed out of thick, inflexible wet neoprene at the beach would mean entering a whole new world of pain, so the crew found an altogether more appealing alternative, one that blended ancient codes with modern conducts. "After the surf we went to the Onsen, the hot spring baths," says Miyatake-san. "Without taking off the wetsuit, we went straight in there. Without hoods, in those temperatures – it was really cold," he says in typical Japanese underplay.

Jack O'Neill may have invented the surfing wetsuit in the 1950s, but, for the first generation of Hokkaido surfers, the luxury of such specialized equipment was many years down the line. "At that time there were no wetsuits for surfers, so we made do with ones for scuba divers. There were no surf shops, but there was a place that sold things like scuba equipment – tanks, suits – so we got them there," says Kasuhiro. "Then a few years after that some surf shops started in Sapporo. Then we could get proper wetsuits and boards from the city. In this area around Muroran, a sports shop sold wetsuits and surfboards. There was also a coffee shop, and the owner was a surfer, so he sold some equipment too. Things gradually got easier, but very slowly." By the fading light of the seventies, two distinct, yet small tribes of waveriders were emerging on the Hokkaido scene – the Sapporo crew, based in the bustling city a couple of hours' drive from the Pacific, and the Itanki Beach crew. But there was a camaraderie between the two, they would band together to share the waves and gradually numbers rose. "Sometimes we'd say to our friends, 'Surfing is really good, why don't you try?'" says Miyatake-san. "So we brought them to the beach and we taught them how to surf."

BRIAN NEVINS

Top
The industrial face of Itanki Beach.

Upper middle
Serene shrine lies at the end of a winding path through the lush forest.

Lower middle
Lizard-like ski jumps look to the sky.

Bottom
Natural form mirrors architectural function.

The sun is smiling on a clean two to three foot swell at Itanki. Light offshores fan the approaching sets and a handful of surfers jostle for the peeling rights as they roll through. To the north sits a sea wall, resplendent in its 'Locals Only' graffiti. To ensure nothing is lost in translation, it has been scribed in English, four feet high. Wetsuits are draped over wing mirrors, couples sit around on the grass watching the surfers, and small groups chat while propped up on sun warmed car bonnets. This Sunday scene has been played out here for the last three decades, only the extras change. Hiraoka Tadanori rests his blue- and- white longboard on the wall and sits with a post-surf sigh of satisfaction. Back in 1980, Tadanori-san was an early defector to the beach scene from the two-wheel lifestyle. "I used to have a motorcycle licence," he explains, absently stroking the nose of his board, "and then I did something that meant I lost my licence," his voice trailling off. "So I had nothing else to do. At that time my younger brother was surfing, so he taught me. When I first tried I thought this was something pretty great." Like many at the time, Hiraoka was restrained in his surfing exploits by the confines of the nine- to five. "There were a few who were students in Muroran who could come every day, but I was working, so I couldn't. Sometimes I could manage one or two hours, maybe, at lunch time. I would jump into my wetsuit quickly, rush in for a surf and then rush back to work."

"Not many college students surfed, it was mostly business people, people who were serious about their jobs. If you lost your job – at the end of seventies to mid eighties – it was difficult to find a new one, so people didn't want to quit. Most surfers had jobs, so they worked Monday through to Saturday. Some surfers were teachers, firemen; I was working at a grocery store. Not like in other places around the world were surfers would be chefs or carpenters, so they could have time to go

RICHIE HOPSON

Shingo Shimokawa
"I opened the shop in 1986. Back then people were surprised that I could make a living out of a surf shop – not now. Though people are still shocked when they see me and my friends, in the depth of winter, bringing a board out and going into the ocean."

RICHIE HOPSON

Hideki Takeda
A skateboarding and
snowboarding legend, Hideki
has been carving powder since
the early days of the sport, on
Team Burton back in '82 and a
Gentemstick rider today.

to the beach!" Surfing first arrived on Hokkaido through the preaching of students returning from Tokyo and found new converts through bikers and young professionals, who, although embracing the surf lifestyle and the surf culture, also had the Japanese work ethic deeply enshrined within them. "You know how people say that Japanese workers work long hours? Well, it's true. At that time it was true, it's still true today. There were a few surfers who worked for a company making fish products, so they had to go to work very early, but they could also leave early, say after three or four, then they could surf. Other than that we only had Sundays off. Today, things are a bit better; we have two days off a week, but thirty years ago we only had one." So Sunday became surf day. "Any condition was good, because we could only surf one day a week! If there were waves, but the weather was bad – even if there was snow – I surfed."

Shingo Shimokawa sits outside his Wave Beat surf shop in Chitose, resting the serious custom chopper onto its stand and leaning back. A huge crack splits the air as an F16 jet hurtles past overhead, rendering all speech useless. Just as the wave of sound passes, another boom reverberates, followed by the sight of another military jet in a steep take-off curve. Kim Jon-il, Supreme Leader of North Korea, has ratcheted up the political tensions a couple of notches by crashing long-range ballistic missiles into the Japan Sea. Just as the noise of the jet abates, a black minibus drives by, engulfing the street in a tsunami of high-pitched sound. It is like the aural embodiment of Hokusai's *The Great Wave*. The van is covered in election posters and teenage girls hang out of each window, dressed in candy pink jackets with white gloved hands clasping microphones, each screaming independently into the PA system broadcasting from the roof of the passing Toyota. The result is a wall of sound even Phil Spectre

would have been baffled by. Shimokawa-san's shop faces onto this bustling street in the town that lies south of Sapporo, half way between the busy metropolis and the Pacific Ocean at Tomakomai. The glass fronted emporium is well stocked with a glittering assortment of hardware and clothing, with a rack of boards he himself crafted in his bay out the back of the premises. Shingo holds a special place within the surf scene on Hokkaido, as the island's first full time shaper. Born and raised in Chitose, Shimokawa-san was recruited by the crusading pioneers. "When I was nineteen, my University friends, who were older than me, got me involved, that's how I started. They asked me to come and check it out – these where the first generation guys, the legends around here, I guess, so I gave it a shot. I tried it and it was really difficult. It didn't go the way I wanted it to, and I think that's why I became crazy about it." Shingo followed the path laid by the early waveriders and headed south. "My first surfing was done in Muroran at Itanki. I didn't really get involved with the surf club there, as we had our own thing here. At that time we didn't have contacts at the beach to tell us what the surf was like, so we had to go to the beach to see. Remember we had no cell phones back then." For Shingo surfing became an instant addiction. "I would go almost every day. It didn't matter back then if there was surf or not, I would be in the water in any case. I would go in the winter, but, back then, the wetsuits weren't up to par – occasionally I would have to double up – wear two. You might be a bit warmer but you couldn't move," he says, laughing.

Standing in the darkened shaping bay, the smooth, sculpted blank is illuminated by two neon strip lights. They cast tell-tale shadows over the contours of the board for trained eyes to interpret. Plan shape, rocker, concave, rails. Shimokawa-san runs his fingers over the foam, then picks up a tiny stringer plane and shaves

Opposite top
This thin ribbon of land running between fractured volcanic cliffs and the Japan Sea allows homes, businesses and roads a precious purchase on the north island coastline. Here it provides a surfcheck.

Opposite middle
Dividing his time between mountain and sea, carpenter Toru Kuwahara unloads in the early morning light outside his workshop in Niseko. "This board is my favourite, it was a wedding present from Taro."

Opposite bottom
Boots and gloves: arsenal essentials even in the misleading spring sunlight.

three fine curls from the central, wooden strip. "Over the years I met a lot of shapers," he explains, "and when I was able to make contact with one who could make a board exactly the way I wanted it, that was a great pleasure. But it wasn't a shaper on Hokkaido, because there wasn't one here. I took up shaping because I wanted the new generation of kids that are going to surf in the future to be able to have that kind of experience and that kind of feeling – to be able to order a board that's exactly what they want and to be able to get it, and I was confident I could do that." For many cold-water surfers, being away from the mainstream can breed a specific kind of resourcefulness and sense of purpose – whether that manifests itself in sourcing suitable wetsuits, or learning the complicated craft of board building, they will often find a way. "So I started teaching myself to shape, mostly by watching other board makers work, then I'd give it a go and bring it to a shaper for a critique. So I started shaping and I also started glassing as well. The shop came first – I opened it in 1986 and I started shaping in about 1994, so I was the first shaper on Hokkaido. Even today, there is only one other, based in Hakodate."

There are those who actively seek out the cold, who revel in the dense blue of the planet's most inhospitable breaks. For Shingo, the cold water of Hokkaido was a means to an end; it was a supreme test to be overcome and mastered. "I always had a fantasy for warm-water surfing but I didn't have the money to travel to these places. I always thought it would be a luxury to surf in just a rash vest, I thought it would be more mellow. So, because of that, I have worked hard and surfed hard year-round. I built up my shop, and that has meant I have been able to go away and enjoy travel; I had to earn myself that kind of experience. My first trip was to Bali; I went for a month and absolutely loved it. I went everywhere, I hit everything I could. I liked it so much I went

Left
A white icing dusts a
sleeping quiver.

BRIAN NEVINS

back for fifteen years, every year. The very first day I was there, it was over six feet at Uluwatu, and there I was surfing in just boardies." He smiles broadly. "It's hard to beat that."

The sat nav screen illuminates the dark cab of the Land Rover. Sitting in the lay-by just off the coastal road, the hammer of the diesel engine is replaced by the ticking of the motor as it cools. On this part of the island the road traces a narrow line between the deep crystalline Japan Sea and the fractured hanging rock faces. At times, there's just enough room for two cars to pass – a single strip of cracked tarmac. Periodically it dives into cavernous, twisting

tunnels only to emerge into the bright light of yet another breathtaking cove. Taro has spent many years scouring Hokkaido's wild and rugged coastline. While early waveriders were inspired by basic maps, today surfing has gone hi-tech. Break locations are logged in the memory of the GPS, swell prediction models are studied every hour, and weather is more a matter of survival than inconvenience. This four-wheel drive is no 'Chelsea Tractor' or 'Soccer Mom mini-van', it is an expedition vehicle, a working tool essential in the life-threatening winter cold. Missions to the north of the island in waist deep snow are challenging in the extreme. While the jet ski has become the trailer toy of choice for many

Top
Hoar frost forms overnight as the air temperature plummets.

Middle
Waist-deep snow is just one obstacle to be overcome by the winter expeditions.

Bottom
The cloud rolls in with this Japan Sea swell.

cutting-edge surfers, here on Hokkaido Taro and his tight crew have an altogether different beast hooked up for their trips into the big white. Huddled under the protective tarp, visible through the back window sits a skidoo, the only way in or out of some isolated spots. The pay-off? Point breaks that peel down huge, mountainous headlands below snow-covered, jagged peaks that shield from frigid northerlies. Few lights cut through the murk here; there are no people for miles. Not far to the north, pack ice covers the Sea of Okhotsk. To surf here you have to really love the cold water, not just suffer it for the pay-off offered by empty virgin waves. The experience means immersing oneself in a dense saline environment, where water temperatures slip below zero, and the wind burns exposed skin. Yet you will not see images of these forays splashed across surf magazines or read of these pioneering exploits on sponsors' websites. These are not undertaken for the warmth of the media spotlight, but for the purity offered by the experience alone.

For Taro, being a cold-water surfer is a holistic experience – it is not just about wearing a thicker wetsuit and enduring; it is about where your mind takes you. "When you go to a tropical place, you see many colours and, with the equatorial air, you feel a resort kind of mentality. Your consciousness and your mind are open, you feel like it's vacation time, your mind is all over the place – not distracted but your mind travels to a lot of places, I think. In the cold water all you see is just a gradation in colour; it's pretty much black and white. There's obviously the cold water and harshness in the air. What happens is that, rather than the mind going all over the place, it focuses into one place; it really concentrates the mind; that matched my mindset. There's something special that I feel, really concentrated in the cold water. When I am in cold water my mind feels very different, much more focused than when I am in tropical conditions. When I have an entire day with perfect waves all by myself, just surfing, I really feel what it is to surf."

At times it feels counter culture has turned marketeers dream vehicle, become a mainline into the consumer vein. While there is a mainstream groundswell in Japan that has assimilated the surfing lifestyle, on

Hokkaido the wheel has turned full circle. Where once they actively recruited, today the waveriders have closed ranks, their coastline has become a closely guarded secret, a resource to be cherished. The incumbent pioneers are blessed with a unique opportunity to enjoy the purity of the experience the way it was during surfing's genesis – away from the hassle, the crowds, the commercialism. The privilege of this position isn't lost on Hokkaido's tight knit community of searchers. "Today in the world it's really hard to find a break that hasn't really been tapped by anybody else," says Taro. "It is a luxurious thing to be able to explore this island and find more new spots than you can actually surf. All over the world you can go deep into the jungles and there are people already surfing there, crowds – so to be able to have this experience… this is what it means to surf. To find new spots where there's no body there and just surf all day. In snowboarding you still can; there are major mountains that are still untouched, there are many places like that left, but it's very rare these days to surf and have that experience. If you head out alone and find a new point, there's no information about it, you don't know whether it's safe or dangerous, whether you can actually surf it or not. There's no one there to save you. It's you and the wave. The whole thing – that's what the experience of exploring is. To me, that's what it means to be a surfer."

Above
"In the cold water all you see is just a gradation in colour, it's pretty much black and white." Taro Tamai.

Author acknowledgments

I would like to thank all those who contributed their time, thoughts, wisdom, support, words and images to this project. I would especially like to thank Demi Taylor who wore many hats on this project and then pig-boarded me over the finish line. You're a star. Also a big thank you to ace photographers Tim Nunn, Richie Hopson and Scott Wicking who delivered awesome images whatever the conditions.

Also to Alan Murphy – the Silver Murpher – for his support through out this long project.

I would also like to thank Bron Taylor airport collection and refuelling, Claire King, Emma Nunn, Steve Peters @ O'Neill Wetsuits for keeping me warm; Tom, Tom, Ernie and Debbie at Finisterre who always push the boundaries, Alex Palmer for web support, Taro Tamai, Noboru Tagawa, Kasagi Hajime, Hisashi Miyatake, Kasuhiro Miyatake, Hiraoka Tadanori, Shingo Shimokawa, Toru Kuwahara, Takashi Osanai, Evan Burkosky, Yuki Miyazaki, Yuki Saito, John Callahan, Gary Rogers, Jo Botham, Andrew Harrison, Jesse Davies, Roger Povey, Aidrian Kelly, Greenie, Pat Kieran, Kevin Rankin, Grant Coghill, Alistair Coghill, Alex Sutherland, Andy Bain, Sheila Finlayson, Angus Lamond, Jon Teitur Sigmundsson, Ingolfur Olsen, Kristjan Petur Saemundsson, Steinar Por Bachmann, Georg Hilmarsson, Valdimar Thorlacius, Mike Howes, Brian Heritage, Charlie Bunger Jnr, Tommy Colla, Jamie Breuer, Tyler Breuer, Andrew Gesler, Alex De Phillipo, Luke Simpson, Johnny Knapp, Nick LaVecchia, Mike LaVecchia, Brad Anderson, Liz Hardy, Jim Leadbetter, Lesley Choyce, Lance Moore, Nico Manos, Jesse Watson, Dorian Steele, Isaac Norman, Andrew Crouse, Connor Marsh, Walter Flowers, Jeff Norman, Mike Rossi, Jay Bowers, Krissy Montgomery, Wayne Vliet, Paul Horscroft, Raph Bruhwiler, Jeremy Koreski, Pete Devries, Tucker Stevens, Zach Wormhoudt, John Hunter, Richard Schmidt, Jay Watson, Charlie Skultka, Kieran Horn, Libby Sterling, Jan Erik Jensen, Marcus Sanders, Lloyd Kahn, Andy Cummins and SAS for keeping up the fight.

Huge appreciation goes to the whole Footprint team, especially Angus Dawson and Liz Harper. Footprint epitomise the real spirit of adventure travel.

Contributing Photographers

Richie Hopson, Tim Nunn, Scott Wicking, Nick LaVecchia, Jay Watson, Jeremy Koreski, Rich McMullin, Tommy Colla, Luke Simpson, Brian Nevins, Cicero deGuzman Jr., Taro Tamai, Kasagi Hajime, Al Mackinnon, David Pu'u, Sharpy, Chris Nelson, Demi Taylor, Tane Skultka, Alex Williams, Greg Martin, Stu Norton, The Gill, Watanabe, Jim Leadbetter, Tucker Stevens Collection, Heritage Surf & Sport, Bunger Collection, Kevin Rankin, Andy Bennets, Pat Kieran, A Maltman, SAS

Footprint credits

Project Editor: Alan Murphy
Design and production: Angus Dawson
Picture Editor: Demi Taylor
Proofreader: Sophie Jones

Managing Director: Andy Riddle
Commercial Director: Patrick Dawson
Publisher: Alan Murphy
Publishing Managers: Felicity Laughton,
Nicola Gibbs
Digital Editors: Jo Williams,
Jen Haddington
Marketing: Liz Harper
Sales Manager: Diane McEntee
Advertising: Renu Sibal
Finance & administration: Elizabeth Taylor

Print

Manufactured in Italy by Printer Trento
Pulp from sustainable forests

The views expressed in this book are the views of the contributors and do not necessarily reflect the views of the author or the publisher. While every effort has been made to ensure that the facts in this book are accurate, the author and publisher cannot accept responsibility for any loss, injury or inconvenience however caused.

Cover image credits

Front cover: Tim Nunn
Back cover: Rich McMullin, Luke Simpson

Publishing information

Cold Water Souls
1st edition
October 2010
Copyright 2010 by Chris Nelson

ISBN 978-1-906098-75-9
CIP DATA: A catalogue record for this book is available from the British Library

® Footprint Handbooks and the Footprint mark are a registered trademark of Footprint Handbooks Ltd

Published by Footprint
6 Riverside Court
Lower Bristol Road
Bath BA2 3DZ, UK
T +44 (0)1225 469141
F +44 (0)1225 469461
footprinttravelguides.com

The moral rights of the author have been asserted.

Distributed in North America by Globe Pequot Press

NICK LAVECCHIA